The World of the Ancient Greeks

JOHN CAMP · ELIZABETH FISHER

The World of the Ancient Greeks

With 376 illustrations, 107 in color

Thames & Hudson

This book is dedicated to our children – Austin, Elizabeth, Katherine and Laura – who have shared our travels and love of Greece.

Many friends, students and teachers, too numerous to list by name here, have contributed to our knowledge of the world of the Greeks. We would like to record special thanks to our colleagues Gregory Daugherty, Dan McCaffrey and Roxane Gilmore for their interest and support. For help with photographs we are indebted to Marie Mauzy of the ASCS, Athens, Hans R. Goette of the DAI and I. Ninou of the Archaeological Society.

On the jacket. Main: kouros from Anavyssos, National Museum, Athens, photo DAI Athens. Front, left to right: votives from temple of Asklepios, Corinth, photo DAI Athens; Cycladic figurine of a harpist from Keros, National Museum, Athens, photo Josephine Powell; relief showing Amphiaraos, National Museum, Athens; the Delphi bronze charioteer, photo Heidi Grassley; temple at Segesta, Sicily, photo John Camp; head of Athena from a coin, Leu Numismatik; horse and jockey, from Cape Artemision, National Museum, Athens, photo Heidi Grassley; Delphi, photo Heidi Grassley. Back, left to right: detail of black-figure vase from Agrigento, Sicily, Metropolitan Museum of Art, New York; detail of a grave stele, National Museum, Athens, photo Heidi Grassley; vase fragment, Allard Pierson Museum, Amsterdam; head of a sphinx, Mycenae, National Museum, Athens, photo Heidi Grassley; detail of a grave stele, National Museum, Athens, photo Heidi Grassley; statue of Leonidas, photo DAI Athens; the Lion Gate, Mycenae, photo Heidi Grassley; the 'Diadoumenos', National Museum, Athens, photo Heidi Grassley; the theatre at Epidauros, photo Heidi Grassley. Spine: gold mask from Mycenae, National Museum, Athens, photo Heidi Grassley. All photos by Heidi Grassley, © Thames & Hudson Ltd, London

Half-title: Two women engaged in a game of knuckle-bones; terracotta statuette from Capua, third century BC.
Title-page: The 'Moscophoros', or Calf-bearer, a statue dedicated on the Acropolis, Athens, c. 560 BC.

First published in hardcover in the United States of America in 2002 by Thames & Hudson Inc., 500 Fifth Avenue, New York, New York 10110

thamesandhudsonusa.com

Library of Congress Catalog Card Number 2002100571
ISBN 0-500-05112-7

Printed and bound in Slovenia by Mladinska Knjiga

CONTENTS

I

WHO WERE THE GREEKS?

II

THE FIRST GREEKS

III

THE HEROIC AGE

IV

THE AGE OF EXPANDING HORIZONS

I

WHO WERE THE GREEKS?

Soft lands breed soft men; wondrous fruits of the earth and valiant warriors do not grow from the same soil.

Herodotus, 9. 122

WHEN WE FIRST can begin to recognize and identify the people known as Greeks, they occupy the rocky, mountainous tip of the Balkan peninsula jutting out into the eastern Mediterranean, together with the many hundreds of small islands scattered around its coast. From here they were destined to spread out and colonize almost all the Mediterranean and Black seas, founding cities which survive today – but the land of Delphi and Olympia is their homeland. It is a land composed of low but steep mountains, which separate numerous coastal valleys and upland plains. The geography does not encourage unity, and during the high point of their history the political structure of the Greeks was based on the *polis*, a small independent city-state which controlled a limited amount of arable land, protected and set off from its neighbours by steep ridges and mountainous terrain. Co-operative, unified action between Greek cities was the exception rather than the rule. Overland communication was not simple and the Greeks were by and large a seafaring people. Setting out from their long and deeply indented coastline they explored their expanding world by ship. It need not surprise us that among the favourite and most enduring early Greek myths we find the stories of Jason's quest with the Argonauts and Odysseus' ten-year voyage home.

The sanctuary of Delphi, situated on the slopes of Mt Parnassos, was the site of one of the great religious festivals that brought together people from all over the Greek world. Religion – a shared belief in the Olympian gods – and language are two of the defining characteristics of the Greeks.

THE ANCIENT GREEKS DEFINED

The human form was a preferred subject throughout the Archaic and Classical periods, 600–350 BC. This kouros *(male youth) dates from c. 500 BC, and is from the Cyclades, possibly Anaphe.*

(Below) The gods of Olympus sitting in council to decide the fate of the heroes in the Trojan War. Frieze from the Siphnian Treasury, Delphi, c. 525 BC.

(Opposite) The Ionic order was developed in the islands of the Aegean and along the west coast of Asia Minor. Characteristic are the light proportions of the columns and the use of elaborately carved mouldings, seen here on the east porch of the Erectheion (c. 430–400 BC), on the Acropolis of Athens.

THE GREEKS HAVE PLAYED a prominent role in the complex mix of peoples who have inhabited the shores of the Mediterranean for thousands of years. Yet in part because of their long history it is no easy task to say with certainty who they were, where they came from, or even how to define them as a people, until well on into the historical period. At that time we can associate many achievements and innovations as being Greek in origin, such as democracy or theatre, while other aspects of western culture have a decided and recognizable Greek identity: athletics, philosophy, architecture, education or sculpture, for instance. These are relatively late achievements, however, and in many cases are shared with other cultures and civilizations. In recognizing the Greeks at the beginning of their long and influential role in the history of the Mediterranean, two aspects set them apart from other people: language and religion.

How a group communicates both draws these people together and excludes others, thereby defining the group as an identifiable, distinct population. The ancient Greeks certainly defined themselves linguistically; the unfamiliar sounds made by a foreigner (bar-bar) gave rise to the Greek word for an outsider: barbarian. Greek has been spoken on the shores of the Mediterranean for at least 4,000 years and seems to have arrived in the peninsula along with new immigrants sometime between 2000 and 1500 BC. It is Indo-European in origin and thus related to many other modern European languages. Several distinct dialects (Ionian, Dorian and Aeolian) presumably reflect early tribal divisions which survived as political divisions in the historical period (see map p. 64).

A system of common belief in one or more specific deities and the practice of traditional rituals in their honour also serve to define and separate a group of people. A belief in the Olympian gods is a characteristic feature of those identified as Greeks and, like the language, it seems to have been introduced into Greece in the years around 2000 BC. The creation myths concerning the origin of the world sound much like those of other people of that time, but Zeus, Apollo, Athena, Poseidon and others became part of a recognizable and distinctly Greek pantheon.

In terms of self-definition, it is worth noting that the word 'Greek' is itself foreign: it is in fact the name used by the Romans to designate the peninsula and its inhabitants (Graecia, Graeci). The people we know as the Greeks in antiquity always referred to themselves as the Hellenes, just as in medieval times they called themselves Romaoi (Romans), and not Byzantines. For Greeks of the historical period Hellas, the original homeland of the Hellenes, was thought to be in Thessaly, in central Greece.

Climate and resources

Greece has a climate that is generally warm and conducive to agriculture. In summer, temperatures frequently reach over 38°C (100°F) and in winter they rarely fall much below 4°C (40°F). Rainfall is unevenly distributed, with far more falling in the west and north than in the south or the islands. Some plants grow relatively well in this dry, temperate climate, such as olive trees, the grape vine, wheat and barley, which were staples of ancient Greek life. Legumes, figs, various nuts and

A black-figure wine cup (kylix) by Exekias, c. 540 BC, found at Vulci, showing Dionysos, god of wine. Both seafaring and the cultivation of vines were important aspects of Greek life.

(Below) A view of a landscape in the Peloponnese. The soil and climate of Greece are conducive to the growing of grain and olives, while rugged hills provide grazing for sheep and goats.

(Right) An olive harvest: three men with sticks, one in the tree, knock the fruit to the ground. Olive oil was a valued commodity, used for food, cooking, fuel for lamps and a form of soap or lotion. Black-figure amphora by the Antimenes Painter, c. 520 BC, found at Vulci.

honey supplemented the diet, while goats and sheep provided milk and especially cheese. Meat was available, though perhaps restricted largely to festival days, and – as no part of the mainland is more than 80 km (50 miles) from the sea – various kinds of fish must also have been a dietary staple.

Many areas of Greece also provided excellent marble or hard limestone for building, fine clays for pottery and other terracotta goods, and a fair amount of gold, silver, lead and iron. Copper generally had to be traded for, as also did tin, which were combined to produce numerous items in bronze, such as weapons, statuary and vessels. Good timber, necessary to sustain the fleets of several Greek cities (especially Athens), was only available in parts of Greece such as Macedonia and Arcadia.

Contact and conflict

The eastern Mediterranean has always been the point of contact, and conflict, between Africa and Europe, as well as between East and West, and memories in this part of the world are long.

THE LOCATION OF HELLAS

As for those, however, who speak of Hellas as a city, the Pharsalians point out at a distance of 60 stades (12 km/ 7½ miles) from their own city a city in ruins which they believe to be Hellas…. Whereas the Melitaians say that Hellas was situated about 10 stades (2km/ 1¼ miles) away from them, on the other side of the Enipeus river, at the time their town was called Pyrrha and that it was from Hellas, which was situated in a low-lying district, that the Hellenes migrated to their own city; and they cite as evidence the tomb of Hellen, son of Deucalion and Pyrrha, in their agora…. So much then concerning the Hellenes.

Strabo, 431–32

A portrait of the writer Herodotus (c. 484–420s BC), a native of Halicarnassus, in Caria. His history of the Persian Wars described, among other things, the cultural and ethnic differences between the Greeks and their neighbours – Lydians, Persians, Egyptians and Scythians.

HERODOTUS

These are the researches of Herodotus of Halicarnassus, which he publishes, in the hope of thereby preventing the great and wonderful actions of the Greeks and Barbarians from losing their due meed of glory; and withal to put on record what were their grounds of feud. According to the Persians best informed in history, the Phoenicians began the quarrel.

Herodotus, 1. 1

Greek migration and settlement in Asia Minor; Persian invasions of Greece; Alexander's conquest of Asia; Roman intervention in the Greek world; the rise of Christianity; the rise of Islam and Arab raids in the Mediterranean; the Crusades to the Holy Land; and the taking of Constantinople by the Ottomans. All these and other events have left their mark, and the factional strife in the Middle East, Cyprus and the Balkans in the twentieth century has deep roots. Throughout this turbulent history the Greeks have survived and often prospered, making unparalleled contributions to western European culture and civilization.

When Herodotus begins his account of the Persian Wars in the fifth century BC, he says the origins of the trouble can be traced back 700 years earlier, with the events leading up to the Trojan War.

Over time, the struggle has surged back and forth across the Aegean: Greeks against Troy;

An Attic red-figure krater (bowl for mixing wine and water) with a scene from the Trojan War – two warriors lead their grandmother Aithra away from the city after it had fallen to the Greeks. Painted by Myson, c. 500 BC.

Map of the Mediterranean and Black seas, showing the major sites mentioned in the text. The inset shows the Greek homeland, with the southern tip of the Balkan peninsula, the Aegean islands and the west coast of Asia Minor.

HISTORICAL OUTLINE

THE HISTORY OF GREECE precedes the arrival of the people we call Greeks by many thousands of years. Humans found the climate and natural resources of the area a congenial place to live in the Old Stone Age (Palaeolithic, 100,000–10,000 BC), when food was acquired by hunting and gathering. With the New Stone Age (Neolithic, 6000–3000 BC) came the ability to produce food by means of cultivation and rearing domesticated animals. Handmade pottery appears early in this period as an innovation in food storage technology.

The years around 3000 BC saw the introduction of bronze, an alloy of tin and copper, which allowed the production of far better tools and weapons. The succeeding years, down to about 1100 BC, are known accordingly as the Bronze Age. This is the period when much of Greek mythology is set.

Archaeology has revealed two flourishing and rich civilizations in Greece, usually regarded as the earliest in Europe, one on the island of Crete (Minoan), the other on the mainland (Mycenaean). Large palaces were built, decorated with handsome frescoes and protected by massive fortification walls. Early

records written in Greek were kept on clay tablets and luxury goods were imported from all over the known world: ivory, faience and glass from Egypt and the Middle East, lapis lazuli from Afghanistan, ostrich eggs from Africa and amber from the Baltic. All this came to an end with the destruction and burning of the palaces

(Left) Gold cup with repoussé decoration, found in a tholos tomb at Vapheio in Laconia, c. 1500 BC. The style of the cup is heavily Minoan and indicative of the close interaction between the Minoans on Crete and the Mycenaeans on the mainland at this time.

(Right) South flank of the temple of Poseidon at Cape Sounion, c. 440 BC, built in the Classical period during the height of Athenian prominence under the guidance of Perikles.

in the thirteenth century BC, a time when Greek tradition also places the fall of Troy.

In the succeeding period, often referred to as the Dark Ages (1100–750 BC), the level of material culture plummeted, though iron makes its appearance in Greece at about this time. Gone are the palaces, fortification walls, writing, virtually all foreign contacts and trade, and all but the most simple artistic expression. Population numbers seem to have dropped dramatically and all available evidence suggests that the Greeks returned to a life of bare subsistence farming, though pottery continued to be manufactured and there are signs of cult activity. There is both archaeological evidence and a literary tradition for the migration of mainland Greeks across the Aegean to Asia Minor, while other Greeks, including a group known as the Dorians, moved into parts of the mainland from the north.

(Right) Athenian white-ground pyxis (cosmetics box), c. 540 BC. Greek pottery was extremely well made in most periods and ornamented in a variety of techniques. The figured pottery of the Archaic and Classical periods is decorated with mythological subjects and scenes from daily life.

Portrait of Alexander the Great of Macedon, whose conquests spread Greek culture far to the east. His successors in the Hellenistic period passed on many aspects of Greek civilization to the Romans.

Beginning around 750 BC there are clear signs of a substantial recovery on the part of the mainland Greeks, the start of a period of growth and expansion known as the Archaic period, which was to last until the Persian Wars in 490–480 BC. A recognizable sense of national identity appears in the eighth century BC, perhaps first expressed in the founding of the Olympic games in 776 BC. It continues and is strengthened by waves of Greek colonists who set out to found Greek cities all over the coasts of the Mediterranean and Black seas. Coming into contact with foreign, unfamiliar, native populations, the colonists became increasingly aware of their common bonds with those left behind on the Greek mainland, however great the local and tribal differences might have been within Greece itself. Contacts with the east led to the introduction of the alphabet via Phoenicia, and after a lapse of 500 years the Greeks became literate once again. To this same early period should be dated the earliest Greek literature – the poems

of Hesiod and the two epics ascribed to Homer, the *Iliad* and *Odyssey*.

In political life aristocracies lost control to tyrants, leaders who seized and held power unconstitutionally, though often as champions of the common people. Individual city-states prospered, often on a nearly equal footing, each following its own inclinations in politics, art and culture. Unified co-operation was rarely recognized as either necessary or desirable, until the threat of the Persian invasion early in the fifth century.

The Greeks repelled the Persians after four major battles in Greece itself, at Marathon (490 BC), Thermopylai (480 BC), Salamis (480 BC) and Plataia (479 BC), but not before the invaders had devastated the city of Athens. Successful leadership in the war left two cities dominant in Greece: Athens and Sparta. The fifth and fourth centuries BC are generally regarded as the high-point of Greek culture, primarily as expressed in Athens, and are known as the Classical period (480–323 BC).

This is the period when Greek architecture, sculpture and vase-painting reached their height, matched by parallel achievements in theatre, philosophy, literature and rhetoric. To this same period in Athens can be dated the uniquely Greek political invention of democracy. A protracted war between Athens and Sparta (431–404 BC) temporarily brought Athens to her knees.

The fourth century BC saw the rise of Philip II and his son Alexander the Great of Macedon. The conquest of Asia by Alexander (334–323

BC) remains one of the outstanding military campaigns of all time and it had a considerable effect on the fortunes of the Greek world. Founding numerous cities on his march, Alexander spread Greek culture all the way across southern Asia, as far as modern Afghanistan. Veterans were encouraged to marry locally and to settle in the new towns. Greek language, religion and customs now reached from Spain to Afghanistan, and from Ukraine to Egypt. This period of uniform, widespread Greek culture, which lasted until the domination of Rome, is known as the Hellenistic period.

On the death of Alexander no one individual was able to maintain control of his conquests, and wars of succession broke out among his followers. The territory was divided into large kingdoms, with the Ptolemies taking Egypt, the Seleucids Syria, the Attalids Pergamon, and the Antigonids Greece and Macedonia. The old individual Greek city-states were in no position to survive unchanged in this new political order and they were either absorbed or forced to cede a measure of independence and join with numerous other cities in new leagues designed to match the greater power and influence of the huge Hellenistic kingdoms.

As early as the third century BC, Rome was drawn into the ongoing wars between the Hellenistic dynasties and the various Greek leagues. Several wars were fought with the kingdom of Macedonia, which continued to cause trouble despite defeats in 197 and 168 BC, and, after defeating the Achaian League in 146 BC, Rome annexed much of Greece and administered it thereafter as though a province.

The Roman period extends from the second century BC until the beginning of the Byzantine era, often dated to the reign of Constantine in the early fourth century AD. During these centuries the Greeks enjoyed a period of relative prosperity, with limited periods of warfare; some areas, such as Asia Minor, grew extraordinarily wealthy. The Romans were great admirers of Greek culture and sought to absorb or emulate much from the Greek world. This admiration was expressed through outright plundering, the luring of Greek artists and intellectuals to Rome, extensive copying of works of Greek art, and through education at the philosophical schools of Athens, Antioch and Alexandria. The Romans thereby served as a major conduit for Greek culture, preserving and transmitting it to the world of Europe.

Bronze statue of Athena, goddess of wisdom and warrior protectress of Athens, c. 350 BC. It was found with three other bronze statues in Peiraieus in a storeroom dating to the first century BC, presumably awaiting shipment to Rome (see also p. 149).

Christianity rose out of the eastern Mediterranean, where Greeks had been living for centuries. It became a prominent religion in the Roman Empire following the conversion of Constantine, who in AD 330 founded a new capital city named Constantinople on the site of the old Greek city of Byzantium. The term *Byzantine* is a modern one, used to describe the Christian continuity of the old Roman empire, particularly in the eastern Mediterranean. The culture of the Greek world continued, even with the abandonment of the Olympian gods, and Greek remained the language of the Byzantine empire.

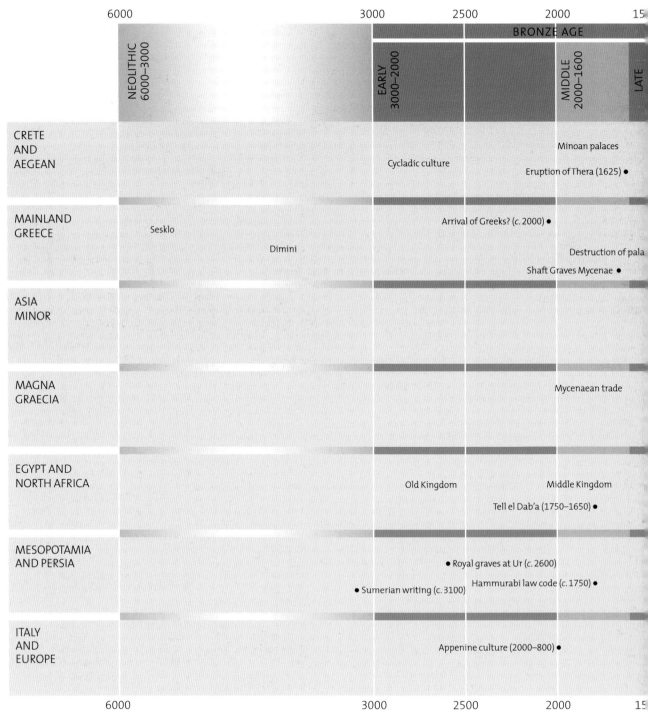

	6000		3000	2500	2000	15
	NEOLITHIC 6000–3000		EARLY 3000–2000	BRONZE AGE	MIDDLE 2000–1600	LATE
CRETE AND AEGEAN				Cycladic culture	Minoan palaces / Eruption of Thera (1625) ●	
MAINLAND GREECE	Sesklo	Dimini		Arrival of Greeks? (c. 2000) ●	Destruction of pala / Shaft Graves Mycenae ●	
ASIA MINOR						
MAGNA GRAECIA					Mycenaean trade	
EGYPT AND NORTH AFRICA				Old Kingdom	Middle Kingdom / Tell el Dab'a (1750–1650) ●	
MESOPOTAMIA AND PERSIA			● Sumerian writing (c. 3100)	● Royal graves at Ur (c. 2600)	Hammurabi law code (c. 1750) ●	
ITALY AND EUROPE				Appenine culture (2000–800) ●		

	6000	3000	2500	2000	15

The rise of Islam in the seventh and eighth centuries brought new opportunities for the preservation of Greek scholarship and science. Despite challenges presented by the spread of Islam and betrayal by Crusaders from Europe and Venice in 1204, Constantinople survived as the capital of the Byzantine empire until its fall to the Ottoman Turks in 1453. Following almost 400 years of Turkish control, the modern state of Greece was carved out of the old homeland at the end of the Balkan peninsula where both Orthodox Greek Christianity and the Greek language have survived to the present day.

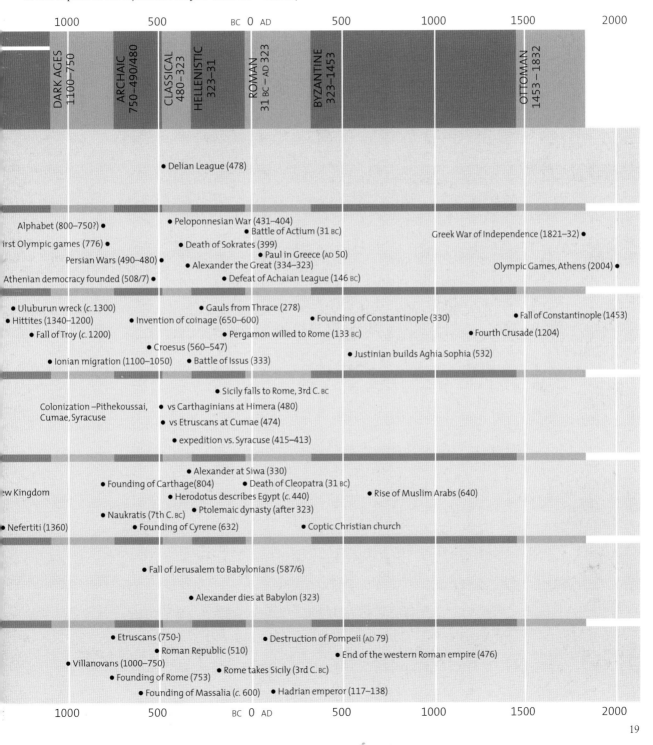

DARK AGES 1100–750

ARCHAIC 750–490/480

CLASSICAL 480–323

HELLENISTIC 323–31

ROMAN 31 BC – AD 323

BYZANTINE 323–1453

OTTOMAN 1453 – 1832

• Delian League (478)

Alphabet (800–750?) •
• Peloponnesian War (431–404)
• Battle of Actium (31 BC)
Greek War of Independence (1821–32) •
First Olympic games (776) •
• Death of Sokrates (399)
Persian Wars (490–480) •
• Paul in Greece (AD 50)
• Alexander the Great (334–323)
Olympic Games, Athens (2004) •
Athenian democracy founded (508/7) •
• Defeat of Achaian League (146 BC)

• Uluburun wreck (c. 1300)
• Gauls from Thrace (278)
• Hittites (1340–1200)
• Invention of coinage (650–600)
• Founding of Constantinople (330)
• Fall of Constantinople (1453)
• Fall of Troy (c. 1200)
• Pergamon willed to Rome (133 BC)
• Fourth Crusade (1204)
• Croesus (560–547)
• Ionian migration (1100–1050)
• Battle of Issus (333)
• Justinian builds Aghia Sophia (532)

• Sicily falls to Rome, 3rd C. BC
Colonization – Pithekoussai, Cumae, Syracuse
• vs Carthaginians at Himera (480)
• vs Etruscans at Cumae (474)
• expedition vs. Syracuse (415–413)

• Alexander at Siwa (330)
New Kingdom
• Founding of Carthage (804)
• Death of Cleopatra (31 BC)
• Herodotus describes Egypt (c. 440)
• Rise of Muslim Arabs (640)
• Naukratis (7th C. BC)
• Ptolemaic dynasty (after 323)
Nefertiti (1360)
• Founding of Cyrene (632)
• Coptic Christian church

• Fall of Jerusalem to Babylonians (587/6)

• Alexander dies at Babylon (323)

• Etruscans (750–)
• Destruction of Pompeii (AD 79)
• Roman Republic (510)
• End of the western Roman empire (476)
• Villanovans (1000–750)
• Rome takes Sicily (3rd C. BC)
• Founding of Rome (753)
• Founding of Massalia (c. 600)
• Hadrian emperor (117–138)

Written Sources and Archaeological Discoveries

Our knowledge of the Greeks comes from a variety of sources. They were a literate people and Greek was used over a wide geographical area. Documents on clay written in a primitive form of Greek go back to the second millennium BC, though alphabetic writing did not appear until the eighth century BC. Once introduced, writing was used extensively all over the Greek world and a vast array of inscriptions are preserved, most written on stone, though clay, bronze, papyrus and lead were also used. These documents preserve laws, treaties, contracts, inventories, sales, public honours, dedications, epitaphs, curses, votes and lists of all sorts. Literally tens of thousands of inscriptions have been recovered and they provide a detailed and vivid picture of life in the Greek world.

Surviving works of Greek literature are another rich source of information. Written on papyrus in antiquity, these works were avidly collected, copied in Hellenistic and Roman times, and kept in large public libraries, official city archives and private collections. The dry climate of Egypt has preserved many fragments of papyrus, often reused in later times to wrap mummies. More durable copies of many other texts were made later on parchment or vellum in monasteries throughout Europe and the Middle East and have survived to the present. The circumstances of survival are very uneven and some great texts that we know once existed have been lost, while some distinctly odd ones have survived. The individuals behind these works are often obscure; in other cases we know a surprising amount about them. Such sources bring the world of the Greeks alive and will be quoted frequently throughout this book.

Archaeological evidence goes a long way in illuminating or supplementing the information available from the written texts. Many remnants of Greek antiquity have always been visible and studied. Even the ancient Greeks came across earlier graves, or prehistoric animal bones so large they were interpreted as the remains of heroes. Early European travellers and foreign residents of Greece tried their hand at excavation, primarily to recover works of art, and the Louvre in Paris, the British Museum in London and the Glyptothek in Munich all have outstanding examples of Greek sculpture collected in the years around 1800, before the formation of the modern Greek state. Other Greek antiquities in European and American museums were acquired even more recently from Asia Minor or Italy. Unauthorized digging and collecting is now illegal in the international community, although a lively trade in dubious antiquities continues.

Inscriptions carved on the wall of a building in the Hellenistic sanctuary of Zeus Lepsynou at Euromos, in Caria.

In Greece, archaeological research was put on a sounder footing with the founding of the Greek Archaeological Service and the Archaeological Society in 1837. Foreign Schools and Institutes of Archaeology followed soon thereafter, beginning with the French in 1846. Since then, archaeologists have brought all phases of Greek antiquity to light.

The centres of the two great Bronze Age civilizations were among the first to be uncovered. Following the discovery of Troy, Heinrich Schliemann turned his attention in 1876 to Mycenae, the citadel of Agamemnon in the *Iliad*, and uncovered among other things a grave circle with six rich shaft graves, full of beautifully wrought bronze weapons, gold, ivories and other luxury goods. And in 1900 Sir Arthur Evans began work at the site of Knossos, on the island of Crete, where over many years he uncovered the extensive remains of a labyrinthine palace. Brightly coloured frescoes

An illustrated fragment from a fifth-century AD manuscript of Homer's Iliad, *probably produced in Alexandria.*

GREEK TEXTS AND AUTHORS

As with inscriptions, the range of literary information is huge and includes:

Myths and legends: Hesiod, Apollodorus, Diodorus
Lyric poems: Sappho, Alcaeus
Epic poems: Homer
Drinking songs: Anacreon, Xenophanes
Histories: Herodotus, Thucydides, Xenophon, Polybios

Biographies: Plutarch
Geographies: Strabo
Travel guides: Pausanias
Tragedies: Aeschylus, Sophokles, Euripides
Comedies: Aristophanes, Menander
Satires: Lucian
Philosophical treatises: Plato, Aristotle
Medical texts: Hippocrates, Galen
Lawcourt speeches: Demosthenes, Aeschines, Antiphon, Lysias

There are also instruction manuals on everything from catapults to horsemanship.

The lyric poets Alcaeus and Sappho from Lesbos, depicted on a vase by the Brygos Painter, c. 490–470 BC, found at Akragas (Agrigento) in Sicily.

depicted a hitherto unknown civilization, which Evans named Minoan after the legendary King Minos. Hundreds of inscribed clay tablets suggested a complex and sophisticated administration.

Large-scale excavations of famous Classical sites were begun by the German Archaeological Institute at Olympia in 1875, and the French School at Delphi in 1892. In Asia Minor the German Institute began work at Pergamon in 1878 and at Miletus in 1899, while the Austrians began at Ephesus in 1895. The pace of archaeological work has continued unabated since then, though the exploration of many great urban sites, such as Thebes, Syracuse or Alexandria, has been impeded by the modern town or city set atop the ruins.

In the twentieth century the discovery of Akrotiri on Thera (Santorini) by Spyridon Marinatos in 1967 and the excavation of a Mycenaean palace at Pylos (1938/9, 1952–) by Carl Blegen and the American School have added immeasurably to our knowledge of the Aegean Bronze Age, while further American excavations of the Athenian Agora (1931–) have revolutionized the study of Athens in all periods. More recently, the discoveries by Greek archaeologists of Macedonian tombs, in particular a rich and unplundered one at Vergina (1977), have yielded unparalleled examples of early wall-paintings and rich caches of luxury goods. Finally, the underwater excavations at Uluburun in southern Turkey (1980s) have produced the cargo of a Bronze Age ship travelling towards Greece laden with all the wealth of Egypt and the Middle East, while the harbour of Alexandria (1990s) is yielding up its secrets. As techniques of recovery and analysis improve, the volume of information available from archaeological discovery seems almost limitless.

In the early nineteenth century the rediscovery of the civilization of ancient Greece took the form primarily of collecting works of art, which often later formed the core of museums in cities throughout Europe, such as London, Paris, Berlin and Munich. Louis Sébastien Fauvel, French consul in Athens, formed a large collection of plaster casts and marble fragments. His house, shown in this lithograph, was situated in the centre of the Athenian Agora.

(Above) A metope from the Parthenon with a fight between a Lapith and a Centaur. This same architectural fragment is depicted in the lithograph of the French consul's house, left, in 1819.

(Right) During the course of the nineteenth century archaeology in Greece became more scientific and systematic. Schools and institutes of archaeology were set up both by the Greeks themselves and by other countries, and excavations were undertaken at many key sites. This photograph taken in the 1890s at Delphi shows the discovery of an early statue.

THE FIRST GREEKS

The islanders too were great pirates. These islanders were Carians and Phoenicians, as was proved by the following fact. During the purification of Delos in this war all the graves on the island were dug up and it was found that over half the occupants were Carians; they were identified by the fashion of the arms buried with them and by the method of interment which was the same as the Carians still follow.

Thucydides, 1. 8. 1

INDIGENOUS PEOPLE HAVE occupied Greece since the time of the Neanderthals. Migrations at various periods have brought in many other groups, recognizable by the distinctive material remains of their cultures – pottery, figurines, technology, burial customs, architecture and the like. Archaeologists have recovered and studied these remains and have attempted to sort out the history and relationships of these different people who at various times occupied the mainland, the islands, Crete and Asia Minor. The literary record of the later Greeks also holds a memory of these early populations, known as Lelegians, Pelasgians, Phoenicians, Carians and others. Somewhere in this complex mix of prehistoric peoples those who spoke Greek and worshipped the Olympian gods arrived, and over the centuries established themselves as the dominant culture in the eastern Mediterranean.

A group of early Cycladic figurines, c. 2500 BC. The pre-Greek islanders show a degree of artistic sophistication – not influenced by any outside culture – distinct from the mainland or Crete. Signs of Cycladic influence, including such statuettes, have been found both on the east coast of Greece and on the west coast of Asia Minor.

PALAEOLITHIC AND NEOLITHIC GREECE

(Right) An architectural reconstruction of the middle Neolithic settlement of Sesklo (5000–4000 BC): a fortified site with small houses made of mudbrick walls standing on foundations of field-stones and covered with thatched roofs. At the top of the hill a larger rectangular building with three rooms arranged axially may be seen as the precursor of the Bronze Age megaron, or great hall (see p. 38).

EXCAVATIONS IN VARIOUS PARTS of Greece have now brought to light considerable information for the Upper Palaeolithic period (40,000–10,000 BC). For the most part, the human inhabitants of the region occupied caves or shallow rock shelters, usually located on the slopes of a ravine or narrow river valley. Migrating animals, in particular red deer, made up a large part of their diet. Hunting and gathering were the means of subsistence and people lived in relatively small groups and almost certainly moved with the seasons to follow herds or collect foodstuffs. More than a dozen Palaeolithic sites have been studied in Greece; the most extensively excavated and published is the Franchthi Cave in the Argolid, in the Peloponnese, which has greatly expanded our information on these early times.

The two great changes of prehistoric times, the domestication of animals and the cultivation of cereals, seem to have occurred far to the east and were imported to Greece

THE FRANCHTHI CAVE

View looking northwest out of the mouth of the Franchthi Cave, with one of the deep excavation trenches in the foreground.

One of the best pictures of Palaeolithic Greece comes from the excavations of the Franchthi Cave in the Argolid, carried out by Indiana University from the 1960s to the 1980s. The cave is 150 m (490 ft) deep, and up to 30 m (98 ft) high, with a pool of clear fresh water at the extreme rear. A collapse of the roof – probably in Neolithic times – in the central and back parts allows in light today, but rendered much of the cave uninhabitable.

Excavations were confined to the front part, where the human habitation deposits are deep. One trench was carried down for 12 m (40 ft), providing a picture of the use of the cave over 20,000 years (23,000–3000 BC), though boulders and rising water prevented excavation all the way down to the original floor. The excavated earth was put through a fine-mesh water sieve and flotation was used to recover organic remains, allowing a picture of the ecological environment to be built up. Tiny bones of lizards, voles and other small creatures – animals sensitive to minor changes in temperature – provided information as to climatic change over the centuries of use of the cave.

Dates were obtained by radiocarbon analysis of organic remains, and a layer of volcanic ash from a known eruption in

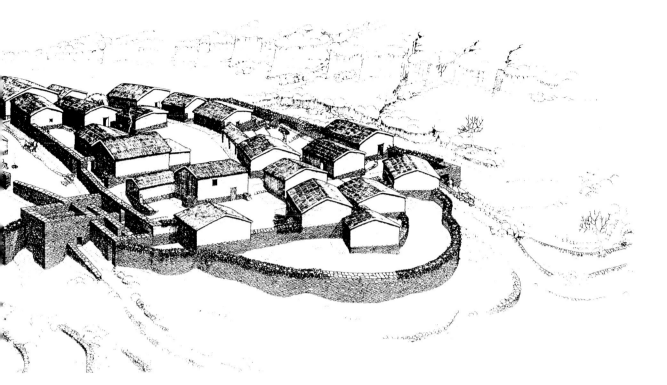

Italy. Full study of the seeds, pollen, stone tools, pottery, molluscs and animal bones is still under way, but the results thus far have been impressive.

The earliest attested use of the cave, from 23,000 to 11,000 BC, corresponds to the period of the last ice age in Europe. The climate was cold, dry and glacial; with so much water locked in great ice sheets, the seashore was some 6 km (4 miles) from the cave and the terrain outside it was probably steppe-like.

Traces of wild cereals, legumes and nuts found inside the cave give an indication of diet. The Palaeolithic inhabitants were hunters and gatherers, originally using chipped stone tools of chert and flint, or bone implements.

A warming trend began in 11,000 BC and the sea level rose steadily thereafter: by 9000 BC the shore was 3 km (2 miles) away, by 3000 BC several hundred metres, and today it is just 45 m (150 ft) away. The landscape probably changed to open woodland and by 7500–7000 BC the inhabitants' diet was varied: traces of wild oats, wheat, barley, pear, lentils, vetch, almonds, pistachios, peas, capers, mustard and coriander have all been found, along with fish, shellfish, red deer and wild boar. The cave was certainly used in spring, summer and autumn, though it is less clear if it was inhabited during the winter.

Around 6500 BC larger fish bones, perhaps from tuna weighing several hundred pounds, were deposited in the cave. That the inhabitants were seafaring widely at this time is suggested by the appearance of obsidian tools. Obsidian is a volcanic glass which holds a far sharper edge than flint or chert and is easier to work; the source for that found in the cave is the island of Melos, some 150 km (93 miles) across the Aegean Sea.

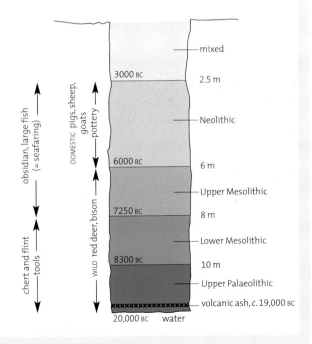

Schematic reconstruction of the sequence of early occupation of the Franchthi Cave, demonstrating the depth of the deposits.

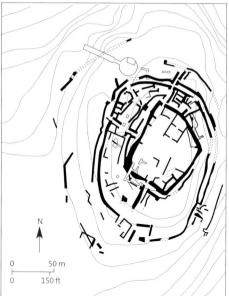

(Right) A middle Neolithic figurine of mother and child from Sesklo, 4800–4400 BC.

(Centre) A late Neolithic vase (4000–3000 BC), with characteristic brown glaze and curvilinear design, from Dimini.

(Below right) Spherical late Neolithic (4000–3000 BC) vase from Lianokladi.

(Opposite) A middle Neolithic cup from Tsani Magoula, Thessaly (5000–4000 BC), with characteristic geometric decoration on a light background.

View (above) and plan (right) of the late Neolithic settlement at Dimini (4000–3000 BC), this was originally enclosed by several fortified circuits and there was a large central building at the top of the site.

PROMETHEUS AND THE ORIGINS OF CIVILIZATION

The Greeks had their own legends concerning their earliest origins: Prometheus, famed for giving mankind fire, was also credited with teaching humans most of the elements of civilization, which he himself had learned from Athena.

First of all, though they had eyes to see they saw nothing useful; they had ears, and couldn't hear; everything they did was confused, like shapeless dreams. They had no knowledge of houses built of bricks and turned towards the sun, nor how to work in wood, but lived underground, like swarming ants in sunless caves. They had no sign of winter or flowery spring or fruitful summer upon which they could depend, until I taught them to note the risings and settings of the stars. Yes, and numbers, the basis of science, I invented for them, and the combining of letters, mother of the Muses' arts,

with which to hold all things in memory. I first brought brute beasts under the yoke to be subject to the collar and pack-saddle, that they might bear in man's place the heaviest burdens. I harnessed horses to the chariot and made them obedient to the rein, as an adornment of wealth and luxury. I and no one else contrived the mariner's flaxen-winged vessel to roam the seas.

Such are the inventions I devised for mankind, poor wretch, yet I have no cunning to rid me of my present suffering....

Hear the rest and you will wonder more at the arts and resources I devised. First and foremost, if ever a man fell ill, there was no defence – no healing food, no ointment, no potion, they wasted away for lack of medicine, until I showed them how to mix soothing remedies by which they now ward off all disorders....

Now as to the benefits to men that lie concealed beneath the earth – bronze, iron, silver and gold – who could claim to have discovered them before me? No one, I'm sure, unless he were a mindless babbler. To sum up briefly, every art possessed by man comes from Prometheus.

Aeschylus, *Prometheus Bound*
447–505

Laconian cup of the sixth century BC, showing Zeus' punishment of the brothers Atlas and Prometheus. Atlas was condemned to hold the heavens on his shoulders, while a bound Prometheus had an eagle or vulture feed daily on his liver, until his rescue by Herakles.

in the years around 6000 BC. Not long after, we also find Neolithic people making durable pots of baked clay.

Neolithic settlements are known from all over Greece, but the rich broad plain of Thessaly has produced the greatest number of sites. Two of the largest settlements, at Sesklo and Dimini, were excavated early in the twentieth century by the Greek archaeologist Christos Tsountas.

Sesklo is the earlier, dating to 5000–4000 BC, with a cluster of one- and two-room houses protected by a winding fortification wall. A larger 'house' right at the summit of the hill might hint at the social structure of the community, depending on whether it is interpreted as the chief's house, a communal lodge or a temple. Lovely pottery, decorated with flame-red patterns, was manufactured, as were numerous clay figurines, often of corpulent females.

Dimini, which lies only a few kilometres to the east, flourished in the late Neolithic period (4000–3000 BC). The low hilltop is surrounded by a series of concentric walls, again with a single large 'house' at the top. Other houses are set between the walls or lower on the slope. Literally dozens of other small sites all over Greece have yielded further information on life in Neolithic times.

THE EARLY BRONZE AGE

An early Cycladic 'frying pan' (3000–2000 BC): the incised decoration with spirals is typical, and such designs often include boats, appropriate for a seafaring island people. The function of these pots remains a puzzle.

Early Cycladic vessel with incised herring-bone decoration, from Antiparos (3000–2000 BC).

MAJOR CHANGES took place in the years around 3000 BC, among them the introduction of bronze. Other cultural innovations in the archaeological record suggest that this new technology was accompanied by new people coming into Greece. Most striking, perhaps, is a change in burial customs, from individual graves to tombs which held multiple burials, presumably the members of a single family or clan. New pottery forms also make an appearance at this time and many of the Neolithic shapes and designs disappear. Houses are larger, often with several rooms and corridors. Settlements are protected by far more substantial and sophisticated fortification walls, with projecting towers. These changes are apparent across the Aegean, at excavated sites such as Lerna, Aegina, Poliochni, Chalandriani, Troy and Klazomenai.

The islands of the Aegean produced a particularly elegant and recognizable 'Cycladic' culture during the early Bronze Age (3000–2000 BC), named after the central group of islands, the Cyclades. In addition to the characteristic architecture and burial customs of early Bronze Age Greece, Cycladic culture is recognized by its pottery and marble vessels and figurines. The islands of Naxos and Paros have large quarries of fine white marble and this was used to make vessels and a large number of human figurines. They generally take the form of female figures, several of them pregnant, with the anatomy and facial features minimally rendered – an abstraction which makes them appear curiously modern. Traces of painted decoration have been detected on many examples. Their function is not well understood, though they are usually recovered from graves and they cannot stand up on their own. A few more complex examples depict male musicians, either standing playing a flute or seated with a lyre. Evidence of this culture is found on most of the islands of the Aegean and along the adjacent coasts of the mainland.

On the large southern island of Crete in this period the inhabitants were apparently in contact with more advanced civilizations in the region, and the art of making vessels in hard stones (granite and basalt) was imported from Egypt.

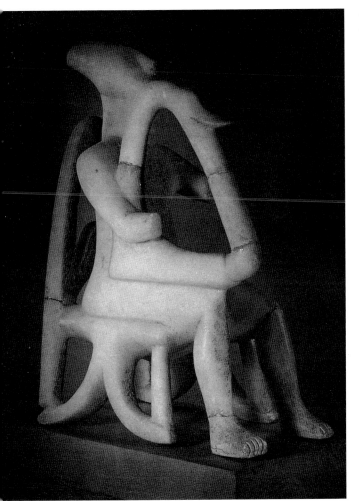

An early Cycladic marble lyre-player from Keros, c. 2500 BC. Figures such as this, and the standing example (right) are usually found in graves, though their precise function is uncertain.

(Below) A typical Cycladic marble figurine of a naked female, with arms held across the body and pointed toes. Late Spedos type, 2600–2400 BC.

The islands of Naxos and Paros are sources of excellent white marble, and Naxos also has deposits of emery, a useful abrasive. Skilled marble-working, as seen in these two vessels, is a feature of early Cycladic culture.

THERA

The island of Thera, or Santorini, some 112 km (70 miles) north of Crete, is still an active volcano. In the 1960s excavations began at the southern end of the island, at a place called Akrotiri, where there are the remarkably well-preserved remains of a prehistoric town, buried under a deep layer of soft pumice and ash. The date of the volcanic eruption which covered this town is still a matter of some controversy. Archaeologists, using traditional methods of pottery chronology, originally dated the eruption to around 1450 BC. More recently, a variety of scientific methods as well as the excavation of layers of pumice at stratified sites on the north shore of Crete seem to indicate that the eruption took place as early as 1625 BC. The devastation was apparently preceded by warning tremors, since few luxury goods and no bodies were found – the inhabitants had time to flee, unlike the many unfortunate victims at Pompeii, caught in the unexpected eruption of Vesuvius in AD 79.

The houses at Akrotiri stand two and three storeys high, their walls decorated with bright and lively painted frescoes depicting a variety of scenes: antelopes, young boys boxing, blue monkeys, fishermen with their catch, women collecting saffron, swallows in a landscape, and miniature scenes showing a river lined with palms and papyrus, a naval procession of many ships from one city to another, and a scene of shipwreck and armed warriors. The interpretation of these pictures with no text has engaged the imagination of several scholars: are they historical, who is depicted and where are they taking place? Of interest in the military

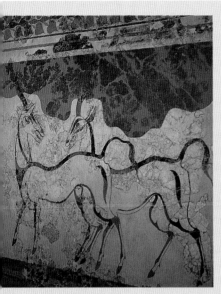

scenes are depictions of soldiers carrying ox-hide shields and warriors wearing boars'-tusk helmets. Actual helmets of this type are a fairly common find in the Mycenaean world, but are very rare in the Cyclades or on Minoan Crete, perhaps suggesting we are looking at

scenes recording a Mycenaean invasion in the Aegean.

The excavations and restoration work, begun under Spyridon Marinatos for the Archaeological Society of Athens, are continuing today under the direction of Christos Doumas.

(Above left) A frescoed room at Akrotiri, with antelopes and youthful boxers; the red skin of the boys is a convention borrowed from Egyptian painting, while the subject matter and naturalistic style are original to the Aegean.

(Above) View of the ruins at Akrotiri. Doors and windows were originally wood-framed and the large storage jars were common. (Below) Frescoes from Akrotiri: opposite, a scene of military action on both land and sea; note the large ox-hide shields and plumed helmets; below, an expedition at sea.

THE ARRIVAL OF THE GREEKS

(Right) A typical cist grave of the Middle Helladic period (2000–1600 BC on the mainland), used for individual burials, often within the settlement itself.

(Below) Three figurines from Minoan Crete. The faience figure of a woman in characteristic costume of flounced skirt and bared breasts (left) is interpreted as a goddess because she holds two snakes and has a feline on her headdress; she was found in the Temple Repositories at Knossos. A clay figurine of a woman with upraised arms (centre) is from a mountain peak sanctuary at Petsophas; and the bronze figurine of a male worshipper (right), with his arms held in ritual gesture, is from Tylissos, 1500 BC.

SIGNIFICANT CHANGES in the archaeological record strongly suggest that a new society established itself in Greece in the years around 2000 BC, the beginning of what is known as the Middle Bronze Age (2000–1600 BC). Many basic aspects of Early Bronze Age culture change radically: architecture, burial customs, pottery and apparently also language. In addition, the domesticated horse makes its first appearance in Greece at about this time. In architecture, the rectilinear house with straight walls gives way to oval houses or houses with a curved or apsidal end. The change, visible at floor level, suggests a different roofing system and perhaps the newcomers were used to another climate or other building materials. The large multiple graves of Early Bronze Age times are replaced by individual burials in small cist graves, often dug within the settlement rather than confined to cemeteries outside the village, as had been the practice before. The introduction at this time of the fast wheel for making pottery resulted in a wide variety of new shapes, while several of the old asymmetrical handmade forms go out of use.

Four of these new arrivals (houses, graves, pottery and horse) leave clear archaeological traces which have been recovered at many sites. Somewhat more complex is the evidence for the introduction of the Greek language at this same time. Here,

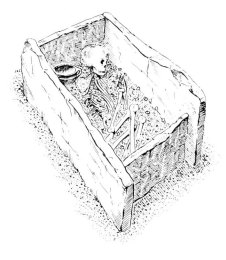

we have to work backwards from the earliest moment we know Greek was in use until we reach the previous major cultural break, when new people arrived, presumably bringing with them their new language.

Greek was certainly being used in Greece around 1250 BC, the date of hundreds of clay tablets written in Greek found at Knossos, Mycenae, Pylos and Thebes (see p. 44). Searching back from then, the first major change in the culture is the one we have just been considering, dating to around 2000 BC.

We do not know the language the Early Bronze Age people spoke, from 3000 to 2000 BC, though several words survived and were adopted by the Greeks. Linguistically speaking, words ending in -ssos, -ttos, and -inthos are not Greek, but are loan words, presumably taken from this earlier language. Significantly, they survive primarily as toponyms such as the names of rivers (Kephissos), mountains (Parnassos, Hymettos) and places (Corinthos, Knossos). The same phenomenon can be seen in North America, where many place names were borrowed from the native population by the European colonists (Massachusetts, Susquehanna river, Chesapeake bay, etc.). It is tantalizing to note that even the word used by the Greeks for the sea, *thalassa* (θάλασσα), is one of these pre-Greek words, perhaps suggesting that the Greek-speakers arrived in 2000 BC by land rather than sea, and therefore presumably from the north.

Middle Bronze Age settlements have been excavated all over the mainland and show that the culture was homogeneous and widespread.

The grey, sharply angled pottery, called Minyan ware by Schliemann in honour of a legendary King Minyas, is a particularly recognizable feature of this society.

Crete and the Cyclades

Compared to the mainland, which shows no particular signs of wealth or foreign contact, Crete and the islands of the Aegean – as in the Early Bronze Age – seem more advanced, wealthy and refined. The regional diversity recognizable between the three areas has led archaeologists to divide the culture along geo-graphical lines, so the Bronze Age on the mainland is known as Helladic, on Crete as Minoan (also named after a legendary king, Minos), and on the islands as Cycladic

On Crete the Middle Bronze Age saw the construction a large palace at the site of Knossos (see pp. 50–51). The pottery, known as Kamares ware, is decorated with light designs, often of marine or floral motifs, on a dark background. Signs of formal cult activity can also be recognized at this time. The people living on Crete worshipped particularly high up on mountain peaks and in caves. Both male and female statuettes have been found, in clay, bronze and ivory. There is no particular reason to suppose that this sophisticated culture was related to the Greek-speakers on the mainland, and indeed the earliest clay tablets from Crete are written in an undeciphered script (Linear A) which seems to record an unknown language, certainly not Greek.

Excavations on the islands of Kea, Melos and Thera have shown that there were close contacts between the Minoans of Crete and the Cycladic culture of the islands, not surprising since both groups were sea-faring islanders. Differences in pottery and other finds allow the two cultures to be distinguished, however. One of the most spectacular excavations in the islands has been at Akrotiri on the island of Thera, also known as Santorini (pp. 32–33).

A clay tablet from Aghia Triadha, Crete, inscribed with Linear A. The language of these inscriptions is unknown, but was not Greek.

KING MINOS OF CRETE

Minos is the earliest of all those known to us by tradition who acquired a navy. He made himself master of a very great part of what is now called the Hellenic Sea, and became lord of the Cyclades Islands and first colonizer of most of them, driving out the Carians and establishing his own sons in them as governors. Piracy, too, he naturally tried to clear from the sea, as far as he could, desiring that his revenues should come to him more readily.

Thucydides, 1. 4

The regional variation in Aegean pottery of the Middle Bronze Age (2000–1600 BC) is clearly visible in these three examples: (top left) Helladic (= mainland) matt-painted ware from Eutresis; (below left) Minoan (= Crete) Kamares ware from Knossos; and (below right) a Cycladic (= island) ewer in the shape of bird.

III

THE
HEROIC AGE

And even as goatherds separate easily the wide-scattered flocks of goats when they mingle in the pasture, so did their leaders marshall them on this side and on that to enter into the battle, and among them lord Agamemnon, his eyes and head like Zeus who hurls thunderbolts, his waist like Ares, and his breast like Poseidon. As a bull in the herd stands forth over all, in that he is pre-eminent among the gathered cattle, even so did Zeus make Agamemnon on that day, pre-eminent among many and chief among the warriors.

Homer, *Iliad* 2, 474–83

BY 1600 BC, GREEK CULTURE on the mainland had advanced considerably, and the differences have led archaeologists – always fond of tripartite divisions – to refer to the succeeding centuries as the Late Bronze Age. The Late Bronze Age culture on the mainland is also often known as the Mycenaean period: the site of Mycenae was one of the first of this era to be excavated (by Heinrich Schliemann in the 1870s), Mycenae has also been shown to have been one of the richest centres at this time, and in the *Iliad* Mycenae was the home of Agamemnon, most powerful of the kings and leaders of the Greeks who went to war against Troy.

The Mycenaean era sits on the cusp between myth and history. By reckoning backwards in terms of generations, the Classical Greeks assigned most of their mythology to this period, the fourteenth and thirteenth centuries BC: the Trojan War, the voyage of the Argonauts, the Oedipus cycle and the Labours of Herakles, to list just a few. Archaeology has confirmed these traditions in a general way – this was certainly a time of large palaces and great wealth, controlled by a warrior society with widespread contacts throughout the Mediterranean. We are close to real history in this period and for the first time we have documents written in Greek.

The Lion Gate at Mycenae: several Mycenaean sites have been excavated which provide a picture of rich palaces protected by massive fortification walls.

THE MYCENAEAN PALACE

SEVERAL PALACES of the Mycenaean age have been excavated – at Mycenae, Tiryns, Pylos and Gla, and parts of that at Thebes. They share certain characteristics in their plan and construction. At their core was a courtyard, open to the sky. From here one passed through a colonnaded porch into a wide vestibule, which in turn gave access to the throne room. This was a large, square room with a low, round hearth taking up most of the centre. The throne would have been on the right wall as one entered. Four columns around the hearth supported an upper gallery around the sides of the room. This whole arrangement is known as a megaron or great hall. On the walls were brightly coloured frescoes depicting mythical creatures, such as griffins, and musicians and scenes of hunting and battle. The plastered floor was also painted with abstract designs and – in the case of Pylos – an octopus. Around this central core were numerous storerooms containing huge quantities of pottery and large stores of olive oil in enormous terracotta jars.

Also nearby or on an upper level were living quarters, provided with facilities for bathing. Excavation of the various palace sites has pro-

The Palace of Nestor at Pylos, looking south. The throne room, with its low, round central hearth is in the centre. Oil jars, set into a bench, are visible in the foreground; it dates from around 1300–1200 BC.

duced furniture inlaid with ivory, gold and silver vessels, jewels of lapis lazuli, pottery with lively painted designs, and carved signet rings in gold or semiprecious stones, creating a picture of luxury and wealth.

These palaces were protected from attack by massive fortifications built of huge unworked boulders. The Classical Greeks, looking at their remains, could only conclude that they were built not by mortals but by the giants known as Cyclopes; this style of wall-building is known accordingly as 'Cyclopean'. The walls were 4.5–6 m (15–20 ft) thick and rose some 6.5–9 m (20–30 ft) in height, remarkable feats of engineering considering the available technology.

Parts of the circuit wall are still left, including the gate, which is surmounted by lions. These also are said to be the work of the Cyclopes, who made the walls of Tiryns for Proetus. Among the ruins of Mycenae is a water channel called Persea, and there are underground buildings of Atreus and his children, where their treasures were kept.

Pausanias, 2. 16. 4/5

Artist's reconstruction of the throne room at Pylos: the central hearth, columns and painted decoration of floor and walls are all certain.

Plan of the palace at Pylos, with the central throne room, or megaron, surrounded by corridors and storerooms. One small storeroom had 2,853 drinking cups.

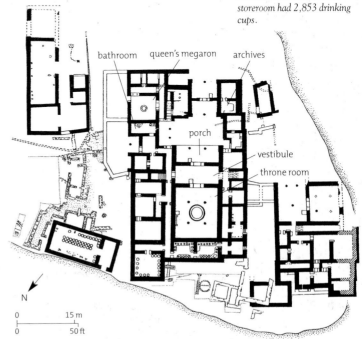

bathroom queen's megaron archives

porch

vestibule

throne room

N

0   15 m
0   50 ft

A part of Grave Circle A (above) at Mycenae, dating to 1600–1500 BC, where Heinrich Schliemann excavated graves containing possibly royal burials with many rich objects, including those seen here: a gold death mask, a bull's-head vessel in silver and gold and a bronze dagger inlaid with a hunting scene.

Tombs and burials

The Mycenaean period is characterized by a shift back to multiple burials and several types of tombs were in use. Common folk were buried with pottery, jewelry, weapons and other grave goods in simple chamber tombs hacked out of bedrock. Royal or aristocratic graves were more elaborate. Early on (1600–1500 BC), the burials were made in deep shafts sunk into the ground and lined with stones. The individual graves were often marked by a stele carved in relief, usually showing a scene of hunting or battle (p. 45). These graves were eventually defined or set off by a low circuit wall; two such 'grave circles' of shaft graves were found at Mycenae, one (A) in the 1870s by Heinrich Schliemann, and the other (B) in the 1950s by John Papademetriou. Unplundered, they contained some of the richest finds ever recovered from the Mycenaean world: gold, silver, ivory, semiprecious stones and bronze, all elaborately worked into death

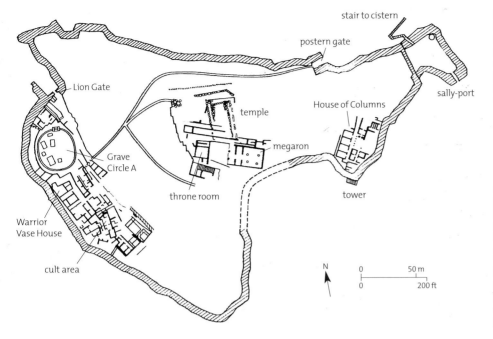

(Left) Plan of the citadel at Mycenae, with the Lion Gate and Grave Circle A at left and the palace complex in the centre. A later extension of the fortification wall and the staircase to a secret water supply (p. 56) are at the extreme right.

(Below left) This Mycenaean piriform (pear-shaped) three-handled jar was manufactured as an export vessel. More jars of this type have been found on Rhodes and in Italy than on the mainland. The naturalistic octopus is borrowed from Minoan prototypes; the drawings (below) chart the increased abstraction of this sea creature by Mycenaean pottery painters over time.

masks, inlaid daggers, swords, furniture and vessels with relief decoration.

These shaft graves were superseded in the fifteenth century BC by more impressive structures known as tholos tombs (plural: tholoi), large round chambers, usually set into a hillside and shaped like bee-hives (pp. 42–43). They were lined with stones, each course slightly overlapping the one below until they met at the top, a system known as corbelling. The largest examples, at Mycenae and Orchomenos, are as much as 14.5 m (47½ ft) across and 13.2 m (43 ft) high, using huge stones, comparable in size to those found in the fortification walls. They required considerable engineering skill and investment of labour, though because they were usually covered by a huge, conspicuous tumulus or mound of earth they were almost invariably plundered in antiquity. Over 150 such tombs have been found throughout southern Greece and as far north as Aetolia and Thessaly. One is also known from Kolophon in Asia Minor.

Arts and crafts

Mycenaean pottery is readily recognizable: well-fired in a wide variety of closed and open shapes and decorated with reddish-brown glaze on a light background. At first (c. 1500 BC), the decorative schemes were borrowed from Minoan Crete; especially popular was the 'Marine style', which favoured scenes of octopods, argonauts, seaweed and other seascapes painted in a

naturalistic style. Mycenaean artists preferred abstraction to realism, however, and over time the subjects become less and less realistic, their use determined by custom but their rendering increasingly decorative, with little attention to detail. A repertoire of distinctive shapes decorated with these stylized designs is found throughout the mainland, and Mycenaean pottery is therefore easily identifiable when found in Italy, Asia Minor, Egypt and the Near East.

The dromos (entrance passage) to a tholos tomb at Mycenae known as the Tomb of Clytemnestra (the unfaithful wife and murderess of Agamemnon, herself killed by her son Orestes). Nine such tholos tombs are known from Mycenae.

Religion and society

Mycenaean religion is imperfectly understood, seen through the representations of deities, a few excavated shrines and references in the Linear B tablets. The tablets refer to several of the well-known 'Olympian' gods of historical times – Poseidon, Zeus, Hera and Hermes – but their cult centres are not the large free-standing temples of later times. Indeed, they are not necessarily allotted a prominent place within the core of the palace. At Mycenae, a set of rooms lower down the hill below the palace was provided with altars for sacrifices and a bench on which had been placed numerous terracotta statues. Similar clusters of large figurines (c. 0.6–1m/2–3 ft high) have been

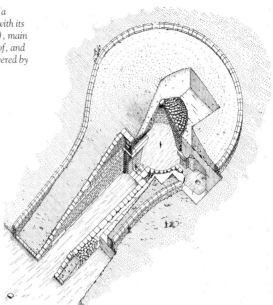

(Right) Cut-away view of a Mycenaean tholos tomb, with its dromos (entrance passage), main chamber with corbelled roof, and small side chamber, all covered by a large tumulus of earth.

They are prominent also in engraved gold rings and carved gemstones and as figurines, usually shown bare-breasted and wearing elaborately flounced skirts (pp. 34 and 48).

The Linear B tablets give some idea of the social structure of Mycenaean society. Numerous officials are named, the highest being the *wanax*, or king. Archaeological evidence, too, suggests a stratified society, with palaces, large sumptuous villas, and small, crowded houses all

Fresco of a Mycenaean lady, or goddess, thirteenth century BC, from Mycenae. Her elaborate clothing, coiffure and jewelry suggest a high position for women within Mycenaean society and/or religion.

found also at Tiryns and on the island of Kea. Tiny terracotta figurines, often with arms upraised, are ubiquitous in the Mycenaean world, but their find-spots in graves and elsewhere mean that they cannot be assigned a universal cult function. Female deities and priestesses figure prominently in cult scenes in the Thera frescoes, as well as in Minoan Crete.

THE DECIPHERMENT OF LINEAR B

When Sir Arthur Evans excavated the great palace at Knossos on Crete he discovered two related but distinct types of early writing, now known as Linear A and Linear B. They were preserved largely on clay tablets covered with symbols incised with a sharp, pointed implement. The tablets, written when the clay was just partially air-dried, survive largely because they were baked hard during the fire which destroyed the palace. Similar tablets inscribed with Linear B script were also found at other palace sites on the mainland, at Thebes and Mycenae, and later at Pylos.

Analysis of the texts allowed certain conclusions to be reached even before Linear B was actually deciphered. That they were largely archival was immediately apparent from the layout and repeated use of a clear numbering system. Pictograms also helped identify what was being recorded: women, animals (pigs, sheep etc.), chariots, vessels of different shapes. The number of symbols (87) was more than required for an alphabet, too few for hieroglyphics, and most suitable for a syllabary.

Charting the frequency of symbols suggested which stood for pure vowels and which for consonants. An initial A, for instance, would be a single symbol appearing frequently, whereas a consonant (such as T) would require five symbols, one for each associated vowel (TA, TI, TO, TE and TU). Intelligent guesses about inflections, declensions, plurals and genders allowed certain symbols to be associated with the same vowel or consonant as

other symbols, and a whole chart of related symbols (which shared either a vowel or a consonant) was drawn up before a word could be read.

Much of this work was done by an enthusiastic and determined young architect, Michael Ventris, along with several other scholars such as Alice Kober, Emmett Bennett and John Chadwick. Ventris had been determined to crack the code ever since he was fourteen, when he heard Evans lecturing on Minoan scripts. Knowing that seven of the symbols were similar to those found in an early script on Cyprus, Ventris assumed the phonetic values (sounds) of the symbols were the same, and tried some out on what were thought might be place-names. The names began to sound like the Greek for known Cretan places (am-i-ni-so = Amnisos) and it became clear to him that Linear B was an early, cumbersome form of writing Greek.

The proof was not long in coming. Soon after his announcement in 1952, more tablets were found at the palace at Pylos. One contained a pictogram of a three-legged vessel or tripod; when Ventris' phonetic values were inserted into the adjacent word it read: ti-ri-po-(de).

Once deciphered, it became clear that the script was used to keep the palace records, which are very complex. There are no historical texts, no literature, no letters, just archives. Preserved are accounts of slave women, flocks of sheep, pigs and goats, lists of bronze vessels, and records of perfumed oil. Also mentioned are several well-known deities, indicating that most if not all of the Olympian gods were worshipped in Greece at this early date.

Tragically, at the age of 30, Ventris was killed in a car crash soon after his great achievement. As the result of his work we now recognize Linear B as the means of writing the Greek language in the Mycenaean world. It was adapted from many of the symbols used in the earlier script used in Minoan Crete, Linear A (p. 35), which thus far remains undeciphered.

	man
	horse
	tripod
	amphora
	spear
	chariot
	woman
	pig
	cup
	sword
	arrow
	wheel

Three examples of clay tablets inscribed with Linear B texts, divided up by ruled lines. The regular placement of horizontal and vertical lines show that something is being counted and recorded.

(Above) Some of the pictograms which often accompany the entries listed and spelled out in the texts.

Examples of texts recorded on Linear B tablets:

Two chariots inlaid with ivory, assembled, painted crimson, equipped with reins, leather cheek-strips (?), (and) horn bits (?).
Knossos: KN sd 0401

One footstool inlaid with a man and a horse and an octopus and a griffin (or palm tree) in ivory.
Pylos: PY Ta 722

Kerowos the shepherd at Asiatia watching over the cattle of Thalamatas.
Pylos: PY Ae 134

making up a large settlement. The economy reflected in the records has been the subject of intense study, particularly for the palaces of Pylos and Knossos.

An elaborate system of distribution and communication operated between the palace and the outlying districts of the countryside. It would seem as though the palace kept a tight control on raw materials and the manufacture of finished products. Detailed records were kept of large numbers of slaves, mostly women weavers and spinners, cloth and clothing, and animals (thousands of sheep in some cases), as well as the distribution of bronze, the management of land, the regulation of the production of perfumed oils, and gifts to the gods.

A warrior society

All the evidence suggests that the Mycenaeans were a warrior society. Their tombs are full of bronze daggers, swords and spear points as well as armour; the frescoes show scenes of warfare and the hunt, while pottery and small objects depict well-armed men. One full set of armour has been recovered from a tomb in the Argolid; it was made of large overlapping sheets of bronze which make it both uncomfortable and cumbersome (p. 114). Other pieces are known from Thebes, and a cuirass is shown on the Linear B tablets. Early Mycenaean helmets were fashioned by sewing rows of boars' tusks on to a leather cap; several examples have been found in tombs and they are shown in pottery and miniature ivories. Shields in the form of a figure-of-eight were made of cowhides stretched over a wooden frame. Scenes carved on grave stelai suggest that hunting and perhaps warfare was carried out from chariots, often with one man driving, another fighting.

In addition to those excavated thus far, traditions indicate that there were several other great palace centres, but differing circumstances have not permitted the full clearing of Thebes, Orchomenos, Iolkos, Athens, Sparta or Ithaka.

(Above) Ivory plaque from Delos showing a Mycenaean warrior wearing a boar's-tusk helmet and carrying a figure-of-eight shield.

(Left) Stele from Grave Circle A at Mycenae (c. 1600–1500 BC), showing a war chariot in use, driven by a single warrior, with a man holding a sword standing next to it.

Detail of the Warrior Vase from Mycenae (c. 1200–1150 BC); compare the crested helmets and small shields with the armour shown on the earlier ivory plaque from Delos (above).

THE MYCENAEAN WORLD

Vessel made of an ostrich egg, indicating some form of extended trade with east Africa in the years around 1650 to 1300 BC. This one is from Thera; others have been found in the shaft graves at Mycenae and on the Uluburun shipwreck.

(Above) A Mycenaean sherd from a three-handled piriform jar from Scoglio del Tonno, c. 1325 BC.

(Near right) A late Mycenaean krater (mixing bowl) from Ephesus in Asia Minor, c. 1300 BC.

(Centre) Wall painting from the tomb in Egypt of Rekhmire, vizier of pharaoh Tuthmosis III of the 18th dynasty, c. 1475–1425 BC. The two young men are from the land of Keftiu; they are bringing an ox-hide-shaped ingot of copper, a conical rhyton, a gold repoussé worked bowl and a dagger in a sheath. These are Aegean Bronze Age objects and the bearers wear embroidered kilts and boots typical of Crete (see p. 14).

As with the later Greeks, the Mycenaeans were an adventurous, seafaring people, not content to leave the Mediterranean unexplored. Foreign goods made their way into the Mycenaean palaces from Europe, Asia and Africa. The nearest source of lapis lazuli, for instance, is in modern Afghanistan, amber was brought from the Baltic Sea and ostrich eggs came from east Africa. It is, of course, not always easy to say who brought the material, nor whether the trade reflected was direct or the goods were passed from hand to hand. Bronze, and especially tin, will have had to have been imported as well. What was given in return has not survived, though Greece has always produced great quantities of olive oil, and the Pylos and Knossos tablets record large numbers of sheep and indicate that numerous women were employed as weavers. Many Greeks in later times made their living as mercenaries, and this too may have played a role in the Mycenaean economy. Some of our best evidence for trade in this period comes from a shipwreck found at Uluburun, off the south coast of Turkey: a ship probably heading westwards towards Greece and carrying vast amounts of precious material sank in the years around 1300 BC.

Mycenaean presence in the east is reflected in pottery of various shapes found at several sites in Asia Minor: Troy, Ephesus, Miletus, Kolophon and Panaztepe, north of Smyrna. At Ephesus, Kolophon and Panaztepe the pottery was found in tombs. The pottery found at Miletus and Ephesus is indistinguishable from mainland pottery, even to the experienced eye, and analysis of the clay is required to determine if the pottery is imported or a local imitation. Further east, in the Levant, Mycenaean pottery has been found at several sites. Especially prevalent are squat containers with narrow mouths which could be securely fastened (called alabastra), and this has suggested that the material carried was perfumed olive oil, which is one of the industries attested at Pylos in the Linear B tablets. And the story of the Argonauts' voyage to Colchis on the eastern shore of the Black Sea hints at a Mycenaean presence there, which thus far archaeology has not confirmed.

Egypt had been in contact with the 'Keftiu' of Minoan Crete for centuries, and the contacts were maintained in the Mycenaean world. Wall-paintings in Egyptian Thebes show tribute bearers carrying recognizably Mycenaean vessels and ox-hide ingots, and Egyptian goods are found at many Mycenaean sites. Small scarabs (easily transported, of course) have been found

in tholos tombs as far away as Aetolia, in north-west Greece, and on the Uluburun wreck.

The Mycenaeans looked west too, and Mycenaean pottery, though fragmentary, has been found in significant amounts at almost 100 coastal sites in Italy, Sicily, Sardinia and Spain. Scoglio del Tonno, near Taranto, and Thapsos, near Syracuse, have produced hundreds of Mycenaean sherds, along with chamber tombs and architecture, which indicate that Mycenaeans were resident there. Just how far Mycenaean influence may have travelled is hard to say, but metalwork found in Germany shows distinct Aegean characteristics.

A BRONZE AGE TREASURE SHIP

Underwater archaeology is logistically demanding and expensive, but the rewards are astounding. A ship which goes down with its cargo represents a time capsule, usually undisturbed by later activities that confuse or even destroy a site on land. In addition, though salt water and sea creatures create their own problems of conservation, many organic materials – such as wood – survive far better under water.

One of the most spectacular underwater finds in the Mediterranean was made in the 1980s and has been excavated by George Bass, Cemal Pulak and their team from the Institute of Nautical Archaeology. It is the wreck of a ship which went down off the rocky coast of southern Turkey and now lies on a steep slope at the dangerous depth of 43–52 m (140–170 ft). From the finds it seems clear that the ship was sailing westwards from Cyprus and the Middle East, carrying a rich and varied cargo of precious goods. There is much raw material: 10 tons of copper ingots from Cyprus, 1 ton of tin, hippopotamus tusks, ingots of blue glass and Canaanite jars full of terebinth resin. The finished goods are equally impressive: a gold scarab of Queen Nefertiti of Egypt, quartz and haematite cylinder seals from Assyria and Babylonia, Canaanite daggers of bronze with inlaid ivory handles, a gold chalice, a faience ram's-head drinking cup, a set of bronze and lead weights (a tiny cowherd with cows, a duck, a frog and a fly), an ivory trumpet and an ivory cosmetics kit in the form of a duck with movable wings for the cover. Perhaps most extraordinary of all was a wooden writing tablet consisting of two leaves joined with ivory hinges, each of the two 'pages' recessed to receive wax which would be inscribed.

(Above) A diver working on a pile of copper ingots on the Uluburun wreck; some 360 ingots, weighing 10 tons, went down with the ship around 1300 BC.

A gold scarab with the cartouche of Nefertiti, c. 1345 BC, queen of the 18th-dynasty pharaoh Akhenaten, found on the Uluburun wreck.

The Mycenaean and Cypriot pottery found on board suggests that the ship went down sometime around 1300 BC. The Mycenaean pottery perhaps indicates that the ship was from Greece, returning home loaded with treasures from the east, but this is not certain.

Much more study is needed before this extraordinary find is fully interpreted, as at least seven cultures are represented. But it is clear that the Uluburun wreck offers a unique picture of sophisticated luxury trade in the Bronze Age Aegean.

CRETE

(Below right) Gold signet ring showing three women before a goddess. Note the typical Minoan flounced skirts and bared breasts, as well as the lily plants and other landscape elements.

(Below) Stone vase from Kato Zakro, eastern Crete, apparently showing a peak shrine with wild goats on the roof. The spirals and 'horns of consecration' (below the bird) are common Minoan decorative elements.

CRETE IN THE LATE BRONZE AGE presents a very different picture from the mainland. Cretan palaces have been extensively excavated at Knossos, Phaistos, Mallia, Kato Zakro and partially at Chania and perhaps Archanes and Kommos. They are much larger than their mainland counterparts and, taking advantage of their island location, the palaces are unfortified, with many more rooms and much more space given over to storage. Administrative records were kept on clay tablets in the undeciphered script known as Linear A (p. 35).

Knossos has pride of place among Minoan palaces, both because it was the first to be excavated, by Sir Arthur Evans in the early 1900s, and because it is by far the largest. It is roughly square, measuring over 100 m (330 ft) on a side – larger than two football fields set side by side. There are well over a hundred rooms on the ground floor and much of the building consisted of several storeys. A central courtyard and a later throne room have been recognized, along with dozens of storage magazines, light-wells, corridors, stairways and bathrooms. The walls of many rooms were covered with wall-paintings showing processions

and scenes from nature, especially birds and plants. Natural scenes also decorated much of their pottery, while other vessels were made of stone, a craft apparently learned from the Egyptians, with whom – to judge from numerous finds – the Minoans seem to have had close contacts.

The huge size and complexity of the Minoan palaces perhaps gave rise to the myth of the labyrinth, a notion which seems borne out by the numerous double-axes carved all over the walls of the palaces: the pre-Greek word for such a double-axe is *labrys*. Bulls figure in a Minoan ritual which may also have contributed to the myth of the Minotaur encountered by Theseus in the labyrinth (p. 55). Numerous Minoan frescoes and carved gemstones show male and female acrobats vaulting nimbly over the back of a charging bull.

In recent years a Minoan-style fresco showing bull-leaping has been found at the site of Tell el-Dab'a in Egypt, further confirming the close connections between these two early

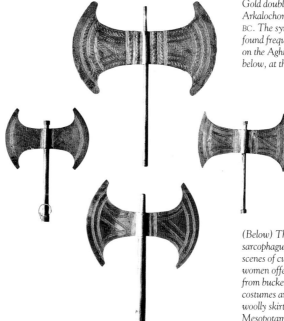

Gold double axes from the cave of Arkalochori on Crete, 1550–1450 BC. The symbol of the double axe is found frequently in Minoan art, as on the Aghia Triadha sarcophagus below, at the extreme left.

(Below) The Aghia Triadha sarcophagus, c. 1450 BC, with scenes of cult activity: men and women offer calves, a boat, liquid from buckets and music. The costumes are unusual, resembling woolly skirts and cloaks seen in Mesopotamian seals and figurines.

A part of the Palace of Minos at Knossos, excavated and partially restored by Sir Arthur Evans early in the twentieth century. The fresco behind the portico shows a charging bull. The columns, with their characteristic Minoan reverse taper, were originally of wood.

(Opposite) Hypothetical reconstruction of the palace at Knossos, seen from the southwest.

KNOSSOS AND MINOS

One of the great islands of the world in midsea, in the winedark sea, is Crete: spacious and rich and populous, with ninety cities and a mingling of tongues. Achaians there are found, along with Cretan hillmen of the old stock, and Kydonians, Dorians in three blood-lines, Pelasgians – and one among their ninety towns is Knossos. Here lived King Minos…

Homer, Odyssey 19, 202–12

Scenes of bull-leaping: a bronze figurine from Crete (c. 1600–1500 BC); drawing from an early Hittite vase from Hüseyindede in central Anatolia (c. 1700–1550 BC); bull-leapers in a Minoan-style fresco at Tell el-Dab'a, Egypt, the arrangement of the overall scene is restored and conjectural, though not the individual figures (c. 1750–1600 BC); and (opposite, below) clay burial larnax from Tanagra, near Thebes (c. 1400–1350 BC).

civilizations. A remnant of the ritual may survive today in the Portuguese version of bull-fighting or bull-baiting, in which unarmed men wrestle a charging bull to a halt.

Though by Classical times it was thought that Zeus had been born on Crete, in matters of both language and religion it would seem that the Minoans were not Greek, despite their considerable influence on the mainland Mycenaean Greeks. This influence is discernible especially in the pottery and art of the palaces, where Minoan marine themes were first copied and then adapted to Mycenaean tastes (p. 41).

Some time around 1450 BC all the Minoan palaces were destroyed, burned and abandoned. The agent of destruction is not always clear, and foreign invasion or some natural disaster such as an earthquake, volcanic ash or a massive tidal wave have all been proposed. Knossos is the only one that was rebuilt, and in this final phase it shows a strong Mycenaean flavour.

HISTORY OR MYTH?

A bust of Homer, dating to the Roman period. Scholars do not agree where he was from, when he lived – or whether he or the Trojan War actually existed; but everyone agrees that he was blind.

THE LATE BRONZE AGE was the chronological setting for most of the stories preserved in Greek mythology. The Classical Greeks believed these legends and regarded them as part of their history; modern scholars have been less willing to accept their veracity. Though some accept at least a 'kernel' of historical truth in Greek mythology, the present trend is to minimize the size of the kernel and its fruitfulness in helping to interpret the past. This despite the fact that archaeology has provided numerous instances where myth and historical reality seem to coincide. Greek myths are wonderfully varied, though many of the most enduring fall into one of three categories: warfare and sieges, quests, and labours.

Warfare and Sieges: Troy and Thebes

The Classical Greeks dated the Trojan War and the events associated with the *Iliad* to the period of the fall of the Mycenaean citadels, around 1200 BC. This story, set during the 10-year siege of Troy, is one of the masterpieces of western literature, its telling attributed to a man called Homer.

In the early nineteenth century there were few people who believed that the story had any basis in fact at all. The discovery of a Bronze Age citadel by Frank Calvert and its excavation by Heinrich Schliemann, however, changed attitudes considerably. Hisarlik, known as Ilion

A reconstruction of Bronze Age Troy, with the early megaron (palace?) on top protected by the Troy II inner wall (c. 2500 BC). The houses between the inner circuit and the outer wall are mostly from Troy VI (1900–1300 BC), as is the outer wall.

in historical times, was believed by the ancients to have been the site of Troy, and the mound, strategically placed at the entrance to the Dardanelles, has certainly produced an appropriately impressive sequence of Bronze Age habitation levels, rich finds and monumental architecture.

Schliemann claimed to have found Priam's city and equated his various finds to the story told by Homer. Subsequent excavations and research have modified many of his claims, and which of the several superimposed cities on the site might be that traditionally destroyed by Agamemnon and his followers is anything but clear. The fact, however, that there was a Bronze Age city at the site, that it was destroyed violently (several times), and that there was

The fortification walls of Troy VI (1900–1300 BC). The use of relatively small blocks, the towers and the sloping face with slight offsets are all unusual features, without parallels in the Aegean or western Anatolia.

52

A BOAR'S-TUSK HELMET
And Meriones gave to Odysseus a bow and a quiver and a sword, and about his head he set a helmet made of hide, stiff within with many tight-stretched thongs, while outside the white teeth of a boar of gleaming tusks were set thick on this side and that, well and cunningly, and within was fixed a lining of felt. This cap Autolycus once stole out of Eleon when he had broken into the well-built house of Amyntor, son of Ormenos; and he gave it to Amphidamas of Cythera to take to Scandeia, and Amphidamas gave it to Molus as a guest-gift, and he gave it to his own son Meriones to wear; and now, being set thereon, it covered the head of Odysseus.

Homer, *Iliad* 10. 260–71

Greek pottery among the ruins all serve to bring the myth a little closer to history.

Homeric scholarship during the twentieth century has also muddied the waters. It has now been shown to most people's satisfaction that the *Iliad* and the *Odyssey* as we have them represent the end of a long tradition of oral recitation, which allowed changes to be incorporated until the poems became crystallized at whatever time it was that they were committed to writing. As writing seems not to have been reintroduced to Greece until 750 BC or thereabouts, the events described in the epics took place around 500 years before the poems were written down.

Some people do not think the epics reached their final written form until *c.* 550 BC, which would make the gap between events and telling even longer, some 700 years. The question then becomes, how much do the epics reflect actual Bronze Age events and society of 1250–1200 BC, and how much do they represent later additions and emendations which crept into the oral performances during the Dark Ages?

There are anachronisms when we compare the epics to the archaeological record. Achilles has his fallen friend Patroklos cremated, whereas cremation seems not to have been introduced until after the fall of the palaces (see p. 154). Similarly, the mention of forging iron seems more appropriate to a somewhat later time. Anachronisms from earlier periods have also been recognized, suggesting to some that the events at Troy may be before 1250 or that

the oral tradition was already well developed when it was used for the *Iliad*. There is a fine description of a boars'-tusk helmet, but the dozen or so actual examples recovered in excavations thus far date to the fourteenth century BC, some 150 to 200 years earlier than 1250–1200 BC. It is worth noting, however, that the helmet described could well have been several generations old when Odysseus acquired it, so the supposed anachronism is not so severe as it first seems.

A pithos (large storage jar) from the island of Mykonos, 7th century BC. The relief decoration shows the Trojan Horse, one of the earliest artistic representations of the story of the fall of Troy. The episode is in the epic tradition, but not actually included in the Iliad.

Her father had been Ops, Peisenor's son, and she had been a purchase of Laertes when she was still a blossoming girl. He gave the price of twenty oxen for her, kept her as kindly in his house as his own wife, though, for the sake of peace, he never touched her.

Homer, *Odyssey* 1. 429–33

The present trend is to assume that much of the life portrayed in the epics refers to post-Bronze Age Greece. This seems perverse in view of the fact that the epics describe large palaces, well-built walls and considerable wealth. They describe a time when men fought in armour from chariots and when Mycenae was the premier citadel of Greece. They portray the Greeks as bold seafarers, cognizant of the western coast of Asia Minor. They refer to writing, which is preserved in the Linear B tablets and the writing boards from the Uluburun wreck. In broad terms, if not in every detail, the epics describe Greece as life was lived in the thirteenth century BC, rather than the insular, poor, illiterate subsistence society which characterized Greece for almost 500 years after the fall of the Mycenaean palaces. In the *Iliad* and the *Odyssey*, we are as close to history as to myth.

The other famous Bronze Age war epic which survives, though only in the later literary traditions, is the story of the Seven Against Thebes, a continuation of the story of Oedipus. This tells of seven warriors from Argos who set out to champion one of the sons of Oedipus when he had been expelled from Thebes by his brother. Each warrior attacked one of the seven gates of Thebes, and each was bested by his Theban counterpart. The associated myths of Amphiaraos and Antigone also derive from this conflict, which was repeated when Thebes was successfully besieged and fell to the next generation of Argive warriors.

Quests: Odysseus and Jason

Odysseus' attempt to return home after the Trojan War cost him another ten years of his life. As described in the *Odyssey*, he wandered the Mediterranean, encountering a bewildering array of unusual people and places. Numerous attempts have been made to pinpoint the specific geography of his travels, which seem to reflect Bronze Age exploration of the Mediterranean. In particular, the dangerous passage between Scylla and Charybdis is often identified as the straits of Messina, the narrow body of water which separates Sicily from the toe of Italy.

ODYSSEUS AND THE BLINDING OF THE CYCLOPS POLYPHEMOS

Odysseus describes how he and his companions blind the Cyclops Polyphemos and then escape from his cave where they had been held captive. The Cyclopes were one-eyed giants, and sons of Poseidon.

So he spoke again and I handed him the flaming wine. Thrice I brought and gave it to him and thrice he drained it in his folly....

He spoke, and, reeling, fell on his back and lay there with his thick neck bent, and all-conquering sleep laid hold of him. From his gullet came forth wine and bits of human flesh as he vomited in his drunken sleep. Then I thrust a stake into the deep ashes to grow hot, and encouraged all my comrades with cheering words so I might see no man flinch through fear. When the stake of olive-wood, green though it

was, was about to catch fire and began to glow terribly, then I came close, bringing the stake from the fire; and my comrades stood around me and a god breathed great courage into us. They took the stake of olive-wood, sharp at the point, and thrust it into his eye, while I, throwing my weight on it, whirled it round, as when a man bores a ship's timber with a drill, while those below keep it spinning with the thong which they hold by either end, and the drill runs around ceaselessly. Even so we took the fiery pointed stake and whirled it around in his eye and the blood flowed around the heated end. All his eyelids and nearby brow were singed by the flame as the eyeball burned and its roots crackled in the fire. As when a smith dips a great axe or adze into cold water amid loud hissing to temper it – for

therefrom comes the strength of iron – even so did his eye hiss around the stake of olive-wood. Terribly then did he cry aloud and the rock rang; and we, seized with terror, shrank back, while he wrenched from his eye the stake, all befouled with blood, and flung it from him, wildly waving his arms.

Homer, *Odyssey* 9. 360ff.

Detail of a large amphora from Eleusis, near Athens, showing the blinding of Polyphemos; c. 675 BC.

The other great voyage of mythical times was Jason's quest for the golden fleece in the *Argo*, together with a band of distinguished heroes. Here, the Black Sea is the large body of water being explored – Colchis (present-day Georgia) is on its eastern shore – as rich in reality as in myth. Attempts have been made to recreate the Argonauts' journey – the so-called 'clashing rocks', for instance, are usually taken to refer to the swift currents encountered where the Black Sea empties into the Bosporus. Though the myth is an old one, and possibly reflects very early Greek exploration of the Black Sea area, it survives only in later literary accounts and representations in art.

Labours: Herakles and Theseus

By far the most popular cycle of myths, both in literature and in art, were the feats of Herakles, the son of Zeus and a mortal woman. His birth was an affront to Zeus' consort Hera, and it was she who contrived to make Herakles' life particularly difficult. Herakles was a phenomenal strongman, pitting his strength and occasionally his wits against a wide range of monsters and beasts, his favourite weapon being a huge club. There were so many feats and such a confused chronology that by the Roman period the Greeks believed there were two different Herakles. Many of his feats were canonized in the Twelve Labours he was required to perform for King Eurystheus in expiation for a homicide (see p. 152). These are shown over and over again in Classical Greek sculpture and vase painting, as well as in small objects.

Many of Herakles' feats took place in the Peloponnese and he is often referred to as the great Dorian hero. He was equally popular in Ionian Athens, however, where numerous buildings on the Acropolis were decorated with relief scenes of his labours, and where the people of Marathon claimed to have been the first to worship him as a god.

Also popular at Athens was a local hero, Theseus, who was the son of King Aegeus, but born and raised by his mother in the Peloponnese. When he was of age, he was sent to Athens to claim his inheritance, meeting and overcoming numerous adversaries on his way. After his arrival in Athens other tasks awaited him, in particular a journey to Crete where he confronted the Minotaur, the bull-headed monster, in the labyrinth. The tribute of young Athenians sent every year to be devoured by the monster may reflect Cretan control or influence on the mainland early in the Mycenaean

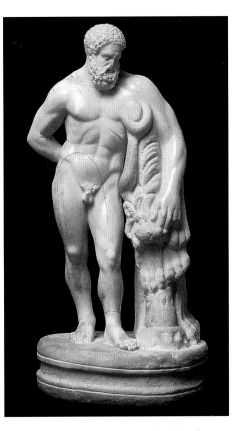

A weary Herakles, resting from his labours; Roman copy of a famous fourth-century BC masterpiece by the sculptor Lysippos, identified by the following ancient description: 'his head bends towards the earth … and his neck is bent downwards along with his head. Of his arms, the right one is taut and is bent behind his back, while the left is relaxed and stretches towards the earth. He is supported under his arm-pit by his club which rests on the earth. So the club supports him while he rests, just as it saved him when he fought. The lion skin is draped upon the club. Of Herakles' two legs one is beginning to make a movement, while the left is placed beneath and firmly fitted on the base', Libanios, Ekphraseis 15. (See also p. 177.)

period and the complexity of the palace at Knossos certainly qualifies it as a labyrinth, while scenes of bull-leaping in Minoan art illustrate a sport which may well have given rise to the legend of the Minotaur (pp. 50–51).

Athenian red-figured cup by the Codrus Painter, c. 450–425 BC, found at Vulci, with the labours of Theseus. The story of the Minotaur in the labyrinth is given prominence in the centre.

THE END OF THE PALACES

IONIANS AND DORIANS

He found by inquiry that the chief peoples were the Lacedaimonians among those of Doric, and the Athenians among those of Ionic stock. These races, Ionian and Dorian, were the foremost in ancient time, the first a Pelasgian and the second an Hellenic people. The Pelasgian stock has never yet left its habitation, the Hellenic has wondered often and afar. For in the days of king Deukalion it inhabited the land of Phthia, then in the time of Dorus son of Hellen the country called Histiaian under Ossa and Olympus; driven by the Cadmeans from this Histiaian country it settled around Pindus in the parts called Makednian; thence again it migrated to Dryopia, and at last came from Dryopia into Peloponnesos, where it took the name of Dorian.

Herodotus, 1. 56

The Dorians, too, in the 80th year after the [Trojan] war, together with the Herakleidai, occupied the Peloponnese.

Thucydides, 1. 12

At SOME POINT in the course of the thirteenth century BC, all the Mycenaean palaces for which we have good evidence were destroyed in a violent manner, and most of them show signs of an intense fire. In general, the pattern of destruction moved from north to south, with Thebes destroyed somewhat before the sites in the Peloponnese. Several of the palaces seem to show signs of warning and advanced preparation. At Mycenae, Tiryns and Athens special measures were taken to bring a secure water supply system within the fortified limits of the palace, as though some sort of siege were anticipated (p. 41).

Evidence and theories

According to the ancient sources these destructions were caused by a migration of Dorian Greeks, 'the descendants of Herakles', returning from the north to claim their rightful inheritance. Despite the ancient traditions, few scholars in recent times seem content to lay the

Egyptian relief from the mortuary temple of Ramesses III at Medinet Habu, Thebes, showing captive Sea Peoples wearing their characteristic feathered head-dresses (1190–1150 BC).

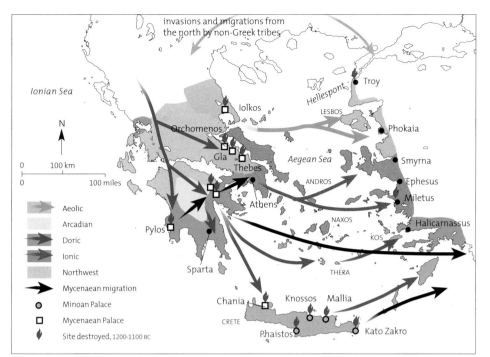

Map showing the destruction of Mycenaean palaces and the subsequent migration of Greeks across the Aegean to the west coast of Asia Minor.

blame on the Dorians. Early on, when the tradition was accepted, several archaeological features were taken as clear evidence that the Dorians had arrived, bringing a recognizable new culture with them. The biggest innovation was the appearance of iron, yet another improvement in the technology of tools and weapons. Other new elements seemed to be the introduction of cremation and individual burials, new pottery and new dress pins. Further research, however, indicated that these novel features were either invented in place or perhaps imported from the east, rather than the north.

This archaeological invisibility of the Dorians has since led scholars to seek other causes to explain the end of the Mycenaean world, and a wide range of theories is now available: earthquake, climatic change leading to famine, social unrest, sea-raiders, new military technology, or some combination of the above. The fact that no one new theory has gained general favour perhaps suggests they are all equally improbable, and no more likely than the Greeks' own traditions of a Dorian invasion. Further research buttressed by archaeological evidence will perhaps clarify the situation.

It should be noted that the destructions in Greece are paralleled by major disruptions throughout the Middle East at about this same time. The Hittite kingdom of Asia Minor collapsed and Egyptian records tell of battles with the 'Sea Peoples' in 1208 and 1179 BC. How and if this is all related is unclear; are the Sea Peoples, for instance, the cause of the downfall of the Mycenaean world, or are they the refugees and remnants of the Mycenaeans fleeing Greece? Philistine pottery found on the coast of the Levant in present-day southern Israel bears remarkable similarities with late Mycenaean pottery; is that where some of the survivors ended up? And what, if any, is the link between the fall of the Mycenaean world and Greek migrations into Asia Minor? These are questions that cannot be answered at present and are the subject of lively debate among archaeologists, linguists, historians and others interested in the early history of the Mediterranean.

A collection of Philistine pottery from Ashdod, dated 1200–1150 BC; both shapes and decoration show strong Mycenaean influence.

IV

THE AGE OF EXPANDING HORIZONS

Whenever Hellenes take anything from non-Hellenes, they eventually carry it to a higher perfection.

Plato, *Epinomis* 987D

THE PERIOD FROM 1100 BC to 750 BC was a time of decline when judged against the material wealth of the preceding Mycenaean age and is often referred to as the Dark Ages. For the most part, the literary sources fail and the archaeological record is largely limited to pottery and scraps of architecture. Yet during these imperfectly understood centuries the foundations of Archaic and Classical Greece were laid. This is the time when the Greeks not only explored but also expanded their world, first in an early wave of migration to the west coast of Asia Minor, and later with a series of colonies established in the west, particularly in Sicily and South Italy, and, later still, in the Black Sea region.

It is to these centuries that we must also date the transformation – through uncertain political stages – from palace to *polis*, as well as the emergence of a Hellenic national identity. At the very end of this period we see the origins of recognizably Greek culture: a literate society, trading widely and beginning to supplement painted pottery with large-scale sculpture in bronze and stone, as well as monumental stone architecture in the form of temples for their gods.

Detail of a funeral shown on a Geometric pedestalled krater from Athens, c. 750–735 BC, with the body laid out on a funeral cart surrounded by mourners and a procession of chariots below. The human figures, horses and birds appear again on Greek painted pottery after a gap of more than 400 years.

AFTER THE PALACES: THE DARK AGES

BY AROUND 1100 BC, despite some slight signs of recovery, the world of the Mycenaean palaces had come to an end. The contrast in the archaeological record is impressive. Gone are the huge palaces with their great circuit walls of megalithic construction. Gone also are most indicators of wealth: the gold and silver vessels, the inlaid daggers, the ivories and the carved sealstones. Tablets inscribed with Linear B disappear and the ability to write is lost for almost 500 years, until the introduction of the alphabet from the east (see pp. 64–65). Pictorial art, so prevalent on the walls, pottery and small luxury items of the Mycenaean world, also disappears for almost 500 years. In contrast to a far-flung trading network which brought goods from three continents, there are now far fewer foreign imports.

In place of the palaces are tiny unfortified settlements with a handful of small houses built with rubble walls and mud, a poor and

The Dipylon Amphora, an example of the fully developed Geometric style of pottery in use in the ninth and eighth centuries BC. The name of this style comes from the use of the geometric patterns – triangles, meanders, zig-zags, diamonds, etc. – as bands of decoration. The occasional human and animal figures are also used repetitively for their decorative effect. This vase dates to c. 750 BC and was found in Athens, where it was used to mark a grave: the central panel shows the funeral itself.

LEFKANDI

A pyxis (small container) of the eleventh century BC from Lefkandi. It shows two griffins feeding their young in a nest.

One of the most spectacular Dark Age sites excavated in Greece is found on the west coast of the island of Euboia. A low, level mound known as Xeropolis ('dry city'), c. 500 m (1,640 ft) long by 120 m (395 ft) wide, Lefkandi sits right by the sea, with access inland to the fertile Lelantine plain. A large, deep trench sunk 8.5 m (28 ft) into the hill by members

A terracotta statuette of a centaur, with geometric decoration, found in two graves, ninth century BC.

uninspired repertoire of pottery, no luxury goods and a subsistence economy. The technology for forging iron seems to make its introduction at this time. And the use of cremation is found alongside the continuing practice of inhumation, though burials are individual rather than in groups. Eventually a wide range of new pottery shapes appears, mostly painted black with restricted bands or panels of decoration. Over time, the decorated areas take over. This decoration consists of geometric patterns including circles, semicircles, zig-zags, dogs' teeth, meanders and swastikas; the word 'Geometric' is accordingly used to define the pottery style and often the entire period it was in use.

of the British School of Archaeology produced an impressive sequence of habitation going back into the Bronze Age. Associated rich cemeteries nearby, excavated by British and Greek archaeologists, have caused many to modify their view of the 'Dark Ages'.

Euboians were among the earliest to colonize in the west. Recognizably Euboian pottery has also been found along the coast of the Levant, and Cypriot and Near Eastern metal objects were found at Lefkandi. The site may well have played a major role in the early contacts with the east which characterize the transition from the Dark Ages to the Archaic period; these contacts might have included the introduction to Greece of the northern Canaanite alphabet, perhaps brought by Phoenicians; some of the earliest examples of Greek writing, scratched on pots, are in the alphabet used in Euboia.

From the four cemeteries come an array of interesting and unusual antiquities: a rare eleventh-century vase in dark clay with two griffins painted in white, and a large terracotta figure of a centaur, the mythical man/horse creature so popular in later Greek art; dated to c. 900–850 BC, its body was found in one grave and its head in another. The most spectacular find, however, was made in the 1980s. A long narrow building, curved at one end, was excavated and dated to the tenth century (1000–950 BC). At 47 m (154 ft) long and 10 m (33 ft) wide, it is the largest building we know of built in

Greece for a period of 500 years, between 1200 and 700 BC. Beneath the floor was an amazing burial consisting of two adjacent shafts. In one were the cremated remains of a man, placed in a bronze cauldron which carried relief decoration of animals and hunters with bows and arrows. Next to him was the extended burial of a female, covered in thin sheets of gold and other jewelry: beads, coils, pendants and rings, together with an iron knife with an ivory pommel. In the adjacent pit were the skeletons of four horses. Just

Drawing of the horse skeletons as found in the second burial pit within the Heroon at Lefkandi, 1000–950 BC.

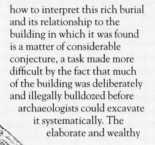

how to interpret this rich burial and its relationship to the building in which it was found is a matter of considerable conjecture, a task made more difficult by the fact that much of the building was deliberately and illegally bulldozed before archaeologists could excavate it systematically. The elaborate and wealthy burial, with sacrificed horses, is somewhat reminiscent of heroic burials described in the *Iliad*; what, if anything, is the relationship between the epic and these funeral rites? What was the relationship between the man and the woman? Was she killed or sacrificed to accompany him? Did the building serve as a house for them, as might seem the case from storage pits found within the curved end, or was it built as a temple or funerary monument? For the present, such questions are easier to formulate than answer. The large scale of the building and the lavish burials perhaps suggest that the occupant was honoured as a hero.

A cutaway reconstruction of the Heroon at Lefkandi, 1000–950 BC. The two dotted squares show the position of the burials within the building, and storage pits can be seen at the curved end.

THE IONIANS

Now these Ionians who possessed the Panionian had set their cities in places more favoured by skies and seasons than any country known to us. For neither to the north of them nor south, east or west, does the land accomplish the same effect as Ionia.... Miletus lies furthest south ... and next come Myus and Priene; these are settlements in Caria and they use a common language; Ephesus, Kolophon, Lebedos, Teos, Klazomenai, Phokaia, all of them being in Lydia have a language which is in common which is wholly different from the speech of the three cities aforementioned. There are three more Ionian cities, on the islands of Samos and Chios, and Erythrai on the mainland. The Chians and Erythraians speak alike, but the Samians have a language which is their own and none other's.

Herodotus, 1. 142

A selection of Geometric pottery from the cremation burial of a rich Athenian lady buried around 850 BC. Compare the limited zones of geometric ornament and lack of figural art (animals, birds, humans) on the large amphora with that shown on p. 60, from about a century later.

SMYRNA (BAYRAKLI)

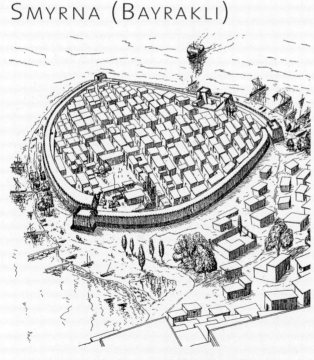

Artist's reconstruction of early Smyrna, tenth–seventh centuries BC. Founded by Tantalos, it was settled by Aeolians and was then taken by the Kolophonians and became an Ionian city.

One of the better-excavated early Greek settlements in Asia Minor is ancient Smyrna, which has been studied by British and Turkish archaeologists since the 1950s. The site is a low mound on a peninsula which originally jutted into the sea at the head of a deep gulf, inhabited at least since the Early Bronze Age. Archaeology would seem to confirm Herodotus' information that Aeolian Greeks first settled the site and were then replaced by Ionians. Pottery from the eleventh and tenth centuries BC includes a fair amount of characteristic Aeolian grey wares, superseded gradually in the ninth century by the typical East Greek pottery found at Ionian sites. The excavations also uncovered some of the earliest architecture surviving from a Greek settlement:

oval houses of mudbrick can be dated to the tenth century BC, while one of the earliest Greek fortification walls was built around the site in the ninth century. By the seventh century a monumental temple to Athena had been built, made up in part of a series of columns decorated with handsome stone capitals and/or bases carved with elegant leaf patterns. This rich and flourishing early city, which is one of several to claim Homer as a native son, was attacked and destroyed by the Lydian king Alyattes in the years around 600 BC.

Crete seems to have fared somewhat better; recovery there seems to have begun sooner than on the mainland. Larger sites, fortifications and simple shrines point to a more corporate, organized society. The excavation of the site of Lefkandi on the island of Euboia (pp. 60–61) has also produced some impressive architecture and signs of wealth and foreign contacts in the form of the rich burial of a man, a woman and four horses within a large building. These weak glimmers of past glories or harbingers of things to come should not, however, obscure the fact that generally, for several centuries after the destruction of the Mycenaean palaces, life in Greece must have been carried on at a basic level and, in comparison both with what went before and what came after, the term 'Dark Ages' is not inappropriate.

Migrations

During the early period of unrest in the eleventh and tenth centuries BC, various people begin to migrate both into and out of Greece. After 100 to 150 years of abandonment, a Greek presence is seen once again at numerous sites along the west coast of Asia Minor. This corresponds to traditions that there was a large migration primarily of Ionian Greeks out of the mainland. Mostly led by Athenians, people from all over Greece are said to have founded twelve cities along the coast, which thereafter became known as Ionia, an area destined to become very wealthy and culturally active in the historical period. At about the same time, Aeolian Greeks from Thessaly and Boiotia settled just to the north of Ionia, in the northwest corner of Asia Minor.

Moving into Greece from the north, the Dorians either were the agents of the collapse of the Mycenaean world or simply filled the vacuum created by the disruptions (pp. 56–57). They settled throughout most of the Peloponnese, then occupied the islands of the southern Aegean, as well as the southwest corner of Asia Minor, just south of Ionia, an area which in historical times became known as Caria.

There are no contemporary written records from this period; later traditions purport to record the movements of people and some other events, but there is little or no reliable

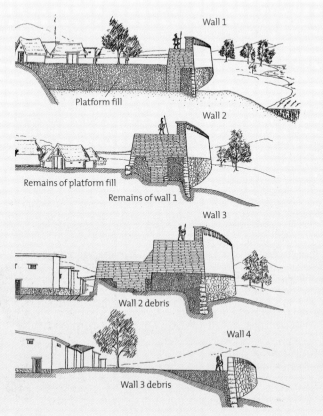

Wall 1

Platform fill

Wall 2

Remains of platform fill

Remains of wall 1

Wall 3

Wall 2 debris

Wall 4

Wall 3 debris

Excavations have recovered the huge siege mound built up by the Lydians to top the walls on the landward side. The city recovered enough the rebuild the temple of Athena, but fell again to the Lydians and then the Persians later in the sixth century. Habitation continued on a reduced scale thereafter, until Alexander the Great refounded the city in the fourth century at a new location several kilometres to the south.

(Opposite right) A carved limestone architectural element used as a base or at the top of one of the columns associated with the early temple of Athena, late seventh century BC.

(Left) Successive fortification walls of the city of Smyrna, consisting of sun-dried mudbrick set upon a stonework foundation (ninth to sixth centuries BC).

THE TWELVE CITIES OF IONIA

For this reason the Ionians made 12 cities and for no other; but it is foolishness to say that they are more truly Ionian or better born than the other Ionians, seeing that not the least part of them are Abantes from Euboia, who are not Ionians even in name, and that there are mingled with them Minyans of Orchomenos, Cadmeans, Dryopians, Phokaian seceders from their nation, Molossians, Pelasgian Arcadians, Dorians of Epidauros, and many other tribes.

Herodotus, 1. 146

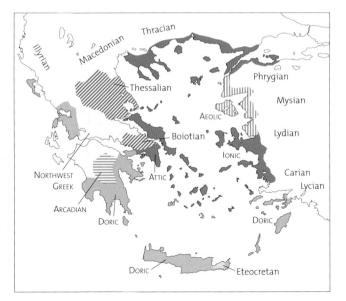

Map showing the distribution of Greek dialects, around 400 BC. Regional differences in dialects (spelling, pronunciation, vocabulary, letter forms) survive until well into the Classical period. These linguistic similarities and differences are used to infer tribal kinship and help to confirm traditions of early movements of people in Greece and the Aegean.

(Below right) Table showing the similarities of many of the letters used in several early alphabets. The Greek alphabet is clearly similar to the Phoenician, though how, when and why it was transmitted to the Greeks are still unanswered questions.

documentary evidence for the social structure of Greece at this time.

From a low point in the eleventh century the Greeks began a long and slow recovery, with increasing foreign contacts and a gradual rise in population visible in the archaeological record, presumably accompanied by a measure of political stability. These conditions seem to have improved incrementally up to the eighth century BC, when we can discern several important events and trends which lead to the full flowering of Classical Greek culture.

By the early years of the eighth century BC we find the Greeks established on the mainland, the islands of the Aegean and the west coast of Asia Minor. Ivories and bronzes excavated at numerous sanctuaries (Olympia, Samos, Delos, Ephesus) indicate trade had opened up once again with the Middle East, and Greek pottery is found at several coastal sites in the Levant.

The alphabet

This contact with the east led to one of the most important of several extraordinary developments in the eighth century. At some point, through the Phoenicians, the alphabet was introduced and Greek began to be written down once again. Just where and how the transmission was effected is uncertain, whether in Greece, the Levant, or as a result of interaction between Greeks and Phoenicians in Italy or Sicily. Just when is also debated, though the earliest extant inscriptions are written on pots dating to the eighth century. In this same era we also find the first firmly established date in Greek history: 776 BC. The Greeks believed that this was the year of the first Olympic Games and it is used as the starting point for reckoning time in many Greek authors. With both the written word and a firm chronological base we stand at the threshold of Greek history.

Name of Greek letter	Proto-Canaanite	Phoenician	Greek	Etruscan	Modern Latin
alpha					A
beta					B
gamma					C
delta					D
epsilon					E
digamma					F
zeta					Z
eta					H
theta					
iota					I
kappa					K
lambda					L
mu					M
nu					N
omicron					O
pi					P
san					
qoppa					Q
rho					R
sigma					S
tau					T

THE GREEK ALPHABET

Ancient traditions show that the Greeks themselves believed that the alphabet was a Phoenician invention, imported into Greece at an early date. Herodotus attributes it to Cadmus, the legendary founder of Thebes. Modern commentators have accepted the eastern 'Phoenician' origins of the Greek alphabet: similarities in names, shapes and order of the letters in the two alphabets are clear. Still hotly debated, however, are questions as to when and where it arrived, as well as how and why it was transmitted.

The Phoenician alphabet has some 22 signs which serve as consonants (with unspecified or no vowels), and seems to have been in use in north Canaan (the area of modern northern Syria) as early as 1000 BC. All 22 symbols were borrowed and used by one or another of the different local Greek alphabets, though the phonetic values of some Phoenician letters were changed to serve as the vowels A, E, I and O.

Our earliest texts in Greek, inscriptions scratched on pots, date to the years around 750–725 BC. They appear on the island of Euboia, at Athens and in the first Greek settlements on the bay of Naples, at Pithekoussai and Cumae. Allowing for the probability that we do not have the very earliest examples, a date around 800–750 BC seems a likely time for transmission.

Both the Greeks and the Phoenicians were great seafarers and traders, and there is ample evidence of Phoenician goods at various places in Greece, including Crete and Rhodes; similarly, considerable amounts of Greek pottery have been found in the northern Levant, especially Euboian pottery at the site of Al Mina in north Syria.

Euboia, the islands of the Aegean and northern Canaan are all therefore candidates for where the transmission might have occurred. Phoenicians and Greeks met and clashed further west as well and the possibility that the alphabet was transmitted in Italy and then brought back to mainland Greece cannot be excluded on present evidence. The Etruscans adopted the same alphabet as well, not long after it appears around the Bay of Naples. Did they get it from the Greeks or directly from the Phoenicians?

Many later alphabets have been the invention of a single individual (Gothic by Bishop Wulfilas in the 4th century AD, Armenian around AD 400 by St Mesrob, and Cyrillic by St Cyril) and it seems possible that the Greek alphabet, as adapted from the Phoenician, is also the work of one man. Several features common to all the early Greek alphabets suggest that the primary transmission was initially a single event, not a process which occurred over time in several places. The first indication, already noted, is the adaptation of several Phoenician symbols to serve as the vowels found in all Greek versions of the alphabet. Secondly, the letter phi has no semitic equivalent; like the vowels, it was invented and used universally by all the Greek alphabets. Third, many early Greek texts are written boustrophedon ('as the ox ploughs'): one line is written with the letters and words left to right, the next right to left, and so on; semitic texts are all written right to left. As with so much else, the Greeks apparently borrowed the alphabet from their neighbours, and then adapted and refined it to suit their own purposes and taste.

These Phoenicians, who came with Cadmus at their settlement of this

country, among many other kinds of learning brought into Hellas the alphabet, which had hitherto been unknown to the Greeks; and as time went on the sound and form of the letters were changed.

I myself have seen Cadmean characters in the temple of Ismenian Apollo at Thebes in Boiotia, graven on certain tripods and for the most part like Ionian letters.

Herodotus, 5. 58–59

(Left) Part of the law code of the city of Gortyn, Crete, c. 450 BC. It incorporates many earlier laws concerning the family, inheritances and slavery. The lines of text and individual letters are written boustrophedon ('as the ox ploughs'), alternating from right to left and then left to right. Several of the unusual letter-forms used here are common on Crete and rare elsewhere.

(Below) The Dipylon Jug, c. 730 BC, from Athens: one of the earliest examples of the Greek alphabet found in mainland Greece.

COLONIZATION

THE FIRST COLONIZERS

THE FIRST COLONIZERS

Of the Hellenes the first to sail over were some Chalcidians from Euboia who settled Naxos with Thoukles as founder and built an altar in honour of Apollo Archegetis…. The following year Syracuse was founded by Archias, one of the Herakleidai from Corinth, after he had first expelled the Sicels from the island, no longer surrounded by water, on which now stands the inner city; and at a later period also the outer city was connected with it by walls and became populous. In the fifth year after the settlement of Syracuse, Thoukles and the Chalcidians, setting forth from Naxos, drove out the Sicels in war and settled Leontini and then Catana.

Thucydides, 6. 3

(Below) A gold fish from a Scythian grave at Vettersfelde (Poland), c. 500 BC. Greeks and Scythians came into direct contact after the colonization of the Black Sea. Herodotus describes many Scythian customs which have been confirmed by recent archaeological discoveries.

(Opposite above) The Doric temple at Segesta, northern Sicily. Sicily, like Asia Minor earlier, was a fertile field for Greek settlers and many large cities prospered there, often matching or surpassing the wealth of the mother-cities.

TO THE EIGHTH CENTURY BC can also be dated the first great wave of colonization, a movement which continued throughout the Archaic period (*c.* 750–490 BC). Starting around the middle years of the century, the cities of mainland Greece began to send out groups of settlers to found new cities. The reasons for this phenomenon are not fully understood and several theories have been put forward to explain it: trade (especially for metals), overpopulation, a love of adventure, political unrest, or drought and subsequent famine have all been championed at one time or another. As with the end of the Mycenaean world, there is as yet no indication that a consensus has been or will be reached, though the limited evidence seems to favour drought and famine as a primary cause. The abandonment of numerous wells in Athens in the late eighth century indicates problems with the water supply in central Greece, the area from which most colonies were sent out. Increased activity at the sanctuaries of several deities associated with rain or water is also to be dated to this time, and a variety of late written sources refer to famine as a factor in the decision to found a colony. Certainly, throughout time, even up to the present day, large-scale migration is a common response to drought and/or famine.

The early colonizing states are found in a band running through central Greece: Achaia, Corinth and Megara at the west, and the islands of Euboia, Andros, Naxos and Paros to the east. At first the Greeks colonized southern Italy and the rich island of Sicily. They then moved on to North Africa and along the south coast of France, eventually reaching Spain. Other colonies were founded in Thrace, to the north. By the end of the Archaic period there

were Greek cities all along the shores of the Mediterranean, except where older civilizations held sway in Egypt, the Levant and central Italy. Nor was the Black Sea overlooked; it came to be heavily colonized, particularly by the great Ionian city of Miletus.

Reflecting the arrival of the colonists by sea, almost all Greek colonies were founded on or very near the coast, a pattern so regular that Greek cities were compared in antiquity to frogs sitting around the edge of a pond. The chief requirements for the new site were predictable: a good harbour, a defensible hill, reliable water supply, and usually some arable land, which sometimes, though not always, was already occupied by indigenous people.

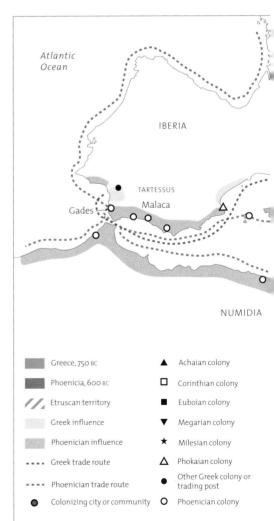

Greece, 750 BC	▲ Achaian colony
Phoenicia, 600 BC	◻ Corinthian colony
/// Etruscan territory	◼ Euboian colony
Greek influence	▼ Megarian colony
Phoenician influence	★ Milesian colony
- - - - Greek trade route	△ Phokaian colony
– – – – Phoenician trade route	● Other Greek colony or trading post
◉ Colonizing city or community	O Phoenician colony

CAUSES OF
COLONIZATION

*Not long afterwards drought
and plague laid hold of the city
… the Corinthians consulting
the oracle [at Delphi] about
relief, the god replied that the
anger of Poseidon would not
relax until the death of Aktaion
was avenged. Learning this, for
he was one of those consulting
the oracle, Archias willingly did
not return to Corinth but, sailing
to Sicily, founded Syracuse.*

Plutarch, *Moralia* 773A–B

*(Below) Map showing the extent
of Greek colonization of the
Mediterranean and Black seas
during the Archaic period,
750–500 BC.*

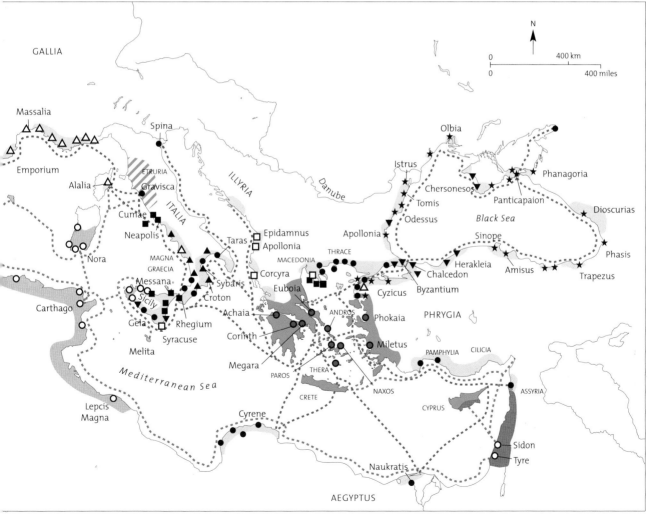

PANHELLENISM

AN IMPORTANT ASPECT of colonization was the rise of the concept of a Greek national identity, or Panhellenism. Throughout the Dark Ages the individual settlements of Greece had been isolated from one another, certainly by geography, perhaps by poverty. Local differences prevailed, whether in dialect or pottery styles, border clashes are attested, and neighbouring states were rarely on friendly terms. Once the Greeks set out to found new colonies, however, and were forced to deal with true foreigners who spoke an entirely different language, practised different customs and worshipped unknown gods, the petty squabbles and minor differences with their neighbours back in Greece seemed to fade, while the overall cultural similarities were highlighted, and eventually celebrated. This is expressed particularly at two sites where all the Greeks were accustomed to gather, Olympia and Delphi; it is probably no coincidence that both sanctuaries came to prominence during the period of intense colonization in the late eighth century BC.

Olympia

The site of Olympia lies within the territory of Elis in the northwest Peloponnese, along the banks of the Alpheios river, the longest in southern Greece. It was the most important sanctuary of Zeus, father of the gods and the most powerful of the Olympian deities. Because of its sanctity, the entire territory of Elis was regarded as inviolate, and all the Greeks gathered here together to worship. Part of the festival included several days of athletic contests which were renowned throughout antiquity and which have of course been revived in modern times. Observing a sacred truce, the Greeks could come together from all over the Mediterranean to compete, to sacrifice, to show off, and undoubtedly to engage in diplomatic and personal business which might be cumbersome if not impossible at any other time or venue.

Within the sanctuary was a row of small, temple-like treasuries built by individual cities to house votive gifts given by that city or its citizens to Zeus. The buildings are little gems of architecture, often highly decorated, and were built undoubtedly to display the wealth and prestige of the sponsoring city, much like the national pavilions at a World's Fair today. It is a measure of the importance of Olympia to the colonizers that over half of these expensive little buildings were sponsored not by neighbouring or nearby states, but by Greek cities founded in faraway Sicily, Italy and the western Mediterranean (for more on Olympia see also pp. 154–58).

(Centre) The remains of ancient Olympia, excavated by the German Archaeological Institute. In the foreground is the terrace carrying the remains of a dozen small treasuries donated by different cities. In the background on the right is the Temple of Hera and on the left the Temple of Zeus.

Early dedications in bronze, especially tripods (left, a leg from a tripod) and figurines (right), attest to a flourishing cult of Zeus at Olympia at the time of the traditional date for the founding of the Olympic Games in 776 BC.

Delphi

Delphi lies on the steep southern slopes of Mt Parnassos in central Greece. It was a sanctuary of Apollo, god of light and music, and drew its fame from the infallible oracle centered there. According to traditions, special priestesses inhaled vapours rising from a cleft in the mountain and succumbed to a prophetic frenzy through which, it was thought, the god Apollo spoke. There was a close connection between the sanctuary, the colonizing movement and its resulting Panhellenism, for colonies were sent out with the advice and sometimes at the command of the oracle. Like Olympia, the site is dotted with little treasuries to honour the god, and again they reflect the pull of the motherland for distant colonists, from as far off as Cyrene in North Africa (Libya) and Massalia (Marseille) in southern France. In a sense, Delphi has an even stronger Panhellenic character than Olympia for it was administered not by any one state, but by a committee, known as the amphikteony, made up of representatives elected from many cities, a rare example of corporate activity in this early period (for more on Delphi see also pp. 158–59 and p. 162).

PANHELLENISM

Now the following is the idea which leads to the founding of cities and to the holding of common sanctuaries in high esteem; men came together by cities and by tribes because they naturally tend to hold things in common and also because of their need for one another; and they met at the sacred places that were common to them for the same reasons, holding festivals and general assemblies. For everything of this kind tends to friendship, beginning with eating at the same table, drinking libations together, and lodging under the same roof; and the greater number of visitors and the greater number of places they came from, the greater is the advantage of their coming together.

Strabo, 419

(Top) A silver coin of Delphi, showing Apollo with his lyre, seated on the omphalos (navel) which was a symbol of Delphi as the centre of the world. The inscription records that the issuing authority was the amphikteony – the international committee that administered the oracle.

Knidos   Massalia   Siphnos

(Above) Reconstructed drawing of three of the many Archaic treasuries at Delphi: Knidos in southwest Asia Minor, Massalia (Marseille in south France) and Siphnos (a small island in the Aegean).

1 Theatre
2 Temple of Apollo
3 Serpent column of Plataiai
4 Sybilline rock
5 Athenian treasury
6 Knidian treasury
7 Theban treasury
8 Siphnian treasury
9 Sikyonian treasury
10 Corinthian treasury

Plan of the sanctuary of Apollo at Delphi. A Sacred Way, lined with dedications and treasuries, zigzagged up from the entrance (lower right) to the temple, where the Pythia (an oracular priestess) was housed and foretold the future.

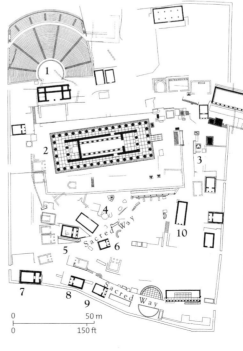

0   50 m
0   150 ft

EASTERN INFLUENCE

(Below) An Egyptian statue of
Mentuemhet, 25th Dynasty,
730–656 BC, from Karnak (left),
and a kouros (young male) from
Anavyssos, near Athens,
c. 550–525 BC (right). Though
comparable, the Egyptian
prototype has been adapted to
Greek tastes.

RENEWED CONTACT with the East had a profound impact on Greek art, dormant for several centuries. The other major seafaring group in the Mediterranean at this time, the Phoenicians, played an active role, just as they had in the Bronze Age, as indicated by the Uluburun wreck (p. 47), the Homeric epics, Phoenician

deities at Erythrai, a tradition of early Phoenician settlement at Thebes and on the island of Thera, and Phoenician place-names for the mining districts on the island of Thasos.

The earliest influence in the Dark Ages is visible in small portable objects, brought back and dedicated in all the early sanctuaries, at Delos, Samos, Sounion, Sparta, Thasos, Delphi and Olympia. In 804 BC, according to tradition, the Phoenicians founded Carthage on the north coast of Africa. Phoenician artifacts and perhaps the artisans who made them have been detected in Crete in the ninth to seventh centuries. This importation and adaptation by Greek artists of decorative objects and motifs can be seen in a wide variety of materials, especially bronzes and ivories, in the early Archaic period. The Corinthians, in particular, had a fondness for the mythical beasts of the east, such as griffins and chimaeras (a creature with a lion's head, goat's body and serpent's tail), and used them liberally to decorate their fine painted pottery in the eighth and seventh centuries. Like the alphabet, imported directly or indirectly from Phoenicia, these influences reflect an important debt owed to the flourishing civilizations of the eastern Mediterranean.

Excavations show a Greek presence at Naukratis in Egypt as early as the seventh century BC, where according to Herodotus trading relations between Egypt and the Greeks were formally established. Greek mercenaries in Egypt are attested in the reigns of both kings Psammetichus I and II. Mentioned in Herodotus, others also left graffiti on the statues of Abu Simbel in Upper Egypt, attesting their presence there in the years around 600 BC.

(Left) A bronze shield from Crete, seventh century BC; both the technique and the frieze of animals show strong north Syrian influence.

(Right) Bronze griffin head from Olympia, seventh century BC, from the rim of a large bronze cauldron.

(Below) Leg of one of the colossal figures of Ramesses II at Abu Simbel, Egypt. Among the graffiti are those left by Greek mercenaries in the late seventh century BC.

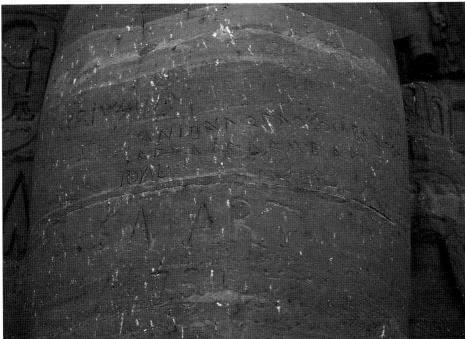

GREEKS IN EGYPT

Amasis [pharaoh of Egypt] became a lover of the Greeks and besides other favours he gave those who came to Egypt the city of Naukratis to dwell in; and for those who came but did not wish to settle he gave land for altars and sanctuaries. Of these the greatest, most famous and most visited is that called the Hellenion, founded jointly by the Ionian cities of Chios, Teos, Phokaia and Klazomenai, the Dorian cities of Rhodes, Knidos, Halicarnassus and Phaselis, and one Aeolian city, Mytilene. It is to them that the precinct belongs and they appoint the wardens of the port. The Aeginetans made a precinct of their own, sacred to Zeus, and so did the Samians for Hera and the Milesians for Apollo. Naukratis was in old times the only trading port in Egypt.

Herodotus, 2. 178, 179

Psammetichus secretly disbelieved the oracle that men of bronze would come to help him. But soon certain Ionians and Carians, voyaging for plunder, were forced to put in on the coast of Egypt, where they disembarked in their bronze armour. An Egyptian came into the marsh country and told Psammetichus that men of bronze were foraging in the plain. Psammetichus understood this as the fulfilment of the oracle; he made friends with the Ionians and Carians and promised great rewards if they would join him; having persuaded them, with the aid of other Egyptians and allies, he deposed eleven kings.

Herodotus, 2. 152

When king Psammetichus came to Elephantine, those who sailed with him wrote this, and they came above Kerkis as far as the river allowed, and Potasimto had command of those of foreign speech and Amasis of the Egyptians; Archon the son of Amoibichos wrote us, and Pelekos the son of Eudamos.

GHI # 7
(Greek inscription carved on the leg of the statue of Ramesses II at Aswan)

THE DEVELOPMENT OF COINAGE

Wealth in the Heroic Age was counted in animals, particularly cattle, as is the case in many primitive societies. The *Iliad* has a long account of a cattle raid by the garrulous old man Nestor, and the prizes offered by Achilles at the funeral games of Patroklos are denominated in oxen.

Then the son of Peleus [Achilles] set within the sight of the Danaans other prizes for the third contest, for wrestling: for him that should win, a great tripod to stand on the fire, which the Achaians valued at 12 oxen, and for him that came second he set a woman of great skill at handiwork, and they valued her at 4 oxen.

Homer, *Iliad* 23. 700–05

It may not have been just convenience, therefore, that led to the form of another sort of early wealth – copper ingots. The four protrusions at the corners make useful handles, but the appearance of the whole is also reminiscent of the shape of an ox-hide.

In later times, iron became a medium of wealth and exchange. It was portable, especially in the form of long spits used for roasting animals. These *obeliskoi* were said to have been dedicated by Pheidon, tyrant of Argos, in the Heraion there, and actual examples were recovered in the excavations of the sanctuary.

Herodotus also describes a group of such offerings at Delphi by the famous prostitute Rhodopis, who flourished in the sixth century BC.

Thus Rhodopis was set free and lived in Egypt where, her charms becoming well-known, she grew wealthy enough for a lady of her profession, but not for the building of such a pyramid. Since to this day anyone can count a tenth part of her possessions, she cannot be credited with great wealth. For Rhodopis desired to leave a memorial of herself in Greece, by making something nobody else had thought of and dedicated in a temple and presenting it at Delphi to preserve her memory. She therefore spent a tenth of her fortune making a great number of iron ox-spits [obelous], as many as a tenth would buy, and sent them to Delphi. These lie in a heap to this day, behind the altar set up by the Chians in front of the temple itself.

Herodotus, 2. 135

The early use of iron spits as currency survived in the terminology of later coinage.

The widely used standard coin was the drachma ('a handful'), with each drachma divided into six obols (spits).

Now [money] was of iron and was dipped in vinegar as soon as it came out of the fire, so it could not be reworked, but remained brittle and intractable by the dipping. Besides it was very heavy and troublesome to carry and a great quantity and weight of it had little value. Probably all ancient money was of this sort, some people using iron spits for coins, and some bronze; whence it comes that even today money retains the name obols and six obols make a drachma or handful, since that was as many as the hand could grasp.

Plutarch, *Lysander* 17

(Left) A collection of iron spits from the Sanctuary of Hera near Argos. Later, there were six obols, or spits, in a drachma: 'a handful'.

(Right) An early electrum coin from Asia Minor.

Archaeological investigation would seem to bear out the Greek tradition that coinage was the invention of the Lydians. Flowing through the capital city Sardis is the Pactolos river, which brought down from Mt Tmolos large quantities of electrum, a naturally occurring alloy of silver and gold. American excavations have revealed small pits along the river which seem to have been used to extract and purify the ore. This was a source of tremendous wealth for the Lydians, giving rise to the old expression 'as rich as Croesus', referring to one of the kings of Lydia. At some time in the seventh century BC it occurred to the Lydians to work the electrum into lumps of standard weight and to stamp them with

(Left) A bronze ox-hide ingot from Aghia Triadha, Crete.

(Right) A red-figured belly amphora by Myson, c. 500 BC from Vulci, showing King Croesus of Lydia on a pyre (as described in Herodotus, 1. 86).

a symbol to identify and guarantee them. This first early coinage greatly facilitated commercial activity, which heretofore must have involved barter or cumbersome weighing out of metals, and the Greeks were quick to adopt it.

A group of early gold and electrum coins was buried in a foundation deposit deep under the floors of the Artemis temple at Ephesus, and a second early hoard made up of coins with very sophisticated stamps has been found more recently at Klazomenai. From the late seventh century BC on, commerce within the Greek world and with its neighbours around the Mediterranean became much easier.

The customs of the Lydians are like those of the Greeks, save that they make prostitutes of their female children. They were the first men known to us who coined and used gold and silver currency; and they were the first to sell by retail.

Herodotus, 1. 94

The Greeks coined mostly silver, though gold issues were not unheard of. Both metals were mined at various places throughout the Greek world: Athens, Thasos, Siphnos, Thrace and elsewhere. Generally the coins carry the head of an important deity on the obverse and some appropriate symbol for the city on the reverse, such as an owl for Athens and Pegasus for Corinth. The use of token issues of bronze, where the value of the metal used was less than the face value of the coin, did not begin until late in the fifth century BC.

The monumental architecture on view throughout Egypt must have had a profound effect when the Greeks began to build their own more modest temples with columns and cut stone blocks in the seventh century BC. Similarly, the stiff striding pose of the *kouros*, which is one of the earliest subjects in monumental Greek sculpture, surely derives from Egypt, albeit adapted to Greek tastes. The triangular headdress of the pharaoh has become locks of long hair falling to the shoulders, and the kilt has been abandoned to accommodate the Greek preference for the male figure shown nude.

One of the most important and influential eastern neighbours of the Greeks in Asia Minor was the adjacent kingdom of Lydia, which lay just inland from Ionia, with its capital at Sardis. In the seventh and early sixth centuries BC the Lydians interacted closely with the Ionians, teaching them luxurious habits while paying homage to Greek gods, especially Apollo at Delphi and Artemis at Ephesus. Cultural interaction did not preclude military conquest, however, and by 560 BC all the coastal Greek cities of Ionia had fallen under Lydian domination. When Lydia herself fell to the Persians in 547/6 BC, the Ionian Greeks also became part of that vast empire.

THE CITY OF SARDIS
Sardis is a great city, and though of later date than the Trojan times, it is nevertheless old, and has a strong citadel. It was the royal city of the Lydians. Above Sardis is situated Mt Tmolos, a blessed mountain, with a lookout on its summit of white marble, built by the Persians, from which there is a view of all the plains below. The Pactolos flows from Mt Tmolos; in early times a large quantity of gold dust was brought down in it, whence arose the riches of Croesus and his ancestors.

Strabo, 625

View of the Hellenistic temple of Artemis at Sardis, capital of ancient Lydia. The gold-bearing Pactolos river flows from left to right just beyond the temple, and the gold-refining area was found a little further downstream.

THE BEGINNINGS OF GREEK LITERATURE

HESIOD ON TRAVEL

If you ever turn your misguided heart to trade and wish to escape from debt and joyless hunger, I will show you the measures of the loud-roaring sea, though I have no skill in seafaring nor in ships. For never yet have I sailed by ship over the wide sea, but only to Euboia from Aulis.... Such is my experience of many-pegged ships.

Hesiod, *Works and Days*
646–62

Your father and mine, foolish Perseus, used to sail on shipboard because he lacked sufficient livelihood. And one day he came to this very place crossing over a great stretch of sea; he left Aeolian Kyme and fled, not from riches and substance, but from wretched poverty which Zeus lays upon men, and he settled near Helikon, in a miserable hamlet, Askra, which is bad in winter, hot is summer, and good at no time.

Hesiod, *Works and Days*
633–40

MILITARY VIRTUE

Some barbarian is waving my shield, since I was obliged to leave that perfectly good piece of equipment behind under a bush. But I got away, so what does it matter? Let the shield go; I can buy another one equally good.

Archilochos, fr. 3
(Compare this attitude with
Tyrtaios of Sparta, p. 85, and
Kallinos of Ephesus, p. 100.)

WHATEVER DATE ONE ASSIGNS to the Homeric epics, written down after centuries of oral composition and performance, Greek literature begins around 700 BC. Perhaps the earliest surviving works are the poems composed by Hesiod, who lived in Askra, a small town in central Greece, not far from Thebes.

Writing late in the eighth century, Hesiod wrote a *Theogony* (Origin of the Gods) as well as an instructional manual on agriculture called the *Works and Days*. Hesiod comes across as a somewhat dour, grumpy individual, unhappy with his hometown and with his brother Perseus, whom he addresses in the *Works and Days*. The grim, hard agricultural life he describes stands in marked contrast to the adventurous, seafaring life of the contemporary Greeks we have been considering, and both pictures are probably accurate. Hesiod himself was no seafarer – the only voyage he undertook was from Boiotia to the island of Euboia, a trip of some half a kilometre, and he did not like it much.

In the writings of Hesiod we find a key to the character of the Greeks which has played a crucial role in their success; they were an intensely competitive people and they were interested in individual achievement. Honour and the desire to be best infuses all of Greek life. This agonistic (*agon* is Greek for contest) approach is praised by Hesiod and laid out in the very earliest lines of western literature.

So there was not one kind of Strife alone, but all over the earth there are two. For the one, man would praise her when he came to know her, but the other is blameworthy; they are wholly different in nature. One, being cruel, fosters evil war and battle; no man loves her. But through the will of the deathless gods men must pay harsh Strife her due honour. But the other is the elder daughter of dark Night and she is far kinder to men. She stirs even the shiftless to toil, for a man grows eager to work when he considers his neighbour, a rich man who hastens to plough and plant and put his house in good order; and neighbour vies with neighbour as he pursues wealth. This Strife is wholesome for man: potter contends with potter, craftsman with craftsman, and beggar is envious of beggar and minstrel of minstrel.

Hesiod, *Works and Days* 11–26

Other, less serious aspects of life are treated by other poets writing soon after Hesiod: hymns in honour of the gods and songs to accompany a drinking party (symposium). They paint a happier picture of life in early Greece, the times when the harvest is in and food, drink and good company are all available to be enjoyed.

A red-figured vase showing a drinking party, the venue and subject of much early Greek poetry, by the Epeleios Painter, c. 510 BC. A krater, the large vessel for mixing wine, stands in the centre.

A mosaic floor from Trier, in Germany, of the fourth century AD, labelled as a portrait of Hesiod and signed by the mosaicist Monnus.

ESIODVS

HESIOD AND THE MUSES

And one day they taught Hesiod glorious song while he was shepherding his lambs under Holy Helikon, and this word first the goddesses said to me – the Muses of Olympus, daughters of Zeus who holds the aegis: 'Shepherds of the wilderness, wretched things of shame, mere bellies, we know how to speak many false things as though true, but when we will we know to utter true things'. So said the ready-voiced daughters of great Zeus, and they picked and gave me a rod, a shoot of sturdy laurel, a marvellous thing, and breathed in me a divine voice to celebrate things that shall be and things that were before.

Hesiod, *Theogony* 22–32

Now, at last, the floor is swept, and clean are the hands of all the guests, and their cups as well; a slave puts plaited wreaths on their heads, while another offers sweet-smelling perfume in a dish; the mixing-bowl stands full of good cheer and other wine is ready, promising never to give out – mellow wine in jars, rich with its bouquet; in the middle the frankincense sends forth its sacred fragrance and there is water, cool and fresh and pure. The yellow loaves lie ready at hand, and a lordly table groans with the weight of cheese and luscious honey; an altar in the middle is banked around with flowers, and singing and dancing and bounty fill the house.

Xenophanes
(fr. l, quoted in Athenaios, *Deipnosophistai* 462c)

(Below) Bronze figure of a banqueter or symposiast, from the rim of a metal vessel, c. 520 BC, perhaps from Dodona. Hundreds of representations, mostly on vases or wall-paintings, show that the Greeks commonly reclined on couches when dining or attending drinking parties (symposia). Such parties seem to have been a common event, at least among the aristocracy (see also pp. 89 and 183).

V

POLIS: THE EARLY GREEK CITY

*The partnership finally composed of several villages is the polis; it has
at last attained virtually complete self-sufficiency and thus while it
comes into existence for the sake of life, it exists for the good life.
Hence every polis exists by nature, inasmuch as the first partnerships
exist, for the polis is the end result of the other partnerships and
nature is an end result in that we speak of the nature of each thing
when it has finished growing, whether a man, a horse or a household.
It is clear that the polis is a natural growth and that man is by nature
a political animal, and a man who is citiless by nature and not by
fortune is either low in the scale of humanity or above it, solitary like
an isolated piece in chess.*

Aristotle, *Politics* 1252b–1253a

BY THE EIGHTH CENTURY BC the *polis* had emerged.
The centuries of the Dark Ages, imperfectly understood, had seen the transition from the Mycenaean
palaces to the small, independent city-states which
were the basic political unit of Greek civilization in the Archaic
and Classical periods. Considerable scholarly discussion in
recent years has centred on the definition of a *polis*, when it
first appeared and how it came about. Essentially the *polis* was
a fortified urban centre, controlling a certain amount of
surrounding territory together with its outlying villages. They
were usually independent, sovereign states, jealously guarding
their borders and minting their own coinage. A critical mass
of population was necessary for the community to survive, but
there was tremendous disparity in the sizes of individual *poleis*.
Beyond these common elements, each *polis* followed its own
destiny and made its own choices, leading to great local diversity
in politics, art, architecture, writing, religion and customs.

*Ruins of ancient Cyrene in North Africa (Libya). Founded in the seventh
century BC, Cyrene became the largest and most successful Greek polis on the
south coast of the Mediterranean.*

THE GREEK CITY

It is twenty stades from Chaironeia to Panopeus, a city of Phokis, if city it can be called that has no government offices, no gymnasium, no theatre, no agora, no water conducted to a fountain, and where the people live in hovels like highland shanties, perched on the edge of a ravine. Yet its territory is marked off by boundaries from that of its neighbours, and it even sends members to the Phokaian parliament.

Pausanias, 10. 4

THERE WAS MUCH VARIATION in the planning of settlements. The old Greek cities of the mainland developed gradually over time and their layout reflects their antiquity and a distinct lack of planning, with winding streets and irregularly shaped houses. Colonies in a sense represent instant cities, and were laid out in a far more regular, planned fashion, with gridded streets and uniform houses built in well-defined blocks. Similarly, newly founded settlements created in the Classical period by gathering together the population of several villages – a process known as synoicism – produced orderly, planned towns.

Urban design

Aristotle provides advice on how to plan and lay out a city, and a man from Miletus called Hippodamus was active as a city-planner late in the fifth century, credited with the layouts of Thurii, Peiraieus and Rhodes. Whatever his innovations, he is too late to have created the regular orthogonal plan shared by many Greek cities; such a layout was developed long before and is found in some of the earliest colonies. Orthogonal plans also occur in earlier Etruscan and Italian settlements.

Whether an ancient settlement, a colonial foundation or a synoicism, all Greek cities shared several common traits. In addition to a fortified lower town, there was usually an acropolis at or near the centre. This was a freestanding hill, separately fortified and easily defended, to provide a place of refuge in the event of the fall of the lower town. As the high point of the city, it was also often chosen as the site for the sanctuary of the principal deity.

The town essentially was divided into three types of space: public, private and religious. Public space would be provided in the form of an agora, the large central square of the city.

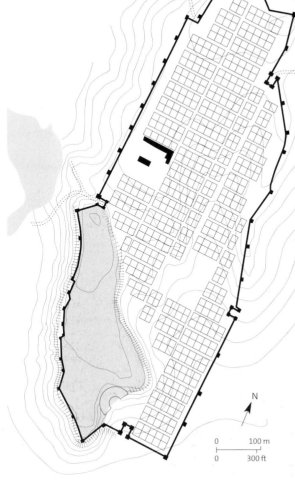

The square itself could accommodate a wide variety of activities: meetings, elections, markets, festivals, athletic contests, processions, theatrical performances, military drill and the like. Not surprisingly, the sides of the square came to be lined with those public buildings necessary to run the city. These would vary from city to city, depending on the type of government: democracy, oligarchy, monarchy or tyranny. In democratic Athens, for instance, the square was lined with a council building, the archives, chief magistrates' offices, the mint, lawcourts and commercial buildings. The theatre of a city also would be a largely public building, and often dedicated to the god Dionysos. It was a logical meeting place when all the citizens needed to gather and deliberate.

Most of the city will have been given over to private houses. These cover a wide range of sizes and amenities and hundreds of houses have been excavated to give a picture of Greek domestic life, particularly at Olynthos and Priene. Religious spaces could be found all over the city, as well as on the acropolis. Usually a sanctuary was walled and its sacred area well defined by boundary stones. Sanctuaries could vary in size from modest altars requiring no more than a few square feet, to huge temples with vast colonnaded enclosures taking up several city blocks.

City walls were a communal concern, built with labour donated by the citizens themselves if the need were urgent, otherwise paid for out of the public treasury, with the proceeds of military campaigns, or from private contributions. Following the landscape for several kilometres, they were an essential and expensive feature of every city. For most sites they represent the

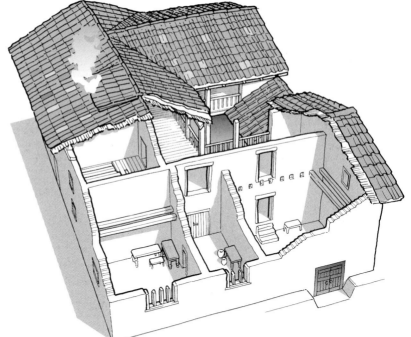

most visible and enduring evidence of organized corporate activity by the *polis*. Greek city streets, on the other hand, were for the most part pretty modest, usually unpaved and surfaced with packed gravel. There were both private and public provisions for water supply; aqueducts were built to deliver water to public fountainhouses from springs far outside of town, while individual houses had wells and/or cisterns. The dead were usually buried outside the walls of the town. Occasionally there are well-defined cemeteries, but more often the burials are placed alongside the roads leading out of the *polis*.

(Above) Reconstruction of a house, based on the 'Villa of Good Fortune' at Olynthos, c. 400 BC. Most Greek houses, like this one, had a central courtyard open to the sky which provided light and air to all the rooms grouped around it. This particular house lay outside the city and is larger and more elegant than the modular houses in the planned part of town.

(Below) Part of the Peisistratid water system of Athens, c. 530–520 BC. Gravity-flow aqueducts and public fountainhouses were often additions made to developing cities.

(Opposite left) Schematic plan of Olynthos. The northern extension was planned at one time and laid out with a rigid arrangement of streets and blocks of similar houses. Destroyed by Philip II of Macedon in 348 BC, it was largely abandoned thereafter, until excavations in the 1930s.

(Opposite right) Fortification walls at Herakleia in Asia Minor. A viable defence was an essential feature of every polis in the Greek world. Only warlike Sparta remained unfortified, until the third century BC when her military reputation waned.

EARLY ATHENS

The city itself is totally dry and not well-watered, and badly laid out on account of its antiquity. Many of the houses are shabby, only a few useful. Seen by a stranger, it would at first be doubtful that this was the famed city of the Athenians.

Herakleides,
Pseudo-Dikaiarchos,
FHG II, fr. 59

PRIENE

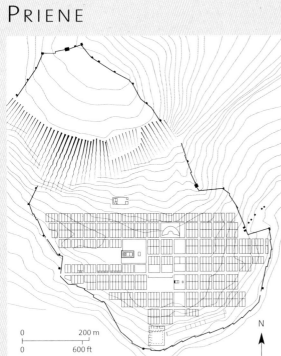

(Above) Plan of Priene: the regular layout is the result of a refoundation of the city in the fourth century BC.

identical units, in precise blocks with regular streets. The temple of Athena, dedicated by Alexander the Great and designed by the architect Pytheos, is one of the finest examples of a Classical Ionic temple.

A rival of the nearby Ionian island of Samos, Priene has little independent history to complement its impressive ruins, though hundreds of inscriptions help to reconstruct the administrative life of the city.

(Below) Remains of the Ionic temple of Athena Polias, principal deity of Priene. Started in c. 350–325 BC, with additions in the second and first centuries BC.

Priene was one of the 12 cities founded in Asia Minor by the Ionians and lay originally not far from the mouth of the Maeander river. The exact location of the early city has not been securely identified. The new settlement, founded in the fourth century BC, was excavated almost in its entirety by German archaeologists (1895–99), and the site gives us our most complete archaeological picture of a Greek city.

All the physical components of a *polis* have been uncovered: fortification walls, a major sanctuary and temple, an agora (marketplace), a fountain-house, a *prytaneion* (town hall), a council chamber, a theatre, a gymnasium, a stadium and dozens of private houses. The houses were laid out as

Political structure

Various forms of government were tried in Greece, and most cities experienced more than one over time. Constitutional monarchy was rare in Greece itself, but not unheard of on the periphery of the Greek world. Aristocracies seem to have been the next development and were still powerful in many Greek cities in the Archaic period. They were often followed by tyrannies; the word is a Lydian one and did not originally carry the negative connotations it acquired as early as the Classical period. It referred to an individual who seized and held power unconstitutionally, and not to how that power was wielded. Often the tyrant rose as a champion of the common people against an entrenched aristocracy.

This new centralized power often led to large building programmes, especially temples and water-supply systems; examples include the Peisistratids at Athens, Theogenes of Megara and Polykrates at Samos (pp. 94–97). Tyrants frequently tried to make their rule dynastic, usually with predictable results; no tyranny lasted more than three generations in Greece. When the tyrant was removed the city usually moved on to one of two forms of government: an oligarchy (rule of the few: *oligos*) or democracy (rule of the people: *demos*). Some cities, such as Sparta, had a mixed constitution, incorporating both democratic and oligarchic aspects.

Each Greek city had its own constitution, and Aristotle and his followers compiled accounts of numerous examples. Except for his *Constitution of the Athenians*, however, none of the others survives except in tiny fragments. From other literary sources we learn a fair amount about the Spartan constitution, the Boiotian, and that of Massalia (Marseille); for the others we are dependent on the patchy information provided by inscriptions. These list the titles of dozens, and occasionally hundreds,

The council house or ekklesiasterion of Priene, built in about 200 BC to accommodate some 640 people. Aristophanes describes an Athenian meeting as follows: 'Even the Prytanes [members of the executive committee] are not here; they will be late, streaming in, pushing and fighting each other for a seat in the front row' (Acharnians II. 23–26).

Manuscript of the Constitution of the Athenians, *attributed to Aristotle and dated c. 325 BC. After giving an account of eleven changes from the seventh to the fourth centuries BC, the work describes the constitution of Athens in force in the fourth century BC, listing officials and their duties. It then goes on to describe the workings of the Athenian lawcourts; the end is not preserved.*

SLAVES AUCTIONED IN
414 BC
*Skonys, house-born, butler
Alexitimos, house-born,
donkey-driver
Potainios, a Car[ian],
goldsmith
Polyxense, a Macedonian.*
                    Attic Stelai, II. 71–80

PIRATES AND SLAVERY
*The exportation of slaves
induced them [Cilician pirates]
most of all to engage in their
evil business, since it proved
most profitable; for not only
were they easily captured, but
the market, which was large
and rich in property was not
very far away, I mean Delos,
which could admit and send off
10,000 slaves on the same day;
whence comes the proverb,
'Sail in, merchant, and unload
your ship; everything has been
sold'. The cause of this was the
fact that the Romans, having
become rich after the
destruction of Carthage and
Corinth [146 BC], used many
slaves; and the pirates, seeing
the easy profit, blossomed in
great numbers, seeking booty
and trafficking in slaves.*
                              Strabo, 668

of magistrates, administrators, publicly owned slaves, councillors and jurors needed to run a large and flourishing *polis*. Government was in the hands of citizens, who made up a tiny percentage of the total population of a city. Excluded were all women, all metics (resident foreigners – including Greeks from other cities) and all slaves. Numerous rights and privileges, as well as duties, devolved upon the citizens and their status was carefully protected. Foreigners could be granted citizenship, but not easily.

Our specific evidence for privileges and duties comes, as so often, from Athens, which during the period of its empire was able to offer its citizens numerous benefits. In addition to the right to vote and to stand for election, privileges included eligibility to sit in the assembly (*ekklesia*), the senate (*boule*) or as a juror in the courts – all paid positions. Attendance at the theatre was also paid for. The state sponsored sacrifices at many festivals, and on such occasions citizens were often given free meals of meat. Subsidized grain was also available from time to time.

As for duties, citizens were expected to serve in the military; after a year of training when they reached 18 they served two years in the border forts and were eligible to be called up for duty thereafter until the age of 59. They were also subject to various taxes, depending on their professions and incomes. And in the democracy, they were expected to stand for public office and serve the city: 'To rule and be ruled in turn'.

Given the variables, estimating the population of any Greek *polis* is an extremely difficult task. We can sometimes get an idea of the relative sizes of communities from the military contingents they sent out, or the taxes they could afford, or the land they farmed, but how many people (women, children, foreigners and slaves) should be factored in for each citizen is unknowable. Some *poleis* may have counted their populations in the hundreds, while Athens had several hundred thousand inhabitants by the Classical period.

Political life in a Greek city was a rough and tumble affair. At one level or another participation in the affairs of the city was expected of all citizens and the costs could be high. Factional strife was a feature of many cities for decades, and the chances of having to spend all or part of one's life in exile were good. Political exile was formalized by the Athenians in the procedure known as ostracism (pp. 122–23), and it is worth noting that all our early historical writers spent time exiled from their respective *poleis*: Herodotus, Thucydides, Xenophon and Polybios.

Economic life

The primary advantages of life in a *polis* were security and the economic opportunities. The city would have a measure of control over the natural resources within its territory, whether metals, marble or timber. Exports and imports were taxed, and restricted in times of trouble. Other taxes would have to be paid and trade in the marketplace was regulated to ensure some

Weighing commodities, on a black-figured belly amphora by the Taleides Painter, c. 530 BC, found in Akragas (Agrigento) in Sicily.

(Left) Public measures for grain, nuts and wine, identified by DE or DEMOSION (public) painted on the vessels. Found in the Athenian Agora (marketplace) and dating to around 500 BC.

(Below left) A red-figured Athenian vase showing a man followed by his slave boy.

Regional diversity

One of the remarkable things about the Greek city-state was its small size. The territory of Athens was 2,500 sq. km (965 sq. miles), about the size of Rhode Island or Luxembourg, and Corinth and Thebes were smaller. Yet each independent city flourished, and though sharing borders each produced cultural material, politics and a lifestyle readily distinguishable from its neighbours. This regional diversity is one of the most interesting aspects of early Greek art. Even to an untrained eye, for instance, the early pottery of Athens, Thebes and Corinth is distinct, though all three cities lie within 80 km (50 miles) of each other. Similarly, the alphabets used in their inscriptions varied from city to city, as did the sculptures which adorned their sanctuaries. So, too, did their calendars and the names of their months, and the weight systems of their coinage, as well as their choices in clothing and personal adornment. The foot length used as a measure also varied, so that a stade race of 600 ft at Delphi was about 15 m (50 ft) shorter than the one at Olympia. As noted, the geography of Greece did not encourage unity; in fact, despite its relatively small size as a political and social unit, each *polis* maintained a strong, individual cultural identity.

Athens was so prominent in the creation and transmission of Greek culture that often other city-states are essentially overlooked. Athens cannot be ignored, and will consume an entire section of this volume. In later times Classical Athens was to become so dominant politically, economically and militarily that local art and culture also began to be overwhelmed by strong Athenian influence and the individual traits of the Archaic cities were lost. The Archaic period was a time when there was something closer to parity among the Greek cities, however, and now is the time to consider the character, contributions and history of some of the other significant cities of the Greek world.

degree of consumer confidence. *Agoranomoi* (market police) monitored the agora, *sitonai* (grain commissioners) watched the price of grain and special testers ensured the purity of coinage circulating in the market. Public standards for weights, liquids, dry measures and even terracotta rooftiles have been found at several Greek cities.

Much of the economy was based on the ownership of slaves – Greeks as well as foreigners, often acquired as a result of military campaigns. Usually captives could be ransomed and sometimes a slave could eventually buy his or her freedom, but generally the life of a slave was a hard one. In Athens, thousands were used to work the silver mines, a huge source of revenue for the city. Some other areas of Greece maintained entire native populations servile – presumably those conquered centuries earlier, during the Dark Ages: the *helots* of Sparta and the *penestai* of Thessaly.

CITIES OF THE MAINLAND

Sparta

One city stood equal to Athens for most of its history: Sparta, which controlled much of the southern Peloponnese, in particular the area called Laconia or Lacedaimon. This is a large valley, well-watered by the Eurotas river and hemmed in on the west by the majestic crags of Mt Taygetos and on the east by Mt Parnon. There is access to the sea towards the south, but Sparta itself lies 35 km (22 miles) inland and the Spartans were not great seafarers.

Sparta was anything but a normal *polis*. In Homer the home of Menelaus and Helen, Laconia was occupied by Dorians moving in from the north in the Dark Ages. When the Dorians arrived they conquered, suppressed and enslaved the local population, known as *helots*, the name said to derive from the coastal city of Helos. Other residents of Laconia, neither enslaved nor Spartan citizens, were known as *perioikoi* ('those who lived around'); they were free, but had limited rights. In the late eighth century Sparta conquered the even richer land of Messenia to the west, though the barrier of Mt Taygetos made control of the territory difficult and the Messenians revolted whenever possible. Faced with a large and hostile servile population at home and restive Messenians to the west, sometime in the seventh century the Spartans adopted a harsh, military lifestyle, much admired in antiquity but never emulated.

The new regimen was attributed in antiquity to a law-giver named Lykourgos, who served as regent for one of the early kings. The constitution, known as the 'great rhetra', was said to have derived from Cretan laws and to have been approved by Apollo's oracle at Delphi. Spartan boys were taken from their families at a

View of Laconia, with Mt Taygetos in the background and the Eurotas river valley in the middle distance. At the right in the foreground is the Menelaion, an Archaic sanctuary of Menelaus and Helen, key figures in the siege of Troy. Late Bronze Age remains have also been found on the hill – 5 km (3 miles) south of Classical Sparta – but nothing which suggests a palace. More substantial Bronze Age remains have been found at Pellana, some 16 km (10 miles) to the north of Sparta.

young age and brought up as warriors by the state. Each full Spartan citizen received an allotment of land, farmed by his wife and the *helots*, while he was expected to eat and sleep in common barracks, spending most of his time on military training. The Spartan citizenry thereby became a full-time professional army, a veritable military machine, far better trained and equipped than the citizen-soldiers of the other cities, who fought only when the harvest was in and with far less practical training. The Spartans were regarded as the premier warriors of Greece, feared whenever they marched out of Laconia – or even threatened to do so.

The Spartan constitution was a mixed one, with both oligarchic and democratic features. There were two kings, each hereditary, presumably reflecting some early compromise between two powerful families. This arrangement had the convenience of allowing one king to lead the army on campaign while the other stayed behind to mind things at home. Five ephors, elected by the citizen assembly, oversaw and had veto power over the kings. There was a council made up of the two kings and 28 elders which made most decisions. The assembly of all

(Above left) A bronze statuette of a warrior, probably Spartan, early fifth century BC.

(Right) Marble statue found on the acropolis of Sparta, early fifth century BC, and often identified as Leonidas, who led the Spartan contingent which was destroyed fighting against the Persians at Thermopylai in 490 BC.

the citizens elected members of the council and had the right to veto legislation, but could not initiate it. The result was a finely tuned system of checks and balances which worked for many generations.

This system of male separation left Spartan women far less supervised than anywhere else in Greece. In addition, as their primary role was to breed more and stronger citizens, they were encouraged to participate and even compete in sports and athletics to an unusual degree. On the whole, Spartan women seem far less restricted than their counterparts in other city states.

Inevitably, the cultural life of Sparta developed differently from other cities, the changes

SPARTAN COURAGE
Stay, young men, shoulder to shoulder and fight; do not turn in flight nor be afraid, but make your heart in your breasts both great and stout, and never shrink when you face the foe. And do not leave your elders, whose knees are no longer nimble, fallen on the ground. For indeed it is a foul thing for an elder to fall in the front, lying before the younger, his head white and his beard hoary, breathing forth his stout soul in the dust....

Tyrtaios, fr. 10. 15–24

SPARTAN WOMEN

Lykourgos believed motherhood to be the most important function of freeborn women. Therefore he insisted on physical training for the female no less than the male, and he instituted races and trials of strength for women competitors, believing that if both parents are strong they produce more vigorous offspring.

Xenophon, *Lacedaimonian Constitution* 1. 4

occurring gradually in the course of the Archaic period. Early on their sculptors produced handsome pieces in local marble, especially supports for basins of holy water (*perirrhanteria*) carved in the form of female figures. Accomplished Spartan potters made distinctive painted vases and brightly coloured roofing systems of terracotta. A productive ivory industry turned out hundreds of exquisitely carved animals and other small votive offerings for their sanctuaries. Early poets wrote hymns suggesting that Spartan festivals were like those enjoyed elsewhere in Greece, but these were later replaced by the martial urgings of Tyrtaios, a warrior-poet. Large-scale lavish public architecture was not a priority, however, and personal wealth was frowned upon. Coinage had no place in Spartan society: valid currency consisted of unwieldy iron spits several feet long.

A selection of Laconian ivories, seventh century BC. The plaque showing the embarkation of a ship, perhaps with Helen and Menelaus (right), and the winged figure with a snake (lower right), were found in the sanctuary of Artemis Orthia; the two warriors and the draped lady (below left) are from Dimitsana in Arcadia.

(Above) Bronze statuette, perhaps of a Spartan woman runner, c. 500 BC, dressed as Pausanias (5. 16. 4) describes contestants in the women's games for Hera at Olympia: 'their hair hangs down, their tunic reaches to a little above the knee, and they bare the right shoulder as far as the breast'.

A bronze hydria (water jar) of Spartan manufacture, c. 600 BC, found at Grächwul, in Switzerland.

(Below right) Remains on the acropolis of Sparta, excavated by the British School of Archaeology.

Protected by its mountains and the reputation of its warriors, Sparta, unique among all other city-states, had no fortification wall until troubled times in the third century BC. Spartan austerity appealed to the Romans looking back on their own simpler Republican days, and the city revived and flourished during the Empire, being much admired by Roman visitors in the first to third centuries AD. Excavations by the British School at Athens have uncovered the Roman theatre, a few remains on the acropolis, and the sanctuary of Artemis Orthia by the banks of the Eurotas river. Here young men were flogged at the altar and expected to endure the ordeal without crying out.

Rescue excavations under the modern city have produced stray finds and some handsome Roman mosaics. In general, however, archaeology has confirmed Thucydides' prediction:

> *For if the city of the Lacedaimonians should be deserted and nothing should be left of it but its temples and the foundations of other buildings, posterity would, I think, after a long lapse of time, be very loath to believe that their power was as great as their fame. ... Whereas if Athens should suffer the same fate, its power would, I think, from what appeared of the city's ruins, be conjectured double what it is.*

(Thucydides, 1. 10)

Thebes

The city of Thebes is in Boiotia, in central Greece. The site occupied a low, very steep hill called the Cadmeia, named after the mythical Phoenician founder Cadmus. Cadmus (semitic for 'from the east') was said to have come from Canaan in a vain search for his sister Europa, who had been taken from Crete by Zeus, disguised as a bull. The oracle at Delphi told Cadmus to abandon his search and to follow a cow and found a city where it lay down to rest. Though Cadmus was himself a foreigner, most of his followers were home-grown, sprung from the planted teeth of a dragon he had killed. Not readily datable, the myth presumably reflects the reality of centuries of early contacts between mainland Greece and the eastern Mediterranean. Much of Greek mythology – the Seven against Thebes and the Oedipus story – is set in Thebes.

In the Bronze Age, Thebes was one of the richest of all the Mycenaean citadels and scattered excavations under the modern city have

(Above) Late Roman portrait of Pindar, the most famous Theban poet. Active in the first half of the fifth century BC, he was known especially for his odes, written in honour of victorious athletes. From Aphrodisias, fifth century AD.

(Left) Attic red-figured cup by the Oedipus Painter, showing Oedipus being questioned by the Sphinx; from Vulci, c. 470 BC. Thebes and Boiotia are particularly rich in mythology, matching the very rich Bronze Age finds occasionally encountered in rescue excavations under the town.

produced frescoes, exquisitely carved ivories, lapis lazuli seals from the Middle East, bronze armour, and Linear B tablets and seals. Historical Thebes was a powerful city in the Archaic period, determined to dominate the other, lesser cities of Boiotia. A large shield is the emblem found on Theban coins and came to be used by many other Boiotian cities.

Both the Thebans and the Boiotians generally were scorned by their neighbours, and the word 'pigs' is applied to them by more than one author. All too often the Thebans chose unpopular political stances, trying for decades to dominate the other free cities of Boiotia, and siding with the Persians during the invasion of 480/79 BC. Their national poet, active in the early fifth century BC, was Pindar, who specialized in victory odes for winning athletes in the Panhellenic games. The Boiotians were fond of music, though their primary use for it was to accompany military drill. Theban flautists were generally regarded as the best in Greece; inscribed victory monuments from all over attest to their pre-eminence.

The excavation of four huge Boiotian cemeteries (Tanagra, Mykalessos, Akraiphnia and Thebes itself) show that the Boiotians imported a great deal of pottery from both Athens and Corinth, but they also produced their own distinctive pottery. In the Archaic period tall goblets decorated with birds are typical. The god Dionysos was said to be Boiotian originally, and his drinking cup with high-swung handles is a characteristic Boiotian shape. Yet another large group of specialized local pottery has been found at the Kabeirion, a Theban sanctuary several kilometres west of the town.

At times Thebes controlled the sanctuary of Apollo Ptoos at the neighbouring town of Akraiphnia and the sanctuary was filled with *kouroi*, the striding nude male figures sculpted in marble. Fragments of over a hundred have been found there, by far the largest concentration anywhere in the Greek world.

Thebes was particularly successful in the fourth century when, for a brief period (371–362 BC), it was the most powerful state in

(Right and below) Examples of Theban black-figured pottery made especially for use in the mystery cult of the Kabeiroi, whose sanctuary lay several kilometres west of Thebes. The cult has Dionysiac elements, but the meaning of the grotesque caricatures is unknown.

(Opposite below) A silver tetradrachm of Thebes, with a Boiotian shield on the obverse.

(Below) Boiotian kantharoi (wine cups), with the characteristic high-swung handles and associated with Dionysos (see left and p. 150), whose cult began in Boiotia. These two are rare examples of pieces actually exported from Boiotia; found in the Agora of Athens, fifth century BC.

The lion of Chaironeia, set up over the Thebans killed in the battle of Chaironeia in 338 BC.

THE SACRED BAND

It is natural that the band should also be called sacred because even Plato calls the lover a friend 'inspired of God'. It is said that the band was never beaten until the battle of Chaironeia, and when Philip was surveying the dead after the battle he stopped where the three hundred were lying, all where they had faced the long spears of his phalanx in their armour and mingled together, he was amazed; and learning that this was the band of lover and beloved, he burst into tears and said 'May he who thinks these men did or suffered anything disgraceful perish miserably'.

Plutarch, *Pelopidas* 18

Greece. The core of its army was a Sacred Band of 300 men, paired homosexuals who went into battle beside their lovers and therefore fought particularly fiercely, both to protect their companion and so as not to dishonour him by displaying cowardice. The fortunes of the city plummeted when it was defeated, along with Athens, by Philip II and the young Alexander the Great at Chaironeia in 338 BC. A huge marble lion marks the graves of 254 men from the Sacred Band who died that day. Three years later, in 335 BC, after an unsuccessful revolt, the city was destroyed by Alexander; though rebuilt a generation or so later, it never regained its former glory.

The Cadmeia today carries the modern town of Thebes and little systematic excavation of the ancient city has been carried out; a small museum houses tantalizing treasures recovered in the course of rescue excavations. Deep down, the Bronze Age levels are relatively well preserved, but Classical Thebes suffered from its destruction at the hands of Alexander, while its ruins are overlaid by the substantial remains of medieval Thebes, a large and rich centre for the production of silk.

Corinth

If geography alone determined greatness, then Corinth would have been the foremost state in Greece, a title the city could never actually claim. It sits astride the narrow isthmus of land which joins the Peloponnese to the rest of Greece and also controlled two harbours: Lechaion, on the Corinthian gulf to the north, looks towards Sicily and the West, while Kenchreai to the east gives access through the Saronic gulf to the Aegean and the East. In short, Corinth dominated both the major land route into southern Greece and the safest sea lanes from the eastern to the western Mediterranean. The acropolis, Acrocorinth, is an extensive, very high and sheer rock with a spring of good water on the top. The lower city, too, is well-watered with springs which come to the surface within the city. Rather than a primary political force, Corinth became what it was destined to be: one of the richest commercial cities of the Greek world. Right at the Isthmus was a sanctuary of Poseidon, god of the sea and earthquakes; controlled by Corinth, it was one of the four great Panhellenic sanctuaries and the site of prestigious games.

(Left) The fortifications of Acrocorinth: the present Byzantine walls – with Frankish, Venetian and Turkish additions – are founded on the original walls of the fourth century BC.

(Below) Silver stater of Corinth, with the winged horse Pegasus on the reverse; fourth century BC.

There are scattered Mycenaean sites in the Corinthia, the territory of Corinth, but no large palace centre has ever been recognized, nor does the city figure prominently in the Homeric epics. Myths associated with the area concern Medea, Sisyphus and the winged horse Pegasus, which became the symbol used on Corinthian coins and those of many of its colonies. Sisyphus was said to be the founder of Corinth and the Isthmian games. Extraordinarily crafty, he was thought also to have been the real father of wily Odysseus and to have cheated death twice.

Temple of Apollo at Corinth, c. 540 BC, with the Acropolis of Corinth (Acrocorinth) in the background; view looking southwest.

(Right) A typical example of Corinthian painted pottery, sixth century BC. The light clay, friezes of animals and background ornaments are all characteristic of the style.

(Opposite above) The Hellenistic phase of the Peirene fountain, which was used from the seventh century BC until the end of antiquity. Long subterranean galleries were cut far into the hillside and directed water to the distribution basins. This and other fountains gave Corinth its ancient epithet: 'well-watered'.

(Below) The territory of ancient Corinth, with its two harbours (Lechaion and Kenchreai) and a dominant position astride the isthmus leading into the Peloponnese.

(Below, centre) The remains of the diolkos, the paved drag-way for ships across the isthmus of Corinth, dating from the seventh/sixth centuries BC. The modern Corinth canal is at left; looking southeast.

He tricked Hades first by locking him into his own handcuffs and shutting him into his house so no one could die. On a second occasion he told his wife not to bury his body, then complained to Persephone in the underworld that he needed to go back to settle the matter, and, when released, refused to return. Once in the underworld for good, he was sentenced to roll a huge boulder endlessly up a hill, punishment for betraying Zeus to an angry father after one of the god's amorous adventures.

Already by the Archaic period the city was rich, and the term 'wealthy Corinth' was current. The city took a leading role in the colonization of the west in the eighth century BC, founding Kerkyra (modern Corfu) along the sea route to Italy, followed by the most successful of all the colonies in Sicily, Syracuse, in 733 BC. At home, the value of Corinth's harbours was increased by the construction of the diolkos, a stone-paved road or drag-way built across the isthmus. Far easier to transport ships and/or cargo those 6 km (3¾ miles) rather than risk the long and dangerous sail around the Peloponnese.

Fine beds of pure yellow clay lie near the city and Corinthian pottery was the most widely traded in the Mediterranean in the seventh and sixth centuries BC. It is usually decorated with friezes of animals or mythical beasts walking around the vase. A variety of shapes are known, but the most common are tiny round or pointed jugs for oil (aryballoi and alabastra). There is no good local marble and much of the finer sculpture is also executed in fired clay. The best building stone is a soft yellow limestone and the first temples of the Doric order in stone anywhere in Greece seem to have been built in the Corinthia in the seventh century BC. Roofing systems of terracotta were also a Corinthian invention. Made of baked clay, they consisted of large flat pantiles with cover tiles overlapping the joints, creating a secure and durable waterproof covering for a temple.

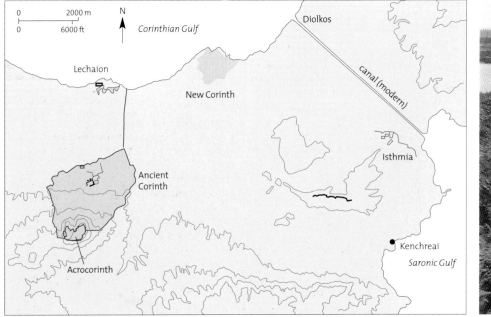

In Archaic times Corinth was first ruled by an aristocratic family, the Bacchiads, who were replaced by a tyrannical dynasty, the Kypselids. With the overthrow of the tyranny an oligarchy was established. Corinth usually followed the lead of Sparta in political matters. In later times, Corinth became the capital of the Achaian League, a position which led to the total destruction of the city by the Romans under Mummius in 146 BC. The city was abandoned for almost a century, until it was

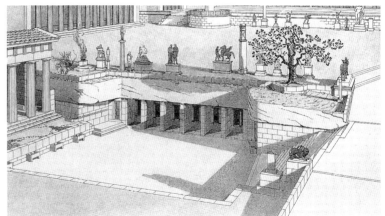

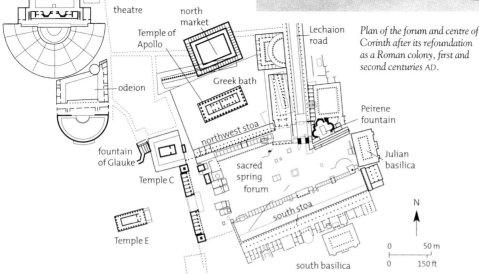

Plan of the forum and centre of Corinth after its refoundation as a Roman colony, first and second centuries AD.

CORINTH

The width of the Isthmus at the Diolkos [drag-way], where the ships are hauled overland from one sea to the other, is 40 stades [8 km/5 miles].

Strabo, 335

The situation of the city, as described by Hieronymos and Eudoxos and others, and from what I saw myself after the recent restoration of the city by the Romans, is as follows. A lofty mountain with a height of 6.5 stades [610 m/2,000 ft] with an ascent of 30 stades [6 km/4 miles] ends in a sharp peak. It is called Acrocorinth and its northern side is the steepest; beneath it lies the city in a level, trapezium-shaped area close to the base of the hill. The circuit of the city used to be as much as 40 stades [8 km/5 miles] and all that was unprotected by a mountain was enclosed in a wall. Even Acrocorinth was included wherever wall-building was possible, and when I went up the ruins of the circuit wall were plainly visible; so the whole perimeter amounted to about 85 stades [17 km/10.5 miles]. On the other sides the mountain is less steep, though here too it rises to a considerable height…. The summit has a small temple of Aphrodite, and below the summit is the spring Peirene, which, though it has no overflow, is always full of clear, potable water.

Strabo, 379

refounded as a Roman colony and provincial capital by Julius Caesar in 44 BC. With Roman patronage and its advantageous geographical position, it soon became a flourishing centre again. Visitors to the city could expect to find entertainment either with the sacred prostitutes at work in the sanctuary of Aphrodite on top of the acropolis, or in the wine-shops of the lower town. So popular was the city that the Roman way of saying you can't have everything in life was 'Not everyone gets to go to Corinth'.

Both Corinth and the Poseidon sanctuary at Isthmia have been excavated by American archaeologists. The forum of the Roman city has been cleared and there is some debate as to whether the earlier Greek agora lay immediately below. From the early city we have the temple of Apollo, which still stands on a low hill north of the forum, two fountainhouses, a huge stoa and a racetrack. The city walls and a potters' quarter have also been explored.

EAST GREEK CITIES

THE WEST COAST OF ASIA MINOR was resettled by Greeks in the early Dark Ages, along with the coastal islands. The twelve cities of Ionia were the most prominent, occupying the central part of the coast, with Aeolian settlements to the north and Dorian cities to the south. The central part of the coast is agriculturally rich and well watered by the Hermos, Kayster and Maeander rivers, and relatively easy contacts with the earlier civilizations of Lydia and Phrygia were possible by means of the river valleys. The Greek cities of Asia Minor prospered, rivalling and often surpassing those of the mainland in both wealth and cultural amenities. East Greek pottery is outstanding, Ionian sculpture and Ionic architecture are widespread, and Ionian poets and philosophers were pre-eminent.

The Ionians were gathered in a loose confederation, with a common meeting-place at the base of Mt Mykale. Here they worshipped at an altar of Poseidon Helikonios and built a small council chamber for their meetings. After numerous campaigns, all the Ionian cities had been conquered by the Lydians by 560 BC and thereafter paid some form of tribute. The Lydian empire, together with Ionia, fell to the Persians in around 546 BC. An attempted revolt in 498 led to a crushing defeat in a sea battle off Lade (near Miletus) in 494 BC, and Ionia remained in Persian hands until Greek victories in 479 BC, after which they were part of the Athenian empire.

Samos

The island of Samos, just off the coast of modern Turkey, had one of the largest and most successful *poleis* of Ionia. In the early fifth century BC the city was capable of manning 60 war galleys, which would have required over 10,000 rowers. Samos flourished particularly in the Archaic period, for part of the time under the

(Below) Samos, seen from the west, with the fortification wall in the foreground and the site of the town and harbour mole at the right.

(Right) Plan of the dipteral temple of Hera at Samos, with a double row of Ionic columns around all four sides.

(Below centre) The temple of Hera at Samos, one of the largest in the ancient world, sixth century BC.

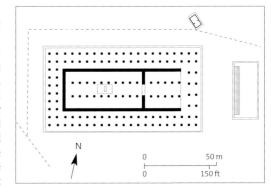

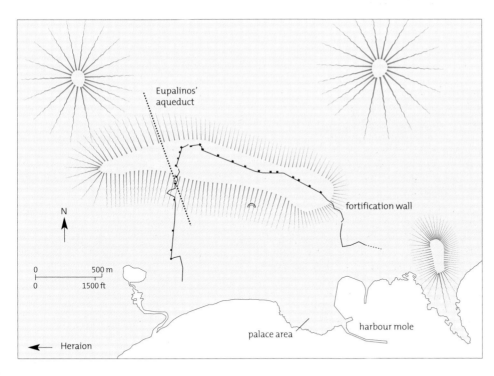

(Above) Silver coin of Samos.

(Left) Plan of Samos, showing the palace area and harbour mole, the fortification circuit and the aqueduct tunnel of Eupalinos.

(Below) Colossal kouros from the Heraion, 5 m (16½ ft) high, dated to the sixth century BC. The inscription above the left knee reads: 'Isches the son of Rhesis dedicated (this)'.

tyrant Polykrates. A famous sanctuary of Hera outside the town was the site of a huge, early temple built in the Ionic style; it was one of the largest in the Greek world, though little survives today. The sanctuary was approached by a sacred way, lined with dedications. Here has been found one of the largest *kouroi* yet discovered, standing some 5 m (16½ ft) high, carved from the local streaky white and blue marble of the island.

Small votive offerings dedicated to Hera attest to a wide trading network throughout the

eastern Mediterranean; carved ivories and beautifully wrought bronzes from all over the Middle East and Egypt have been recovered. Samos was also the site of one of the great feats of early Greek engineering: an aqueduct tunnel 1,036 m (3,400 ft) long, driven through a mountain to reach the city. It was designed by Eupalinos, a local engineer, who began digging

(Right and opposite) Samples of carved ivories found in the German excavations of the Heraion of Samos, seventh/sixth centuries BC. The kneeling youth is part of an ivory lyre.

EUPALINOS' AQUEDUCT

Herodotus describes three marvels of engineering at Samos, undertaken in the sixth century BC during the reign of the tyrant Polykrates. His description has been confirmed by German archaeologists.

I have written at length of the Samians because they are the makers of the three greatest works to be seen in any Greek land. First of these is the double-mouthed channel pierced for 150 orgyias (900 feet) through the base of a high hill. The whole channel is 7 stades long, 8 feet high and 8 feet wide. Throughout its length runs another channel, 30 feet deep and 3 feet wide, in which water from an abundant spring is carried through pipes to the city of Samos. The designer of this work was Eupalinos, son of Naustrophos, a Megarian. The second is a mole in the sea enclosing the harbour, sunk 20 orgyias (120 feet) and more than 400 yards long. The third Samian work is the temple, which is the greatest I have ever seen; its first builder was Rhoikos, son of Philes, a Samian.

Herodotus 3.60

The aqueduct of Eupalinos, c. 550–525 BC. The water was carried in clay pipes at the bottom of the smaller, deeper channel.

from both ends at the same time and yet managed to make the two tunnels meet at the correct elevation deep within the mountain.

Many tyrants provided their cities with aqueducts, but none are as impressive as that commissioned by Polykrates for Samos. The city walls are also extensive and well-preserved, though much of the ancient town itself lies under modern Tigani. The Heraion, tunnel and fortifications have all been excavated and studied by German archaeologists.

Miletus and Didyma

Miletus was built on a promontory near the south side of the mouth of the Maeander river. Site of a significant Mycenaean presence, the area was settled as a Greek city in the Dark Ages by Athens, with which it maintained close ties. It was a great colonizer, founding 30 cities, most of them around the Black Sea.

The Archaic city was a centre of early philosophy, home of Thales (who predicted an eclipse in 585 BC), Anaximander and

A PICTURE IN THE TEMPLE OF HERA

After this, Darius, being well pleased with his bridge of boats, gave Mandrokles the Samian a gift of ten of everything; from a tenth of this largesse Mandrokles had a picture made showing the whole bridge over the Bosphorus, with Darius sitting aloft on his throne and the army crossing. This he set up in the temple of Hera.

Herodotus, 4. 88

(Below) The Hellenistic/Roman theatre of Miletus, with seating for about 15,000 people.

(Above left) View along the south side of the temple of Apollo at Didyma. According to the building accounts each column cost 40,000 drachmas, the salaries of 100 men working for over a year.

(Above right) The temple of Apollo at Didyma. One of the largest temples in the Greek world (along with Samos and Ephesus), it was started in around 300 BC and was still under construction in the second century AD.

Anaximenes. A leader in the Ionian revolt against Persian rule, Miletus was sacked by the Persians in 494 BC.

It was rebuilt in the fifth century and was the hometown of Hippodamus, famous in antiquity as a city-planner. Most of the remains visible today are of the Hellenistic and Roman periods, times when Miletus once again enjoyed great prosperity. They were brought to light by German archaeologists, who continue to work on the site today.

The most famous oracle of Apollo in Asia Minor was located in Milesian territory, at Didyma, some 30 km (18 miles) to the south of the city. A sacred way lined with sanctuaries and votive monuments connected town and shrine. In around 494 BC the Persians destroyed a large Archaic temple of the Ionic order; they carried off the priestly family, the Branchidai, along with spoils from the temple, including the cult statue of Apollo and a dedicatory bronze knucklebone which weighed close to 90 kg (200 lb). A new temple was started late in the fourth century, with help from Alexander and his successor Seleukos; among the largest of Greeks temples, construction work continued for hundreds of years, throughout the Hellenistic and Roman periods.

THE SKILL OF THALES

Thales, so the story goes, because of his poverty was taunted with the uselessness of philosophy; but from his knowledge of astronomy he had observed while it was still winter that there was going to be a large crop of olives, so he raised a small sum of money and paid deposits to rent all the olive-presses of Miletus and Chios, which he got for a low price as there was no competition; and when the season arrived, there was a sudden demand for many presses at the same time, and by sub-letting them at whatever price he liked he realized a large sum of money, thereby proving it is easy for philosophers to be rich if they choose, but this is not what they care about.

Aristotle, *Politics* 1259a

HIPPODAMUS OF MILETUS

Hippodamus, son of Euryphon, a Milesian (who invented the division of cities and laid out the Peiraieus, and who also became somewhat eccentric in his general mode of life owing to a desire for distinction, so that some people thought he lived too fussily, with a surplus of hair and expensive ornaments and many cheap, warm clothes, not just in winter but also summer, and who wished to be a man of learning in all natural sciences) was the first man not engaged in politics who attempted to speak on the best form of constitution.

Aristotle, *Politics* 1267b

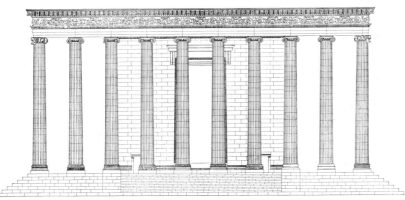

Restored elevation of the temple of Apollo; it was hypaethral (open to the sky) and therefore had no roof. The bronze cult statue by Kanachos was housed in a separate small building within.

ONE OF THE SEVEN WONDERS OF THE WORLD

Our genuine admiration for the magnificence of the Greek genius is roused by the temple of Artemis at Ephesus, which was built in 120 years by the exertions of all Asia. The temple was placed on a marshy site, that it might not suffer from earthquakes, while on the other hand, to prevent any weakness or shifting in the foundation on which the huge weight of the temple was to rest, a substratum of pounded charcoal covered with fleeces was laid. The full length of the temple is 425 feet and its width is 225. There are 127 columns, 60 feet in height, each made by a different king. Of these, 36 are sculpted, one of them by Skopas. The head architect was Chersiphron.

Pliny, *Natural History* 36. 21

ARTISTIC RIVALRY

Bupalos and Athenis were masters of great renown in their craft in the time of the poet Hipponax, who certainly lived in the 60th Olympiad [540–537 BC]. Hipponax was conspicuous for his ill-favoured countenance, which incited the sculptors in wild jest to display his portrait for the amusement of their friends. Incensed at this, Hipponax lampooned them so bitterly that some believe they were driven to hang themselves, though this cannot be true.

Pliny, 36. 11–12

... hold my cloak, I'm going to hit Bupalos in the eye.

Hipponax, fr. 120

KALLINOS OF EPHESUS

For it is a splendid honour for a man to fight on behalf of his land, children and wedded wife against the foe. Death will occur only when the Fates have spun it out. Come, let a man charge straight ahead, brandishing his spear and mustering a stout heart behind his shield, as soon as war is engaged.

Kallinos of Ephesus, fr. 1

(Top) View of the ruins of Ephesus, second to fourth centuries AD. *The Roman city had streets paved with marble and a theatre which held 24,000 people.*

(Above) Archaic coin of Ephesus.

Ephesus

Ephesus was famed in antiquity for the Artemesion, considered one of the Seven Wonders of the world. Excavations by British and Austrian archaeologists deep in the swampy low-lying site of the sanctuary have produced hundreds of rich gold, glass and ivory votive objects, along with some of the earliest known Greek coins and remains of much earlier, smaller temples. A huge Archaic Ionic temple of marble was under construction in the mid-sixth century BC; King Croesus of Lydia donated several of the sculpted column drums. This temple was burned down in 356 BC and replaced by another giant temple, which according to Pliny took 120 years to build. Housed in the temple was a strange eastern-looking cult statue of Artemis, her torso covered with numerous breast-like protrusions.

Ephesus lies near the mouth of the Kayster river, which eventually silted up and ruined the harbour of what was originally a seaside city but is now several kilometres inland. Only traces of the Archaic city have been found, deep below the Hellenistic and Roman city which, like Miletus, was extensive and prosperous: agoras, baths, a library, a stadium, long city walls and a huge theatre have all been uncovered, along with material from the period when Ephesus was an important Christian site. The apostle St John brought the Virgin Mary here and he is buried in a vast basilica on a nearby hill, while the town boasts several ruined churches and was a major pilgrimage centre until its decline in the seventh century AD.

THE SITE OF EPHESUS
King Antiochus was very anxious to get possession of Ephesus because of its favourable site, as it may be said to stand in the position of a citadel both by land and sea for anyone with designs on Ionia and the cities of the Hellespont, and is always a most favourable point of defence against Europe for the kings of Asia.

Polybios, 18. 40

(Left) Site of the Artemision at Ephesus, with a single column of the fourth century. The columns at upper right are part of the basilica of St John, sixth century AD.

(Below left) Restored view of the fourth-century Artemesion with sculpted column drums (p. 177). The temple was a place of asylum and the largest bank in Asia.

(Below) Copy of the cult statue of Ephesian Artemis. The cult was said to be pre-Greek, imported by the Amazons; this would help to explain the unusual appearance of the goddess.

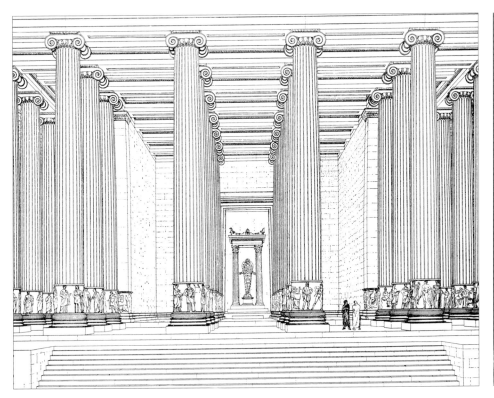

WESTERN GREEK CITIES

Traditionally, the Greek cities of Italy, Sicily and the western Mediterranean are later than their counterparts in Ionia, and their character is somewhat different. In origin they were colonies sent out by individual cities rather than the result of large migrations. They were usually sent with the advice of the oracle at Delphi, and maintained close relations with the mainland. The impetus for these foundations is still debated, but the fact that Demeter is very widely worshipped all over Sicily reminds us of the welcome agricultural wealth of the island.

To judge from their temples and other amenities, the western cities, like their eastern counterparts, soon grew far more prosperous than their mother-cities in Greece. Many of these early temples stand far better preserved today than anywhere else in the Mediterranean. For the most part the temple architecture reflects the Dorian origins of the colonies and are built in the Doric order. Rome took Sicily at a relatively early date, in the third century BC, and Cicero's attacks on the greedy plundering of the governor Verres give a vivid picture of the tremendous wealth and works of art still to be found in the Greek cities as late as the first century BC.

Akragas (Agrigento)

Set along the south coast of Sicily, Akragas was a foundation from Gela in c. 580 BC. In the early Classical period a group of Doric temples stood dramatically along the top of a high ridge. Within the town itself a temple to Olympian Zeus was laid out, one of the largest in the West. Instead of columns it had solid walls, decorated with huge standing figures of giants (*telamones*) supporting the entablature. The city was also well supplied with water by means of an extensive early aqueduct system, the tunnels of which have been traced far back into the hills.

The temple of Concord at Akragas (Agrigento), fifth-century BC, the best-preserved Doric temple surviving from antiquity. The temple of Hera can be seen further along the ridge.

Selinus (Selinunte)

Further west along the south coast in the seventh century was Selinus, which was something of a frontier town. Beyond Selinus, the western end of Sicily was occupied by Phoenician settlers at Motya. Much of the early history of the entire island concerns the conflict between Greeks and Phoenicians. Selinus was destroyed by the Phoenicians in 409 BC, and rebuilt. Like Akragas, the city had an impressive array of early Doric temples, which survived the sack

and are still well preserved today. Among them is temple G, a vast peripteral temple and the largest Doric temple ever built. The profiles of the capitals at the western end are more rounded and primitive than their counterparts at the east and indicate that the building was worked on for decades. The quarries for this huge temple have been found some 13 km (8 miles) to the northwest of the city, still full of immense column drums only partially freed from the bedrock.

(Above) Temple E at Selinus, fifth century BC.

(Left) Metope from the frieze of temple C at Selinus: Perseus beheading the gorgon Medusa, sixth century BC.

(Right) The Motya Charioteer, found in the Phoenician town at the west end of Sicily; marble, first half of the fifth century BC. The statue is thought to be plunder from a Greek city, perhaps Selinus in 409 BC. The high belt and long robe suggest the identification as a charioteer; compare another charioteer, also Sicilian and of the same date, found at Delphi (p. 158).

SYRACUSE

You will often have been told that Syracuse is the largest of Greek cities and the loveliest of all cities. Gentlemen, what you have been told is true. Its position is not only a strong one, but beautiful to behold in whatever direction it is approached, by land or sea. Its harbours are almost enfolded in the embrace of the city buildings. At their meeting place, that part of the town which is called the island, being cut off from the rest by a narrow strip of sea, is reunited with it by a connecting bridge. So large is the city that it is described as four great cities joined together. One of these is the island, flanked by the two harbours. In this district is the house of our governors, once King Hieron's. Here also are a number of temples, two much finer than the rest: that of Diana and the other of Minerva, a place rich in treasures before Verres arrived. At one end of the island is the spring of fresh water called Arethusa, an incredibly large spring, teeming with fish, which would be swamped by sea waves but for the protection of a massive stone wall.

There is a second town called Achradina, containing a large agora, some fine stoas, a richly-adorned prytaneion, a large bouleuterion, the noble temple of Olympian Zeus, and the rest of the town, filled with private houses and divided by one broad street crossed by a number of others. The third town is Tycha, called that from the ancient temple of Fortuna which once stood there: this contains a spacious athletic ground and several temples and is also crowded and thickly inhabited. The fourth town, the most recent, is Neapolis; on the high point stands the great theatre, and two splendid temples, one of Ceres and one of Libera, with a huge and beautiful statue of Apollo Temenites, which Verres would have carried off if he could.

Cicero, *Verrines* 2. 117ff.

Syracuse

By far the most successful colony in Sicily was Syracuse, founded from Corinth in 733 BC. The city lies in the southeast of the island, on a headland overlooking a deep, well-protected harbour. The Arethusa spring rises at the base of the acropolis and her image decorates Syracusan silver coinage.

Several early Doric temples stood on the acropolis and are now embedded in the fabric of the modern town, including the cathedral which was once a temple of Athena. A section of the town, an unusually long altar, the theatre and an outlying fort, Euryalos, have all been excavated and studied.

The tyrants of Syracuse were the most powerful on the island for much of antiquity, not just in the Archaic period, and directly ruled several lesser cities in Sicily. During the Peloponnesian War the Syracusans withstood an Athenian siege in 414/13 BC and ultimately captured a fleet of some hundred ships, the biggest single Athenian loss in the war.

The city continued to be the largest and most powerful in Sicily throughout the Classical and Hellenistic periods, until it fell to the Romans late in the third century BC. The famed engineer and scientist Archimedes made his home in Syracuse and, in addition to his famous bath and immortal cries of 'eureka', invented assorted devices to hinder the Roman fleet during the final siege of the city.

The theatre at Neapolis, Syracuse, third century BC, with the great harbour in the background.

Painted terracotta plaque of the gorgon Medusa with Pegasus, Syracuse, seventh/sixth century BC.

(Above) Tetradrachm of Syracuse with the head of Arethusa, the nymph who gave her name to the principal fresh-water spring of the city.

(Opposite) The temple of Athena at Syracuse, fifth century BC, is now embedded in the fabric of the modern cathedral.

(Above) An early coin of
Poseidonia (Paestum), with an
image of Poseidon with his trident.

(Right) A banqueting scene
painted on the interior of a
sarcophagus, the Tomb of the
Diver, at Poseidonia, c. 480 BC.

Doric temples at Poseidonia
(Paestum). In the foreground is the
temple of Hera II, fifth century BC,
beyond is the temple of Hera I
(basilica, sixth century BC).

Poseidonia (Paestum)

The city of Paestum will serve as an example of
the Greek cities built along the coast of Italy
itself. There were several such colonies:
Taras (Taranto), Thurii, Kroton, Sybaris and
Metapontum, to list but a few. Itself a colony of
Sybaris, founded in c. 600 BC, Paestum was set
on low-lying ground. Silted up and surrounded
by swamps, it was forgotten in the Middle Ages,
and three Doric temples within the city are
remarkably well preserved. The town itself, with
its circuit wall, has been excavated, as has an
extramural sanctuary near the borders of the
polis. The early temples here are Doric as well,
and were decorated with sculpted metopes (frieze
blocks) showing scenes from Greek mythology.
Many of the early Italian and Sicilian temples
had sculptural decoration and the invention of
this concept, popular in Greece in the Classical
period, should probably be attributed to the
Western Greeks. From the cemeteries comes a
rare example of Classical Greek monumental
painting: a sarcophagus painted inside with
scenes of banqueting and a diving boy.

(Left) A coin of Massalia, with the lion emblem of the city.

Massalia (Marseille)

Further afield, we come to the south shore of modern France, where the Phokaians established the colony of Massalia in around 600 BC. According to tradition, the Phokaians themselves came originally from Phokis, the area around Delphi before taking part in the Ionian migration and founding Phokaia on the west coast of Asia Minor. They became the boldest of Greek seafarers and Herodotus records that their 50-oared ships were the fastest and widest-ranging in the Mediterranean.

In founding Marseille, the Phokaians chose a setting similar to their home in Asia Minor, with a spectacularly deep, well-protected harbour. Remains of the ancient city, including the wall and part of the harbour have been found. From there other colonies were sent out along the coast: Nikaia (victory = modern Nice), Antipolis (Cap d'Antibes) and Monaco (Herakleia Monoikos), to the east, and as far as Hemeroscopion in Spain to the west. Their goods, if not the colonists themselves, moved up the river valleys into central France and Greek items are found in strongly Celtic areas. And it was more than just pottery – one of the finest monumental Archaic Greek bronze vessels (p. 187) was found in a tomb at Vix, on the Seine river. A huge krater (mixing-bowl), 1.64 m (5½ ft) high and weighing 208.6 kg (460 lb), it represents a major import and was discovered with black-figured pottery and gold jewelry.

The Massiliotes also dedicated an exquisite marble treasury in the sanctuary of Athena Pronaia at Delphi. They claimed to have been the earliest Greeks to have come into contact with the Romans and the two cities certainly enjoyed a close relationship throughout antiquity. Exploration westwards put them in contact with the inhabitants of present-day Spain and Portugal, with whom they also maintained friendly relations.

The harbour of modern Marseille, ancient Massalia. Traces of the ancient harbour are still preserved.

GREEK EXPLORATION

The Phokaians were the earliest of the Greeks to make long sea voyages; it was they who discovered the Adriatic Sea and Tyrrhenia, and Iberia, and Tartessos, not sailing in round freight-ships but in 50-oared vessels.

Herodotus, 1. 163

SILPHIUM

Silphium juice is mentioned by Antiphanes in Unhappy Lovers, speaking of Cyrene: 'I will not sail back to that place from which we were carried; I want to say goodbye to all that: horses, silphium, chariots, silphium stalks, steeple-chasers, silphium leaves, fevers, and silphium juice'.

Athenaios, *Deipnosophistai* 100f

Archaic silver coin of Cyrene, depicting a silphium plant, highly prized for its medicinal properties.

Next after these we will speak about laser-wort, a remarkably important plant, the Greek name for which is silphium. It was originally found in the province of Cyrenaica. Its juice is called laser, and it takes an important place in general use and among drugs, and is sold for its weight in silver. It has not been found in that country for many years, because the tax-farmers who rent the pasturage strip it clean by grazing sheep on it, making more profit that way. Only a single stalk has been found there within our memory, which was sent to the emperor Nero. If a grazing flock ever chances to come on a promising young shoot it is recognized immediately, for a sheep after eating it at once goes to sleep, while a goat has a fit of sneezing.

Pliny, *Natural History* 19. 15

The leaves of silphium are used in medicine to purge the uterus and to bring away the dead unborn baby; a decoction of them is made in white aromatic wine to be drunk after the bath in doses of one acetabulum. The root is good for soreness of the windpipe, and is applied to collections of extravasated blood; but it is hard to digest when taken as food, causing flatulence and belching. It is injurious to the passing of urine, but with wine and oil most beneficial for bruises, and with wax for scrofulous swellings. Warts in the seat fall off if fumigated with it several times.

Pliny, *Natural History* 22. 48

Cyrene (North Africa)

Herodotus tells the story of the foundation of Cyrene late in the seventh century BC. A drought on the volcanic island of Thera led the inhabitants to consult the oracle at Delphi. They were told to take one of every pair of brothers and have them found a new colony in Libya. After several unsuccessful attempts, the settlers were led to Cyrene, destined to become the primary Greek city in North Africa. The city was known, perhaps disproportionately, for horses and silphium, a highly prized medicinal plant, now extinct. The area was also rich in grain. In the years around 330 BC, when the *poleis* of mainland Greece were suffering from the effects of drought,

Cyrene was able to provide 805,000 medimnoi of grain (1 medimnos = 30–33 kg/66–73 lb) to help relieve the resultant famine. Excavations by Italian, British and American archaeologists have revealed much of the extensive Greek and Roman city, dating from the seventh century BC to the end of antiquity: the Greek agora, the Roman forum, sanctuaries of Apollo and Demeter, a sacred spring, a Doric temple to Zeus and the theatre.

All these cities and dozens more were established around the shores of the Mediterranean by 500 BC. Soon thereafter there arose a double threat to this great expansion of the Greeks: the Persians in the east and the Phoenicians and Etruscans in the west.

(*Left*) A view of the extensive north necropolis at Cyrene. Several thousand tombs of all types have been recorded at Cyrene, dating mostly from Archaic to Hellenistic times, with continued use in the Roman period. The north cemetery has several of the finest rock-cut tombs, many carved with elaborate architectural façades.

(*Below*) A Laconian cup showing King Arkesilas of Cyrene overseeing the weighing out of a commodity, possibly wool or silphium, c. 560 BC and found at Vulci.

(*Below left*) Athenian head vase, c. 500 BC. Representations of black Africans and imported exotica show there was interaction between Africans and Greeks, presumably through Egypt and Cyrene.

THE FIGHT FOR SURVIVAL

Bronze helmet dedicated at Olympia by the Athenian general Miltiades after the victory over the Persians at Marathon in 490 BC. The inscription reads: 'Miltiades dedicated this to Zeus.'

War with Persia

Troubles with Persia came to a head when the Ionian Greeks in Asia Minor revolted from Persian rule in 499 BC and called on their mainland brethren for help. Only two cities responded – Eretria, on the island of Euboia, and Athens, both of which sent warships. At first things went well: the Greeks marched inland and took and burned the provincial capital of Sardis. In 494 BC, however, a Greek fleet was defeated off the island of Lade, Miletus was sacked and the revolt collapsed. The Persians turned their attention to punishing Eretria and Athens.

Marathon (490 BC)

In 490 BC a large Persian fleet sent by King Darius sailed across the Aegean; after landing the Persians took Eretria within a matter of days. They then sailed across to Attica, reaching the broad plain of Marathon, some 40 km (25 miles) east of Athens. The Athenians, supported by only 600 allies from the small Boiotian town of Plataia, marched out and defeated the much larger Persian army, suffering 192 casualties while killing 6,700 Persians. The battle is often regarded – probably correctly – as a turning point in Western history. It is always hard to guess a future that never happened, but it seems likely that had the Athenians lost, their history and many of their contributions to Greek culture, including democracy, would not have evolved as they did.

As a result of their triumph at Marathon, Athens could claim a status among the other cities which only Sparta had claimed hitherto. Numerous monuments – buildings, paintings, and sculpture – were erected in Athens, at Marathon and at Delphi to remind both the

Athenians and the rest of the Greeks of the Athenian victory and pre-eminence. And the name of the battle of Marathon survives in the modern race which recreates in its length the run of the messenger sent back to Athens to announce the victory.

Thermopylai (480 BC)

The Persians retired, but only to plan a larger campaign. When they returned it was with both a huge land army and a fleet, led now by King Xerxes. The two moved together along the coast of northern Greece, unchecked until they reached the mountain barrier between Thessaly and Phokis. Here, at Thermopylai, the narrow pass between the mountains and the sea was blocked by several hundred Greeks, led by the Spartans. For several days the Greek line held against much greater but ineffective numbers until a traitor showed the Persians a way through the mountains. Characteristically, the Spartans sent their Greek allies away and stayed themselves to fight to the death.

Salamis (480 BC)

Pouring into central Greece, the huge Persian army destroyed the towns of Phokis, accepted the capitulation of most of the Boiotian cities, and took Athens, which had been abandoned. The Athenians had ferried women, children and non-combatants to the island of Salamis and the Peloponnesian city of Troizen and took to their fleet of 200 ships. A crucial sea battle was fought in the narrow stretch of water between Athens and Salamis, and the Persian fleet was smashed. The creation of the Athenian fleet and the trickery necessary to ensure the battle was fought at Salamis were attributed by Herodotus to Themistokles, who is also credited with the vision that Athens' future must be as a sea power. He had fortified the port of Peiraieus and persuaded the Athenians to invest a huge find of silver from the mines at Laureion in 484/3 BC in a fleet of 200 triremes – which was to prove crucial at Salamis.

The stronger and bigger the fleet, the more democratic Athenian society became as the many oarsmen demanded a greater say in the affairs of state. Themistokles was thus seen as something of a threat by the more conservative politicians of Athens. His native craftiness helped him arrange the ostracism of his main rival, Aristeides, trick the Persians at the battle

NAVAL WARFARE

An Athenian black-figure cup showing a merchant ship (left) and a trireme (right); late sixth century BC.

Seafaring seems to begin in the Aegean in the years around 8000 BC. Pictures of ships are incised on the Early Bronze Age pottery of the Cycladic islands in around 2500 BC, fleets of oared ships with sails are depicted on the Thera frescoes in around 1600 BC, and trading vessels from the late Bronze Age (14th/13th centuries BC) have been excavated. Naval power was a tremendous asset in an area so tied to the sea. Tradition records that the earliest sea battle took place between Corinth and Kerkyra in the seventh century BC. In the seventh and sixth centuries the Phokaians were famed as sailors, sending their 50-oared ships to explore the western Mediterranean and beyond. The sea battle at Salamis in 480 BC, when the Greeks defeated the Persian fleet, was a major factor in the liberation of Greece. In the Classical period the Athenians maintained a fleet of several hundred ships and a naval alliance directed first against the Persians then against the Spartans and their

allies. In the fourth century BC the harbour at Peiraieus was equipped to accommodate 372 war-ships.

Various people or cities were said to have had control of the seas at different times, and lists of ancient *thalassocracies* survive in late and imperfect texts of Eusebius and others. Despite uncertainties, a version of the ancient tradition of who controlled the seas would be as given in the table below. The lower, later part of the list seems to be historically accurate and accords fairly well with information provided by Herodotus. After 480 BC Athens was the dominant naval power in the eastern Mediterranean and remained so for the fifth and much of the fourth centuries. In the Hellenistic period the island of Rhodes had the most effective navy.

The basic fighting ship was the trireme, so named because

Lydians	118 years	1174–1056 BC
Pelasgians	51 years	1056–1005 BC
Thracians (Europe)	33 years	1005– 972 BC
Uncertain (Thracians)	53 years (?)	972– 915 BC
Rhodes	24 years	915– 891 BC
Phrygia	27 years	891– 864 BC
Cyprus	28 years	864– 836 BC
Phoenicia	54 years	836– 782 BC
Egypt	34 years	782– 748 BC
Miletus	28 years	748– 720 BC
Caria	51 years	720– 669 BC
Lesbos	93 years (?)	669– 576 BC
Phokaia	44 years	576– 532 BC
Samos	15 years	532– 517 BC
Sparta	2 years	517– 515 BC
Naxos	10 years	515– 505 BC
Eretria	15 years	505– 490 BC
Aegina	10 years	490– 480 BC

it had three banks of oars, powered by between 170 and 200 rowers. They carried sails when cruising. The prow was provided with a bronze ram designed to pierce and sink enemy ships. A squadron of 20 hoplites would be carried on board for close-in fighting. Triremes sat low in the water and could obtain great speed over short distances; as with hoplite formations, their effectiveness depended largely on good training.

The appearance of these ships is well known from vase-painting and sculpted reliefs, and several shipsheds have been excavated, so that the dimensions of a trireme can be worked out as *c.* 30–35 m (98–115 ft) in length and 6–6.5 m (20–22 ft) in width. Our understanding of the ancient warship has been greatly enhanced by the building and manning of a full-scale trireme, the *Olympias*, in the 1980s.

The Olympias, *a modern reconstruction of a trireme.*

THE BATTLE OF SALAMIS

*Now from our side arose in
answer the mingled clamour of
Persian speech; time allowed
no delay, but instantly ship
dashed its bronze-sheathed
beak against ship. It was a ship
of Hellas which began the
charge and sheared off the
entire curved stern of a
Phoenician barque. Each
captain drove his ship straight
against some other ship. At
first, indeed, the Persian line
held its own; but when the
mass of ships was crowded into
the narrows and no one could
render aid to another, each
crashed its bronze-faced beak
into another in the line and
shattered its oars. The Hellenic
galleys, seeing their chance,
hemmed them in and battered
them on every side. The hulls
of our ships rolled over, and the
sea was hidden from sight,
strewn as it was with wrecks
and slaughtered men.*

Aeschylus, *Persai* 406 ff.

*(Above right) The tripod
monument for the victory at
Plataia, inscribed with the names
of the participating Greek cities.
Set up at Delphi, 479/8 BC, its
remains now stand in the
hippodrome of Constantinople
(Istanbul).*

*(Below) Plans of the four major
battles of the Persian Wars.*

of Salamis and delay the Spartans while Athens
was refortified after the Persian Wars. Eventually the Athenians tired of him and exiled him
around 472 BC. Pursued by Athenian and Spartan agents, he eventually made his way to Asia
Minor and talked his way into the good graces
of the Persian king, promising to advise him on
how to deal with the Greeks. He was settled
comfortably in Magnesia and lived there for
several years. When the Persian king eventually
called for his advice, however, he committed
suicide rather than betray his homeland.

After the defeat of their fleet at Salamis, the
Persian army withdrew to central Greece, but
not before burning and destroying virtually
every building in Athens. The total devastation of the city in 480/79 BC represents a break
with the past which is usually used to mark the
transition from the Archaic to the Classical
periods.

Plataia (479 BC)

The final great battle of the Persian Wars in
Greece was fought near the city of Plataia, in
Boiotia. Dozens of cities, led by Sparta and
Athens, routed the Persians yet again, driving
them out of Greece for good. The war continued for many more years, but the scene shifts to
the eastern Mediterranean. In Greece, monuments were set up all over to commemorate
these great victories over a powerful and feared
enemy. At Delphi, a huge bronze column consisting of the bodies of three coiling snakes
served as the support for a golden tripod dedicated to Apollo. The lower part of the serpent
column today survives in the hippodrome at
Constantinople/Istanbul, and the head of one
snake is in the museum in that city. Sparta was

deemed the premier land power, while Athens
was recognized as dominant on the high seas.
The rivalry of these two cities was to be a major
theme in the history of Classical Greece.

War in the West: Phoenicians and Etruscans

While the mainlanders and Ionians were coping with the Persians, the Greeks in Italy and
Sicily were fighting their own battles against
well-established foes.

The most successful Phoenician colony was
Carthage on the North African coast (in modern
Tunisia). From here the Phoenicians sent out

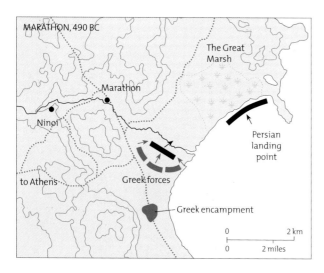

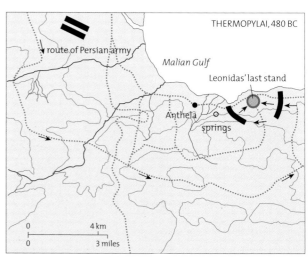

(Below) Etruscan bronze helmet dedicated at Olympia, the inscription reads: 'Hieron, son of Deinomenes, and the Syracusans dedicated this to Zeus after their victory over the Tyrrhenians at Cumae' (474 BC). This was one of several sea battles between the Syracusans and the Etruscans.

traders and settlers throughout the western Mediterranean. A particular area of conflict was Sicily, where Phoenicians tenaciously held the west end of the island, a constant goad to the Greek cities further east. A major battle was fought in the same year as the Persian invasion, 480 BC, at Himera on the north coast of the island, in which the Greeks under the leadership of Gelon, tyrant of Syracuse, were triumphant. The inscribed base for the golden tripod sent by Gelon to Delphi to celebrate this victory still stands in a prominent position just east of the temple of Apollo. This conflict continued into the fourth century BC, with the Carthaginians destroying Selinus in 409 BC (p. 103), and the Syracusans answering with the destruction of the Phoenician settlement of Motya in western Sicily in 397 BC.

The Etruscans, who occupied the area of central Italy north of Rome, were very receptive to Greek culture in the Archaic period. Many of the finest examples of Greek painted pottery now in European museums were found in Etruscan tombs; the Etruscans wrote their own language in an alphabet close to that used by the Greeks; and there are numerous indications of considerable trade between the two areas. Herodotus claims that the Etruscans actually came originally from the northeast Aegean (just as Virgil claims that the earliest Romans came from Troy), though the present thinking is that they were an indigenous people, who developed out of the earlier Villanovan culture of central Italy.

Despite these commercial and possibly political ties, relations between Etruscans and Greeks became strained where they overlapped. Several significant sea battles were fought, particularly around the Lipari islands north of Sicily, near Corsica, where the Phokaians were discouraged from attempting to found a colony, and around the early settlement at Cumae near the bay of Naples. Both sides celebrated victories, the Greek ones commemorated with monuments and dedications of captured armour at Olympia and Delphi. In 474 the Syracusans also won a sea battle over the Etruscans near Cumae and dedicated more armour at Olympia. In general, the Etruscans managed to keep Greek settlements away from the west-central coast of Italy and the offshore islands, but were themselves restricted elsewhere.

VICTORY AT HIMERA

After this Gelon built noteworthy temples to Demeter and Kore out of the spoils, and making a gold tripod of sixteen talents he set it up in the sanctuary at Delphi as a thank-offering to Apollo.

Diodorus Siculus, 11. 26

Gelon, the son of Deinomenes, the Syracusan dedicated the tripod and the Nike (Victory) to Apollo. Bion, the son of Diodoros, the Milesian made it.

GHI # 17
Inscribed on the base at Delphi

VICTORY AT CUMAE

Grant I pray, O Son of Kronos, that the battle cry of the Carthaginians and Etruscans may stay home in peace and quiet, now that they have seen their overbearing insolence off Cumae has brought lamentation to their ships; such were the losses they suffered when vanquished by the lord of the Syracusans, a fate which flung their young warriors into the sea, freeing Hellas from grievous bondage.

Pindar, *Pythian* 1. 71–75

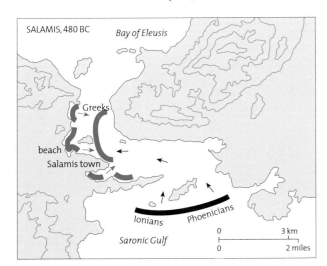

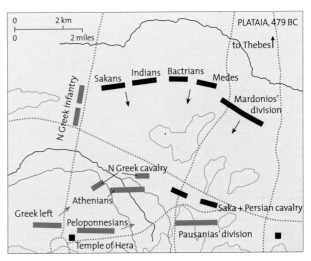

GREEK WARFARE THROUGH THE AGES

The mechanics and equipment of warfare among the Greeks changed over time and can be assessed from literary sources, archaeological evidence and representations in art, all of which are plentiful. There is a fair amount of variation, presumably reflecting different periods, different sources and different types of soldiers. As always, training and experience seem to have been the deciding factors in many military engagements.

Bronze Age

From Mycenae come grave stelai showing warriors and hunters in chariots (p. 45) – just as the kings and heroes are described in the *Iliad*. In the epic the chariots are used largely as transport to the field of battle, after which the nobles duel on foot. A set of heavy armour, made up of overlapping plates of bronze, has been recovered from a tomb at Dendra in the Argolid, and similar pieces have been found on the Cadmeia of Thebes. They date to the early fourteenth century and are very similar to armour shown in the pictographs on Linear B tablets. They also bring to mind Homeric descriptions of fallen warriors, whose armour 'crashed about them'. The Dendra armour is heavy, though modern reconstructions have shown that it is not as cumbersome as it looks. Two types of Bronze Age helmets are known. The earlier, described as an heirloom in the *Iliad* and found in tombs of the fifteenth and fourteenth centuries BC, is made up of dozens of boars' tusks sewn on to a leather cap. Later, helmets with a high crest were in use, made up of different materials; bronze cheek-pieces have been found and full helmets are shown on a vase from Mycenae depicting soldiers on the march (p. 45).

Different types of shields are known as well: large rectangular shields made of cow-hide are depicted on the Thera frescoes (p. 32), whereas the frescoes at Mycenae show cow-hide shields in a figure-of-eight form. The Warrior Vase from Mycenae shows the type

Set of Mycenaean bronze armour found in a tomb at Dendra; early fourteenth century BC.

of smaller round shield, perhaps of bronze, that became common later on. Throwing spears with bronze tips, bronze swords and bronze daggers were all used as weapons and have been recovered in large numbers from many Mycenaean tombs.

Archaic and Classical

At some point in the Dark Ages, presumably in the eighth century BC, the practice of war changed somewhat. Long ranks of similarly armed soldiers, usually eight rows deep (a *phalanx*), replaced the individual duels described in the earlier epics. The warriors were now known as hoplites, after the armour and equipment (*hopla*) that they used: a crested helmet, a metal breastplate (often with a metal or leather skirt below), metal greaves on the lower legs, a large round shield and a long spear used for thrusting rather than throwing.

The ranks would close up with their shields overlapping and the resultant battle must have looked like an armed rugby scrum, with a great deal of massed pushing and shoving until one side gave way. Cavalry was also used, but in smaller numbers, and usually for scouting, skirmishing, concealing troop movements and pursuit once a line had broken. Lighter-armed troops, slingers and archers were all employed on occasion.

A bronze figure of a mounted warrior wearing a Corinthian-type helmet and short tunic. It was found at Grumentum in southern Italy and dates to the first half of the sixth century BC.

(Opposite) Hoplites were the core of Greek armies: in this detail from the late seventh-century BC Chigi vase, two groups clash in battle.

(Below) The Macedonian phalanx armed with long spears – held out straight in front by the five first rows – played an important role in the successes of Philip II and his son Alexander the Great.

Hellenistic

The use of a phalanx of unusual depth and equipped with especially long spears (*sarissas*) seems to have been the invention of Philip II, father of Alexander the Great, and a characteristic of the Macedonian army.

It was actively supported by cavalry, which was supposed to turn the enemy line.

Fortifications were an effective deterrent for centuries and early on cities more often fell through trickery or treachery rather than effective siegecraft: the story of Troy provides an excellent example. Tremendous patience and/or huge siege mounds were often necessary to reduce a city in Archaic or Classical times. Siegecraft advanced considerably throughout the fourth century BC and was matched by ever more elaborate fortifications. Bolt-throwing catapults, stone-throwers and immense movable siege towers became common weapons in the Hellenistic period. Diodorus Siculus describes a *helepolis* ('city-taker') built by Demetrios for the siege of Rhodes in 304 BC. It was a wooden and iron tower about nine storeys (43 m/140 ft) tall, 23 m (75 ft) on a side at the bottom, tapering to 10 m (30 ft) at the top. It was mounted on wheels which could be turned, and it required 3,400 men to push it up to the walls. The missile throwers inside the nine levels of the tower were protected by movable shutters made of hides stuffed with wool, designed to absorb the shock of incoming catapult balls.

Examples of the sort of artillery ranged against such siege towers has been found on the acropolis of Pergamon. It had an arsenal in which the excavators found 961 round stone catapult balls in 13 sizes, the largest measuring 41 cm (16 in) across and weighing 75 kg (165 lb).

VI

CLASSICAL ATHENS

That which gave most pleasure and adornment to the city of Athens, and the greatest admiration and even astonishment to all strangers, and that which now is Greece's only evidence that the power and former wealth that she claims is no fiction or lie, was [Perikles'] construction of the public and sacred buildings.

Plutarch, *Perikles* 12 and 13

ATHENS AS A CITY was paramount in many of the achievements of Greece we admire and emulate today: architecture, theatre, art, philosophy and government. It should be noted that not just native Athenians made the city great. Its tremendous size created unparalleled opportunities, and people were drawn there from all over the Mediterranean. A startling 40 per cent of identifiable gravestones from Athens are for foreigners, both Greek and otherwise. All these contributed to a culture which set a standard against which most other societies are judged today. Statesmen and playwrights, historians and artists, philosophers and orators, such as Thucydides, Aeschylus, Sokrates, Pheidias, Demosthenes and Praxiteles, flourished here in the fifth and fourth centuries BC, when Athens was the most powerful city-state in Greece. Here, too, the political institution of democracy took root under the guidance of Solon, Kleisthenes, Themistokles and Perikles. Even when her political, economic and military significance waned, Athens remained an influential cultural and educational centre for centuries, drawing teachers and students of philosophy, logic and rhetoric until the sixth century AD.

A view of the Acropolis of Athens from the northwest, with the Agora, the marketplace and civic centre of the city, in the foreground.

THE RISE OF ATHENS

The tyrannicides, Harmodios and Aristogeiton, who killed Hipparchos; Roman copies in marble of the bronze originals that were set up in the Agora of Athens in 477 BC.

THE EARLY HISTORY OF ATHENS is much like that of the other Greek centres, with a flourishing, but unremarkable, presence in the Bronze Age. Theseus was the local hero and archaeology has revealed rich though not spectacular tombs and a large fortification wall around the Acropolis, presumably protecting a palace which later building has completely obliterated. Also like the other centres, Athens declined into a Dark Age; the Dorians passed by into the Peloponnese and Athens was very active in the Ionian migration.

Aristocratic families ruled in the Archaic period, until tensions led to the appointment of Solon to draft more equitable legislation early in the sixth century BC. Continuing unrest allowed a man called Peisistratos to set himself up as a tyrant later in the century. His reign was characterized by the construction of temples and a water-supply system (p. 79), and his sons are credited with attracting notable poets to their court. When one son, Hipparchos, was killed in a love-feud, the reign of the survivor, Hippias, became much harsher, and in 510 BC the Athenians drove him out with Spartan help.

The Acropolis of Athens, seen from the southwest. On the left is the Propylaia and temple of Athena Nike, in the centre the Erechtheion, and on the right the Parthenon.

After two years of strife, Kleisthenes created a new form of government – democracy, designed to break the monopoly on power held by the aristocratic families. Athenian military successes in Boiotia and Euboia in 506 BC and against the Persians at Marathon in 490 BC set Athens among the first cities of Greece. This reputation was enhanced by the success of the Athenian fleet at Salamis in 480 BC, though Athens itself had to be completely rebuilt as a result of the total destruction of the city by the Persians.

The fifth century saw the continued rise of the city at the head of a league of somewhat reluctant allies in the islands and Ionia. Under Perikles, the Athenians undertook a programme of construction of new temples on the Acropolis and in the outlying territory of Attica, building the finest surviving examples of Greek architecture. The widespread Peloponnesian War with Sparta engaged Athenian energies throughout the last third of the fifth century, until her defeat in 404/3 BC. After a brief decline, Athenian fortunes rose again in the fourth century BC, until a defeat at the hands of Philip of Macedon at Chaironeia in 338 BC. Thereafter Athenian history, like that of all the Greek *poleis*, is written with reference to the larger Hellenistic kingdoms and leagues which resulted from Alexander's conquests and premature death.

Despite the loss of political, military and economic power, Athens remained the cultural and educational centre of the Mediterranean for centuries. Hellenistic princes and, later, Roman noblemen came to study philosophy, rhetoric and logic, as well as to visit the old monuments. The city was adorned with concert halls, libraries and philosophical schools until her pagan traditions proved too threatening to the ruling Christian order and in AD 529 the emperor Justinian forbade any pagan to teach philosophy in Athens.

A bust of Solon, the lawgiver, dating from the Roman period.

GOVERNMENT AND LAW

A PRELIMINARY STEP towards democracy in Athens was made under Solon, early in the sixth century BC, when he established the right of appeal to a popular court which was to include all levels of the citizenry; hitherto magistrates had had the power to adjudicate most cases, with no further appeal. The next crucial step occurred in 508/7 BC under the leadership of Kleisthenes, about whom we know almost nothing. All Athenians were divided into ten newly created tribes from which they derived most of their benefits as citizens. They fought in tribal contingents, served in the *boule* (council) in tribal units, held certain common property with their fellow tribesmen and shared a common tribal hero. This last meant sacrifices and feasting with their tribesmen as well. All these political, military and social contacts forged new bonds of loyalty to the tribe rather than any one aristocratic family, whose members were dispersed among the new tribes. On these basic foundations the structure of a democratic society was erected in incremental stages over the decades, championed by leaders such as Themistokles and Perikles. The creation of democracy was a long process, rather than a single event, and Athens was not entirely democratic: women, slaves and foreign residents had little or no say in how the state was run.

The basic outline of the Athenian democracy and how it worked is laid out for us in *The Constitution of the Athenians*, attributed to Aris-

(Below) Architects of Athenian democracy: Themistokles (left) and Perikles (right).

(Centre) The Agora of Athens, marketplace and civic centre of the city. The temple of Hephaistos and Athena overlooks the square from the west. The site was excavated by the American School of Classical Studies at Athens.

totle and dated to around 325 BC (p. 81). There were three parts to the government: legislative, administrative and judicial. Legislation was passed by two bodies, the *ekklesia* (assembly) and the *boule* (council). The *ekklesia* consisted of all male citizens, who would meet about every ten days to vote on legislation approved by the *boule*. The *boule* was made up of 500 members, 50 members from each of the ten tribes: they served for the period of one year and met every day except festival days. On occasion, a special board of lawmakers (*nomothetai*) would be empanelled to draft new laws.

Numerous officials ran the city administratively on a day-to-day basis. The chief magistrates were the nine archons: the Eponymous archon (after whom the year was named); the King Archon (*basileus*), responsible for religious matters and the laws; the War Archon (Polemarch), responsible for some military matters as well as foreigners; and six *thesmothetes* (keepers of traditional laws).

A host of lesser officials and boards were responsible for various aspects of public concern: fiscal matters, grain supply, water supply, weights and measures, police, and the like. In keeping with democratic ideals, the highest officials were chosen by lot rather than elected. Money, water supply and military matters are simply too important to leave to the luck of the draw, however, and a handful of positions were filled by election: certain treasurers, the water commissioner and tribal generals. These were the real positions of power. We speak of 'Periklean Athens' yet Perikles was never the chief magistrate; he was elected general of his tribe year after year and influenced public policy from that position.

Tokens for allotment of offices, 450–425 BC (above). Most Athenian offices were allotted rather than elected, and clay tokens with irregular joints were one way of matching individuals or groups with their official duties.
To prevent tampering, juries in courts were chosen from a large body of eligible citizens by allotment machines (below), from excavations in the Agora.

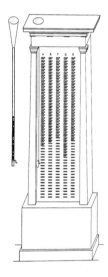

The lawcourts were tremendously important; administrators might decree and assemblies could legislate but – as today – it was up to the courts to determine if the law was constitutional and how it was to be interpreted. The decision, however, was referred to a popular court, made up of regular citizens, rather than to a handful of specialized jurists. The minimum Athenian jury was 201 members, 501 was by no means unusual, and juries of 2,501 are known, so any court decision was in effect a mini-referendum. The big difference between then and now is that there was no attempt at a separation of powers; all three branches of the government were made up of regular citizens, almost all of them allotted.

If these various procedures and offices are still familiar to us today, one aspect of Athenian democracy has not survived: ostracism. When the Persians landed at Marathon in 490 BC, they were guided by Hippias, the old tyrant of Athens, hoping to be reinstated in power once the Persians were victorious. Events turned out differently, but the reappearance of their old tyrant made the Athenians somewhat uneasy about the security of the democracy they had been enjoying for 18 years, and they employed the procedure of ostracism to protect it.

All the Athenians would vote once a year on the question: is anyone aiming at a tyranny? If a simple majority voted yes, then the citizens met again, two months later, bringing with them their *ostrakon* (potsherd), on which they had scratched the name of the man they felt represented a threat to the democracy. The man with the most votes lost and he was exiled for ten

A selection of ostraka from the Athenian Agora, inscribed with the names of Athenian leaders (484–443 BC): (clockwise from upper left) Aristeides son of Lysimachos, Themistokles son of Neokles of Phrearrhios, Perikles son of Xanthippos, and Kimon son of Miltiades. Written by individuals, they shed light on the literacy of the average Athenian. Close to 10,000 examples have been found in the Agora and in the German excavations of the Kerameikos.

DEMOCRACY

Democracy crowns Demos (the People of Athens): relief on a law against tyranny. The decree forbids any legislative body to sit and consider proposals made by a tyrant and ensures that whoever kills the tyrant shall not be prosecuted for murder. The law was passed in 336 BC, after the defeat at Chaironeia in 338 BC, at a time when the Athenians were concerned about the strength of their democracy.

years. In the early years of the fifth century most of the prominent Athenian politicians took one of these enforced ten-year vacations, courtesy of the Athenian people: Xanthippos, Aristeides, Themistokles, Kimon, and many others.

Excavations have been carried out in the Agora of Athens since 1931. The area was densely inhabited from medieval to modern times and some 400 houses have been demolished in order to allow the uncovering of the ancient civic centre. The buildings are generally in a poor state of preservation, but careful work by American archaeologists together with the rich written sources for Athens have allowed the reconstruction of a remarkably complete picture of the birthplace of democracy. Buildings recovered include the *bouleuterion* (seat of the council of 500, or *boule*), the *tholos* (headquarters for the executive committee of the *boule*), the archive building, the Royal Stoa (office of the King Archon), several law-courts and a mint. Many of the 7,500 inscriptions on marble preserve the texts of laws, treaties, public honours and the records of numerous magistrates.

Bronze ballots used by Athenian jurors to record a verdict, fourth century BC. Jurors were given two such ballots (inscribed 'public vote'), one with a pierced axle (for guilty), and one with a solid axle (acquittal); the juror could conceal his vote by holding the ballot with thumb and forefinger covering the axle.

Small objects used in the day-to-day administration of the courts include allotment machines to pick the juries, water-clocks to time the speeches, bronze ballots used by the jurors in rendering a verdict, and tokens to pay the jurors. Other public antiquities recovered include the archives of the cavalry, sets of official weights and measures, and hundreds of *ostraka* used to vote overly ambitious politicians out of office.

One of the most precious gifts of ancient Greece, which seems to have been an invention of the Athenians, is the concept of democracy: the notion that all people can and should govern themselves (*demos* + *kratos* = 'power to the people'). Throughout most of history, people have been ruled by a single individual or a small group, with limited control over the decisions which govern their lives. New was the idea that individuals should have equal access to political power, and to rule and be ruled in turn. In Athens, citizens served in turn as magistrates, councillors and jurors. With the exception of one or two magistracies concerned with festivals, the entire government changed every year; this required and resulted in detailed record-keeping, often on stone. Though usually dated to 507 BC and the reforms of Kleisthenes, the creation of democracy should probably be thought of more as a process than an event, the end result of several important developments which took place over time.

1. Early in the sixth century BC Solon gave the people the right of appeal before the courts (rather than aristocratic magistrates) and allowed everyone to sit as jurors on those courts. As in the American system, the judicial branch had final say over executive and legislative decisions, so juries manned by all the people are the bedrock on which democracy was founded.

2. In 508/7 BC Kleisthenes created ten new tribes, each tribe drawing members from all over Attica, thereby breaking the hold of the old aristocratic families, whose power was based on geography and control of the different parts of Attica. Citizenship, along with most rights and privileges (political, military and social), were now largely in the hands of the tribes and the bonds of loyalty to the clans were gradually dissolved.

3. In promoting Athens as a naval power, Themistokles changed the political landscape of the city in the early fifth century. The thousands of rowers who now provided Athens with its military clout expected a greater share of political power, at the expense of those who made up the smaller land army: wealthier individuals who could afford a full set of armour.

4. Political power is a fine thing, but only if you can afford to wield it. In the mid-fifth century, during the administration of Perikles, pay was introduced for sitting on the council and in the assembly, as well as for jury duty, so poor citizens could actually afford to participate in the public life of the city.

By the fourth century the full democracy had come into being, as described by Aristotle in his *Constitution of the Athenians*. Many Athenians, among them several philosophers, had considerable doubts as to its worth. By modern standards, of course, it was hardly democratic. Women were excluded from voting and Athens was a slave society. Also unrepresented were thousands of citizens of other Greek cities who lived and worked in Athens. A tiny percentage of the total population of the city actively participated.

Despite these flaws, the concepts of full and equal citizenship, a communal civic awareness and a sense of the corporate identity of the *demos* (people) developed over time and led to an entirely new Athenian society, one which endured in reality for two hundred years and which has remained an ideal for twenty-five hundred.

COMMERCE AND BUSINESS

THE MARKET IN ATHENS

*You will find everything sold
together in the same place at
Athens: figs, witnesses to
summonses, bunches of grapes,
turnips, pears, apples,
witnesses, roses, medlars,
porridge, honeycombs,
chickpeas, lawsuits, puddings,
myrtle, allotment machines,
irises, lambs, water-clocks,
laws, indictments.*

Athenaios, *Deipnosophistai* 14,
640 b–c (quoting Mnesimachos,
fourth century BC)

IN ADDITION TO SERVING as the civic centre, the
Agora was also the main marketplace of
Athens. Temporary booths and stalls would
be set up in the great open square, and more
permanent shops were located nearby.
Several small shop buildings have been found
in the excavations, providing evidence of
active and varied commerce: potters, banks,
coroplasts (makers of terracotta figurines),
sculptors, bronze-workers, iron foundries, shoemakers, bone-workers and wineshops have
been uncovered.

Other goods poured into Athens from all
over the Mediterranean, and Peiraieus, the port
of Athens, was a huge commercial centre. The
main harbour was lined with colonnades,
where a vast array of material was displayed and
sold. The port was a huge city itself, with two
agoras and two theatres, and many groups of
Athenian state officials were in fact divided,
with half assigned to monitor trade in the
Agora uptown and the other half to supervise
commerce in Peiraieus. Like most ports,
Peiraieus was a cosmopolitan place and many of
the metics (resident aliens), both Greeks and
foreigners, lived there, some of them in groups
large enough to import their own gods: Cypri-
ots (Aphrodite), Egyptians (Isis) and Thracians
(Bendis). Many did very well indeed; one of
the largest tombs in Attica, built of marble

*(Above right) Red-figured cup by
the Foundry Painter, c. 480–470
BC, found at Vulci, showing a
sculptor's workshop (note the head
of a statue at lower right).
Industrial establishments in the
form of bronze-casting pits, iron
foundries and pottery kilns have
been discovered all over Athens.*

*(Right) A terracotta group of
women making bread; from
Boiotia, fifth century BC.*

and decorated with sculpted friezes and three lifesize statues, is that of a businessman from the Black Sea town of Istria.

Along with the foreigners, the other engine which drove the economy were the slaves. Exact numbers are hard to come by, but there must have been tens of thousands. Their status varied tremendously. At the low end of the scale were those who worked in the silver mines of Laureion who could expect a short and toilsome life. Temple building accounts indicate that some slaves worked as artisans side by side with Athenian citizens and resident aliens, and

were paid the same daily wage of 1 drachma – though we are not told how this was split with their masters.

Other slaves were owned by the state and essentially served as bureaucrats; their lot must have been better, though if they erred their punishment was flogging rather than the fine levied against citizen officials. At the top of the scale, surprisingly, were some prominent bankers who controlled vast financial resources. Slaves could and did buy their freedom occasionally, though that, of course, did not necessarily make them Athenian citizens.

GREEK AGORAS
(King Cyrus of Persia speaks)
'I have never yet feared men who have a place set apart in the midst of their city where they perjure and deceive each other'.... This threat he uttered against all the Hellenes, since they have agoras and buy and sell there; the Persians themselves use no market-places, nor do they have any.
Herodotus, 1. 153

KEEPING TRACK OF TIME

A working replica of a unique example of a klepsydra *(water-clock) from the Athenian Agora, c. 400* BC. *The painted inscription records that it belonged to the tribe of Antichis and held two* choes *of water. It runs for about six minutes and larger examples did exist – as is clear from references in the preserved courtroom speeches of Demosthenes, Aeschines, Lysias and others.*

Timekeeping has been a concern of mankind since the earliest days; the Greeks were no exception, and both extended and short periods of time had to be kept track of.

For long periods of time the Greeks favoured genealogies and generational counts, allowing 30 years per generation on average – not unlike the string of 'begats' early in the Bible. Such genealogies allowed the Classical Greeks to count backwards over the centuries, to the earlier heroic times of Herakles, Theseus and Jason, and the bold deeds associated with the war against Troy, the adventures of Odysseus and the Calydonian boar hunt.

Local dates would be computed on the basis of local heroes, kings, magistrates or priesthoods. Time reckoning for historical purposes became somewhat standardized in the

eighth century BC with the foundation of the Olympic games, generally dated to 776 BC. This served as a starting point, which most Greek cities acknowledged, for recording subsequent events, and allowed correlations between the dating systems of individual cities. The almost simultaneous traditional date for the founding of Rome, 753 BC, provided another means for historians in antiquity to correlate events.

On a local level, most Greek cities had their own yearly calendar, with their own sequence of months, sometimes corresponding to that of other cities, usually not. They used both lunar and solar cycles for different purposes, such as religious as opposed to civic activities, and when the two calendars fell sharply out of alignment extra days or even months would be added

(intercalated) until they were synchronized again, cruder versions of our own added 29 February every leap year. These different calendars in use simultaneously are often hard to reconstruct, but were presumably no harder for an ancient citizen to grasp than our ability to think simultaneously of the calendar year, the fiscal year and the school year, each with its own starting point and particular divisions. The Athenian year began roughly in mid-summer, so a date shown as 425/4 BC means the twelve months from July of 425 BC to the end of June 424 BC.

On a daily basis, the passage of time was marked by the movement of the sun and was often recorded by sundials. In antiquity, however, time was kept in temporal (rather than equinoctial) hours, which means that the period of

sunlight every day is divided into 12 hours, which in turn means longer hours in summer and shorter hours in winter. The earliest extant sundials date to the third century BC.

Also used were water-clocks, which grew increasingly sophisticated in the third and second centuries BC and worked whether the sun shone or not. They were used especially when time less than an hour was to be reckoned. A unique terracotta example found in Athens was used to time speeches in the law-courts, each speaker being given the same amount of water for his speech. We also hear of a prostitute known as Klepsydra (water-clock) because she used one to time her customers. The technology and mathematics of both sundials and water-clocks were borrowed from Egypt.

More precise timekeeping seems not to have been a concern and we therefore have no sense of 'records' for running events at something like the Olympic games. Great runners were recognized by their ability to win races for many years at numerous festivals.

In the next year – the year in which there was a lunar eclipse one evening – and the old temple of Athena at Athens was burned, Pityas being ephor in Sparta and Kallias archon in Athens …
Xenophon, Hellenika 1. 6. 1 (defining 406 BC)

125

RELIGIOUS LIFE

(pp. 142ff.)

The Acropolis of Athens, crowned by the Parthenon (447–432 BC); the colossal statue of gold and ivory of the goddess Athena housed in the temple is known from copies in clay, marble and metal. The most complete and best preserved, the Varvakeion Athena (below), dates to the second century AD.

THE ATHENIANS, like all Greeks, worshipped a wide variety of Olympian gods and local heroes (pp. 142ff.). Several sacred calendars preserved on stone list the various festivals and sacrifices necessary to keep the city on an even keel vis-a-vis higher powers. Though many cults were for limited groups of people, several festivals were celebrated by the whole city. Such events were both the occasion for a holiday – often of several days' duration – and an important vehicle of social cohesion.

Athena and the Acropolis

Of all cults, the most important for Athens was the worship of Athena, the patron deity of the city. The whole of the Acropolis was given over to her cult – focal point of the religious life of the city, the citadel dominated the skyline of Athens. It may well be, however, that the citizens visited the shrine only rarely, on the festival days of specific gods.

A host of temples and private dedications erected in the sixth century BC were swept away in the destruction of Athens by the Persians in 480 BC. Their fragments were buried in great pits on the Acropolis and they were replaced in the second half of the fifth century BC by three marble temples and a monumental gateway. Athens was then at the height of her power and wealth and able to command the best materials, craftsmen and artists, and these buildings are generally regarded as the outstanding examples of Classical Greek architecture. Built during the administration of Perikles, the overall conception of the project was the work of the Athenian sculptor Pheidias, whose earliest work was the colossal bronze statue of Athena Promachos ('champion'), which was set up on the Acropolis around 460–450 BC as a thank-offering for the battle of Marathon. Pupil of earlier masters, he was the premier sculptor of fifth-century Athens and is said by Plutarch to have had creative responsibility for the building programme generally, as well as being directly responsible for the chryselephantine statue (see below) which stood in the Parthenon.

The Propylaia

The entrance to this great sanctuary high above the city was a lavishly expensive marble gateway known as the Propylaia. Built using both the Doric and Ionic orders, it was completed in five years (437–432 BC) under the direction of the architect Mnesikles. A picture gallery occupied the northern wing, while the southern one led to the Athena Nike sanctuary; the central hall had five large doors which gave access to the Acropolis itself.

The Parthenon

Centrepiece of the building programme was the Parthenon. Using eight Doric columns across the front, rather than the canonical six, the architect, Iktinos, was able to make a more monumental temple without actually expanding the size of the individual elements. Inside, this allowed sufficient room both for an interior colonnade and a colossal chryselephantine (gold and ivory) statue of Athena, over 9 m (30 ft) tall and fully armed. Athena was also celebrated in the sculpted pediments high up on the building. At the east end her miraculous birth from the head of her father Zeus was depicted. Her mother Metis was the goddess of wisdom and, fearing that she might produce someone smarter than himself, Zeus swallowed her, leading to the splitting headache nine months later. Sharing the pediment were all the gods of Olympus watching this amazing arrival of their sibling. At the west end the pediment showed the contest between Athena and her uncle Poseidon to see which would be the patron

THE GLORIES OF ATHENS

The materials were stone, bronze, ivory, gold, ebony, cypresswood; and the arts or trades that wrought and fashioned them were smiths and carpenters, moulders, founders and braziers, stone-cutters, dyers, goldsmiths, ivory-workers, painters, embroiderers, turners; also those who brought them to town, merchants, marines and ship-masters by sea, and cartwrights, cattle-breeders, waggoners, rope-makers, flax-workers, shoemakers, leather-dressers, road-makers and miners by land.

Plutarch, *Perikles* 13

And so the works arose, no less impressive in size than exquisite in form, the workmen striving to surpass the material and design with the beauty of their workmanship, yet the most wonderful thing of all was the rapidity of their construction.

Plutarch, *Perikles* 13

On the left of the gateway is a room containing pictures. Among the works which time had not effaced were Diomedes and Odysseus, one at Lemnos carrying off the bow of Philoctetes, the other carrying off the statue of Athena from Troy. Among the paintings here is also Orestes killing Aegisthus and Pylades slaying the sons of Nauplius, who came to the rescue of Aegisthus, and Polyxena about to be slaughtered at the grave of Achilles ...

Pausanias, 1. 23. 6

(Above) A section of the Parthenon frieze, showing figures of the Athenian cavalry.

A reclining male figure, possibly Dionysos, Herakles or Ares, from the east pediment of the Parthenon.

An inscription recording the treasures kept in the Parthenon crowned by a relief showing Athena and Erechtheus on either side of an olive tree; c. 410/09 BC.

deity of Athens, a contest obviously won by Athena. Other sculptures showed scenes from Greek mythology illustrating the triumph of civilization over barbarians, a reference to the Greek victories over the Persians: Greeks over Amazons (west end), Greek against Centaurs (south side), Greeks at Troy (north side) and Gods over Giants (east end). An interior frieze shows a great procession usually identified as part of the Panathenaic festival in honour of Athena. The building and its sculpture are in effect a celebration of the city of Athens itself, a monumental votive offering to its patroness. It served both to house the huge statue and also as the state treasury of the city; it was not, however, a particularly religious building. There is no contemporary altar, which is the focal point of most Greek religious activity, nor is there an attested priest or priestess of Athena Parthenos.

The Erechtheion

The most important cult building on the Acropolis was built later than the Parthenon; it lies on the north side of the citadel and replaces an earlier sixth-century BC temple. The traveller Pausanias, who came to Athens in around AD 150 and was especially interested in religious matters, writes only two sentences on the Parthenon but needs two full pages on the Erechtheion and its cults. The building housed a cult statue of wood, crudely carved and so old it was said to have fallen from heaven. It is of unusual form for a temple, with free-standing columns at the east, engaged columns at the west, and two porches of completely different scale and form stuck on the north and south walls. Within it were a multiplicity of sacred spots, and at least eight deities are associated with the building: Athena, Poseidon, Erechtheus, Zeus, Dione, Hermes, Kekrops and Butes. Its peculiar plan may well derive from the need to accommodate all these sacred areas, and the Erechtheion is just what it looks like: a temple built by committee, with numerous priests insisting that their sacred ground be respected. The architect, building literally in the shadow of the Parthenon, wisely decided not to compete directly, and chose the lighter, more ornate Ionic style (p. 168) for his building, thereby avoiding comparison with its Doric neighbour. In addition to elaborately carved mouldings, there was a sculpted frieze of white marble figures pinned to a grey limestone background, and the south porch uses heavily draped female figures (caryatids) instead of columns to support the roof (see also p. 6).

Athena Nike

The third temple of Athena was a tiny one, set on a bastion just outside the entrance to the Acropolis. It was of the Ionic order, with four columns projecting from east and west. Sculpted friezes showed an assembly of gods and battle scenes. The cult statue inside is described as holding a pomegranate in one hand and a helmet in the other. The usual way of showing victory (*nike*) is as a winged female figure, but as Athena was shown here there are no wings and the statue therefore became known as the 'wingless victory'. The little marble temple is the third temple of Athena Nike to occupy the bastion; remains of the earlier ones, including an inscribed altar, were found buried deep below.

Other cults

Athena was worshipped on the Acropolis in a variety of other guises. Just inside the gateway there was an altar and statue of Athena Hygieia (health), and numerous other dedications preserved different forms of her name such as Ergane (worker) and Promachos (champion). In addition to Athena, other deities were worshipped on the Acropolis as well, honoured with temples, altars or statues: Zeus Polias, Poseidon, Artemis, Earth (Ge), and the numerous deities lodged in and around the Erechtheion.

The Caryatids (female figures serving as columns) on the south porch of the Erechtheion (c. 430–410 BC). Their specific identification is uncertain.

(Below) The small Ionic temple of Athena Nike on the Acropolis, c. 435–425 BC.

The Panathenaia

The principal festival of Athena, the Panathenaia, was held each year in summer (roughly July), in the first month of the Athenian year, on Hekatombaion 28, traditionally recognized as her birthday. From modest beginnings it grew with Athens into a huge national celebration with several different parts. The focal point was a great parade in honour of the goddess.

The parade is described by Aristophanes, and most scholars – though not all – think it is also depicted in the Parthenon frieze. It consisted of priests and cult officials, the elders of the city, attendants carrying baskets, stools, parasols and metal trays of offerings, musicians (flutes and citharas), people carrying olive branches, sacrificial animals (bulls and rams), and large contingents of cavalrymen and their horses. The procession set out from the main city gate, traversed the Agora, and wound its way up to the Acropolis. Here the statue of the goddess was presented with a newly woven garment (*peplos*). In later times this robe was prominently displayed by hanging it as the sail on a ship which was dragged along as part of the procession. A sacrifice of 100 bulls was held and all that meat was carried down into the lower city for a huge communal feast.

By 566 BC a set of athletic games had been added to the programme and the festival was

(Below right) A Panathenaic amphora, made to hold the olive oil given as a prize for many events. One side always shows the striding warrior Athena, though in around 360 BC she turns and starts moving left to right. Painted inscriptions date the vases to a specific year.

held with particular grandeur every four years. The athletic contests were in some ways similar to the great Panhellenic festival games held at Olympia, Delphi, Isthmia and Nemea (pp. 154–59); the differences, however, are striking. First, while the victors at the other games received only a wreath, prizes of value were

(Below) A marble relief found in the Agora of Athens (c. 400 BC), commemorating a victory by the tribe Leontis in the anthippasia, *a cavalry display which was one of the team events held as part of the Panathenaic games.*

given at the Panathenaia. These took the form of cash, gold crowns or a bull. Most common, however, were jars of oil taken from Athena's sacred olive trees. The jars were specially made, dated and painted on one side with the figure of a striding Athena, and on the other with a representation of the event for which the oil was a prize. Easily recognizable, hundreds of these prize jars have been recovered all over the Mediterranean. Other differences in the Panathenaic games were that prizes were given for more than just first place, there were some events open only to Athenians and others open to everyone, and many of the events had a

Sections of the Parthenon frieze, often interpreted as the Panathenaic procession. With a total length of 160 m (524 ft), it shows hundreds of figures. Over the central door was an enigmatic scene (bottom row) involving five mortals flanked by seated deities. Other sections depict a cavalcade of horsemen and bulls being led to sacrifice. The identification as the Panathenaic procession was made in the eighteenth century by the British architects Stuart and Revett, though no ancient source identifies the scene for us, and the interpretation has recently been challenged. The frieze, part of the Elgin Marbles, was taken to England in the early nineteenth century and is now in the British Museum.

The reverse of a Panathenaic amphora, showing the event for which the oil it contained was the prize, in this case a footrace. Panathenaic amphoras continued to be painted in the black-figured style for centuries, long after the technique went out of favour for other pottery.

They say that the Rarian plain [at Eleusis] was the first to be sown and the first to bear crops, and therefore it is the custom to take the sacrificial barley and to make cakes for the sacrifices out of its produce. Here they show the threshing floor of Triptolemos and the altar. But my dream forbad me to describe what is within the wall of the sanctuary; and surely it is clear that the uninitiated may not lawfully hear of those things the sight of which is denied them.

Pausanias, 1. 38. 6

A caryatid from the inner propylon (gateway) at Eleusis (c. 50 BC). She carries a cista (container for secret cult objects) on her head.

strongly military character (dances in armour, a javelin thrown from horseback). Perhaps most striking, there were many team events, in contrast to Olympia and elsewhere, where all events were for individuals. One wonders if this reflects the democratic values of the Athenians and an attempt to avoid the aristocratic character of the Panhellenic games, with their glorification of the individual.

The Eleusinian Mysteries

At some time around the seventh century BC, Athens gained control of one of the most important cult sites in Greece, Eleusis, and incorporated it into the Athenian state. Eleusis lay 22.5 km (14 miles) west of Athens and was connected to the city by a sacred way which led to the sanctuary of Demeter. She was the principal fertility deity of the Greeks, responsible for good crops.

Unlike the other gods, her rites were secret and held at night; her cult building at Eleusis, the Telesterion (Hall of Mysteries), was therefore not like other temples. It was a huge enclosed hall, capable of holding thousands of celebrants. Because the penalty for revealing the mysteries to anyone who was not an initiate was death, the secret was well kept; even today we do not know for certain what rites were carried out in the Telesterion. We know only that they were regarded as crucial for successful crops each year.

(Right) General view of the Telesterion (Hall of Mysteries) from the south. No fewer than seven separate building phases can be made out in the course of the 1000 years the hall was in use.

(Left) Part of the frieze of the inner propylon, c. AD 50. The inscription, a rare example of Latin used in Athens, records the dedication of the building by Claudius Appius Pulcher. The Doric frieze carries sculpted symbols of the Eleusinian cult.

(Right) Plan of the sanctuary of Demeter at Eleusis in the mid-second century AD; the cult was extremely popular throughout the Roman period and several emperors were initiated into the mysteries.

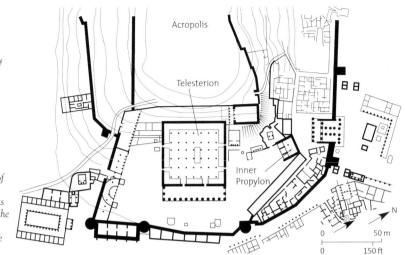

Acropolis

Telesterion

Inner Propylon

N

0   50 m
0   150 ft

THE DIONYSIA AND GREEK THEATRE

THE THIRD GREAT FESTIVAL of the Athenians was the City Dionysia, held every year in the month of Elaphebolion (roughly March). This celebrated the worship of Dionysos, god of wine and good times. He was an import from the Boiotian town of Eleutherai and was therefore known as Dionysos Eleuthereus. The focal point of the festival was, as at the Panathenaia, a great procession and the sacrifice of dozens of bulls – perhaps as many as 240.

Offerings of wine and bread were made, and phalluses were carried in the parade. This was followed by a revel (*komos*), with singing, dancing and too much wine.

The sanctuary of Dionysos, with temples, a stoa and votive offerings, lay at the base of the Acropolis on its southern side. Set into the hillside was a huge theatre, scene of

(Left) Terracotta theatrical masks of the third century BC, from Athens (top) and South Italy, two great centres of ancient theatre.

(Right) An ivory statuette of an actor with mask and platform shoes (kothornoi); all parts were played by men.

(Below) A Dionysiac scene – a revel or komos with music and dancing, depicted on a kylix (cup) by the Brygos painter, c. 490 BC.

GREEK THEATRE

Roman portraits of the three great Athenian tragedians: (from left to right) Aeschylus (who fought at the battle of Marathon), Sophokles (who was a general in the Athenian army) and Euripides (who retired to a cave on the island of Salamis to write his plays).

Drama as we know it had its origins in Greece, and Athens in particular. The early comedies, tragedies and assorted choral performances can be seen as the ancestors of modern showbusiness. Such spectacles must have had tremendous impact in antiquity; they were the principal source of entertainment for people in a society not suffering from sensory overload.

Theatre is thought to have begun with songs and dances in honour of Dionysos, patron god of wine. In the years around 534 BC Thespis (hence thespian) added an individual actor to the chorus and the performance moved beyond the simple singing of a hymn or story. A second actor was added, and eventually a third. Throughout, however, the singing and dancing of the chorus remained a focal point of the play, and Greek theatres have a large dancing-ground known as the orchestra.

The acting was all done by men, in costume and wearing large masks. It is not entirely clear that women were even allowed to attend the performances, though it seems on balance that they were.

Greek mythology was the usual source of inspiration for ancient playwrights. As the bad news often continues down through more than one generation, the tragedies in Athens were presented in the form of three plays (trilogies), to allow the full telling of the story. The only complete trilogy to survive is the *Oresteia*, by Aeschylus: the *Agamemnon* covers the murder of Agamemnon by Clytemnestra in revenge for his sacrifice of their daughter Iphigenia, at the start of the Greek expedition against Troy; the *Choephoroi* tells of Orestes' murder of his mother Clytemnestra; and the *Eumenides* concerns the trial and acquittal of Orestes for matricide.

Sometimes more contemporary events were portrayed, as in the lost play by Phrynichus on the fall of Miletus in 494 BC, or Aeschylus' play *The Persians*, based on the battle of Salamis in 480 BC (see p. 112).

In all, some 33 tragedies survive, written by the three great poets of fifth-century Athens: Aeschylus (7 plays), Sophokles (7 plays) and Euripides (19 plays). Much of the play consisted of dialogue and narrative; most of the action, particularly the bloody bits, took place off-stage (hence the original meaning of obscene).

Comedies were performed as single plays and were definitely contemporary, lampooning prominent citizens and politicians mercilessly and coarsely. Eleven plays of Aristophanes survive from the end of the fifth century, and large parts of four plays by Menander from the fourth century.

The costumes, sets, costs of training the chorus, musicians, and the like, made the productions expensive undertakings, assigned to wealthy individuals to pay for as a form of taxation. The plays were performed as part of the festival of Dionysos and prizes were awarded to the winning producer (*choregos* = leader of the chorus), playwright/poet and actor.

Theatres were a feature of almost every Greek city (see also pp. 172–73), consisting of an auditorium – usually set into the slope of a hill – a large orchestra and a scene building. The largest theatres held over 15,000 spectators, so good acoustics and good projection by the actors were essential.

Over time, as the actors became more important and the chorus less so, the scene building with its raised stage was moved forwards into the area of the orchestra. The end result, of course, is the modern theatre with its tiny, sunken 'pit' for the orchestra.

Scenery consisted originally of painted panels on a rather simple structure, but this received more attention as the stage developed. In the Roman period scene buildings were three storeys high, with architectural embellishments and often lavish sculpture.

Agora inscription (I 7151) winners in tragedy:

When Timokrates was archon [364/3 BC]
(? was the winning playwright)
With the Oinopion and Hekabe
Arexis as the lead actor

Theodorides was second
With the Medea and Phaethon
Androsthenes as the lead actor

Kleainetos was third
with the Hypsipyle and Ph…
Hipparchos as the lead actor

Arexis won as best actor.

The theatre of Dionysos at Athens, birthplace of western drama (and therefore most showbusiness). The surviving building, which seated 15,000 to 17,000 people, dates from the 330s BC, with Roman additions (first/second centuries AD) to the orchestra and stage.

the performances held as an important part of the festival. These included odes in honour of Dionysos (dithyrambs), tragedies, satyr plays and comedies. Contests of these theatrical performances were held for several days immediately after the *komos*, all as part of the sacred rites of Dionysos. The dramatic performances evolved over time and were regarded in antiq-

uity as an Athenian invention. They seem to have begun originally as choruses, singing and dancing in honour of Dionysos. In the years around 534 BC a man called Thespis was credited with adding an actor who interacted with the chorus, and drama as we know it began. Over time other actors were added, and full tragedies and comedies were being produced by

the fifth century BC. Some of the works of the most successful Classical playwrights survive: tragedies by Aeschylus, Sophokles and Euripides, and comedies by Aristophanes.

Actors played both male and female roles, clad in elaborate costumes and large masks. The costs of the performances were considerable (costumes, training, salaries, etc) and were paid for by the wealthiest citizens of Athens. The winning producer (*choregos*) had the right to set up a conspicuous monument displaying the bronze tripod which was the prize for a winning performance. Prizes were also offered for best actor and best playwright and numerous victor lists survive, essentially recording the Academy Award winners of centuries long past.

A choregic monument set up by Lysikrates, the winning producer in 336 BC, to display his prize, a bronze tripod, on the roof. The frieze above the columns shows a scene of Dionysos changing a ship full of pirates into dolphins. (The same pirates as dolphins are shown on the sixth-century cup on p. 10.)

INTELLECTUAL LIFE: EDUCATION AND PHILOSOPHY

(Above) Roman portraits of Sokrates (left; 469–399 BC), and Aristotle (right), founder of the Lyceum and tutor to Alexander the Great, a copy of an original of the later fourth century BC.

(Centre) Young boys practising music and writing; a red-figured cup by Douris, c. 470 BC, from Vulci.

ARISTIPPUS SHIPWRECKED
The philosopher Aristippus, a follower of Sokrates, was shipwrecked on the coast of Rhodes, and, observing geometric diagrams drawn in the sand, he shouted to his companions: 'Good hope here, I see human footsteps'. He went at once to the city of Rhodes and to the gymnasium. There he disputed on philosophical topics and was so richly rewarded he fitted out himself and his companions with clothing and other necessities.

Vitruvius, 6 praef. 1

IN ADDITION TO ITS GREAT DRAMATISTS and the invention of theatre, Athens soon became prominent in other intellectual spheres, in particular philosophy. Some of the earliest philosophers practised in the East Greek world, especially in Miletus (Thales, Anaximander, Anaximenes), and Pythagoras was to become very influential in the West. But Athens, with her wealth, educational concerns and a tradition of vociferous public debate ensured by Athenian democracy, drew many outstanding teachers throughout the Classical and later periods.

Very influential was a local Athenian, Sokrates. Active in the last quarter of the fifth century BC, many of his dialogues are preserved in the writings of Plato and Xenophon. He taught wherever he happened to be, often in and around the public buildings of the Agora or in nearby shops. His teaching of the young men of Athens led eventually to charges of impiety and corruption of the youth of Athens and he was condemned to death and made to drink poison. After him, Plato and then Aristotle preferred to teach in well-established institutions, the gymnasia of the city.

Education and the gymnasium

The word gymnasium derives from the Greek word for naked (*gymnos*), which is how the Greeks practised and performed athletics. This habit was for other cultures a defining feature of Greeks everywhere, and gymnasia have been found in Greek cities as far away as Afghanistan. The earliest attested gymnasia date to the sixth century BC, and several were flourishing by the fifth (pp. 156–57). They provided instruction and facilities for running, wrestling, boxing, jumping, archery and throwing the discus and javelin, much of it useful for training young men in the basic military skills.

Where young men gathered to exercise their bodies was the place also to exercise their minds, and gymnasia became centres of learning much more than just facilities for sports and athletics. In Athens this was formalized with the founding of two philosophical schools in direct association with famous old gymnasia, the Academy and the Lyceum.

The Academy

By the sixth century a gymnasium had been founded just over a mile northwest of the city at the shrine of a local hero, Hekademos. In the fifth century it was provided with water and turned into a welcoming grove, and here, in 386 BC, Plato established his philosophical school, known hereafter and into the present day as the Academy. A boundary stone of the gymnasium was found *in situ* in the 1960s but most of the Academy lies under the urban sprawl of modern Athens. Plato's extensive recording of Sokratic dialogues and treatises on laws and society remain the basis for much of Western philosophy.

The Lyceum

Aristotle founded the second great philosophical school in 335 BC. He established it at another Athenian gymnasium, which was centred around the cult of Apollo Lykeios. This lay southeast of the town, like the Academy outside the walls. It has not been excavated either, though inscriptions and literary sources suggest it should be sought largely under the National Gardens of the modern city. Aristotle was not Athenian, but was born in Stageira in Macedonia. He was hired by King Philip II as a tutor for his son, Alexander, and their school has been found near modern Naousa in northern Greece. Aristotle also spent time on the island of Lesbos and at Assos on the mainland opposite, before returning to Athens. He was interested in all the natural world, as well as politics; most of our understanding of the Athenian political system comes from his *Constitution of the Athenians*, while other surviving treatises cover a wide variety of topics.

Other philosophers

Dozens of other philosophers followed to teach at Athens, which became the university town of the Mediterranean throughout the Hellenistic and Roman periods. Even when other great centres of learning arose, such as Alexandria, Antioch and Massalia, Athens retained its pre-eminence for centuries, catering first to princes of the Hellenistic kingdoms and then to the sons of Roman nobility.

A well-known, almost legendary, fourth-century philosopher was Diogenes, the Cynic, who emigrated from Sinope on the Black Sea to Athens, where he lived in poverty in various public buildings of the city (the archive building, the Stoa of Zeus and the Pompeion). He believed that happiness depended on satisfying one's natural needs as easily as possible. He held that whatever is natural cannot be dishonourable or indecent and could therefore be done in public, which he accordingly did. From this shameless behaviour he became known as κυον (dog), from which the term Cynic arose.

Among the most influential Hellenistic philosophers was Zeno, who came to Athens from Kition in Cyprus in the years around 313 BC. Like Sokrates, Zeno preferred to teach in the centre of town, choosing as his favoured classroom the famed Painted Stoa, which stood along the north side of the Agora square. From his regular meetings here, Zeno and his followers became known as the Stoics. His doctrine, developed after following Cynic and Sokratic teachings, was that the only real good is virtue, which is based on knowledge which is in harmony with logic. The only evil was not to be virtuous; everything else, including pain, poverty and death, is indifferent. If a man is in harmony with reason, he is possessed of the only real good and thus is independent of the vicissitudes of fortune and accordingly happy.

Also active at this time was Epicurus, born in Samos of Athenian parents. In 307/6, after teaching in Asia Minor, he moved to Athens, where he bought a house and garden, which became the centre of his school. In contrast to the public venues sought out by Sokrates, Diogenes and Zeno, Epicurus and his followers removed themselves, living together privately in his house. Adherents included both women and slaves. Some of his writings survive and many of his precepts are recorded by the Roman poet Lucretius. The purpose of philosophy was to secure a happy life, and pleasure was the beginning and end of living happily. Pain resulted from unsatisfied desires, which could be limited by seeking less pleasure and being satisfied with what one had. Avoiding the competitive life freed one from jealousy and failure, while avoiding intense emotional commitment spared the pain of emotional turmoil. Man was mortal, there was no providential god, pleasure was central, the creation of the cosmos was accidental and the world could be explained by natural causes: these precepts made Epicurianism especially distasteful to Christianity.

Diogenes the Cynic (note the dog). When Alexander asked him what he could do for him, Diogenes is said to have requested that he move and stop blocking the sunlight. Roman copy of a Hellenistic original.

ATHENIAN EDUCATION
After this they send them to school and charge the master to take far more pains over their children's good behaviour than over their letters and harp playing.

Plato, *Protagoras* 325D

Zeno of Kition in Cyprus, founder of the Stoic school of philosophy in Athens.

PRIVATE LIFE

FEMALE VIRTUES

If I am to speak of womanly virtues, referring to those of you who will henceforth be widows, I will sum it up briefly: Great is your glory if you do not fall below the standard which nature has set for your sex, and great also is hers of whom there is least talk among men, whether in praise or in blame.

Thucydides, 2. 45

THE IDEAL BANQUET

From Elis comes the cook, from Argos the cauldron, from Phlius the wine, from Corinth the bedspreads, from Sikyon the fish, from Aegion the flute-girls, from Sicily the cheese, from Athens the perfumes, and from Boiotia the eels.

Athenaios, *Deipnosophistai* 27d (quoting Antiphanes)

IN ADDITION TO THE GREAT TEMPLES and bustling public buildings of the city, literary texts and excavation have shed much light on the private lives of Athenians as well. Athenian houses, like Athens itself, were built in an irregular, almost random, manner and we do not find many ordered square city blocks or a regular arrangement of rooms as in the planned communities of, among others, Olynthos and Priene (pp. 78–80). Most houses, however, have several features in common. The walls were usually built of plastered sun-dried mud-brick set on a rubble or cut stone socle (base), the floors would be of clay or packed earth and timbers supported a roof of baked terracotta tiles. Often there was a second storey.

Houses looked inwards, with light and air provided by a central courtyard open to the sky. A formal dining room, reserved for men and called the *andron*, was to be found near the entrance, often paved with a mosaic floor and built with an off-centre door to allow the maximum number of dining couches. The function of other rooms is often harder to determine, though literary sources indicate that if large enough the house would have a separate women's quarter. By modern standards the

rooms were dark and sparsely furnished, with wooden couches, chairs, stools and chests. A well and/or cistern in the courtyard would provide most of the water for household use, while clean drinking water might be carried from the nearest public fountainhouse. General household waste was disposed of casually; nightsoil was carted away and disposed of beyond the city walls, though there is some debate whether the *koprologoi* were officials or private contractors.

By and large Athenian women spent their time at home in pursuits which have occupied them for centuries: child-rearing, cleaning, cooking and weaving. Generally a woman was under the legal authority of a father, husband or brother. They were citizens, but with few civic rights – their citizenship of significance only in determining the status of their offspring. Occasions to leave the house were limited, perhaps confined to a daily visit to the fountainhouse. The other occasions when they were free to move about was during some of the big festivals, usually those concerned with fertility, and especially those in honour of Demeter. Here women were essential and fully responsible for the rites, often lasting all night and without male participation or supervision.

(Left) Grave stele of Ampharete. The inscription reads: 'My daughter's beloved child is the one I hold here, the one whom I held on my lap while we looked at the light of the sun when we were alive and still hold now that we are both dead.' From the Kerameikos cemetery, Athens, late fifth century BC.

(Right) Detail from a black-figured hydria (water-jar), c. 540–520 BC, with a woman collecting water from the spouts of a public fountainhouse. The daily scene is described by Aristophanes: 'Rising at dawn, what trouble I had to fill this pot at the fountain. What a mob, what noise, what a rattling of water pots! Crowded with slaves and servant girls.'

THE PELOPONNESIAN WAR

A defining period in Athenian history was the war fought between Athens and Sparta during the last third of the fifth century BC. It pitted Athens and a large group of (sometimes reluctant) allies in the Aegean islands and the west coast of Asia Minor against Sparta and the cities of the Peloponnese and much of the Greek mainland. The story is told by Thucydides, who was himself an Athenian general until exiled in 424 BC. His account is generally regarded as one of the outstanding examples of historical writing.

Thucydides, an Athenian, wrote the history of the war waged by the Peloponnesians and the Athenians against one another. He began the task at the very outset of the war, in the belief that it would be great and noteworthy above all the wars that had gone before, inferring this from the fact that both powers were then at their best in preparedness for war in every way, and seeing the rest of the Hellenic race taking sides with one state or another, some at once, some planning to do so.
Thucydides, 1. 1

The Peloponnesian war was protracted to a great length, and in the course of it disaster befell Hellas the like of which had never occurred in any equal space of time. Never had so many cities been taken and left desolate.... Never had so many human beings been exiled, or so much human blood shed, whether in the course of the war itself or as the result of civil dissensions. And so the stories of former times, handed down by oral tradition, but very rarely confirmed by fact, ceased to be incredible; about earthquakes, for instance, for they prevailed over a very large part of the earth and were likewise of the greatest violence; eclipses of the sun, which occurred at more frequent intervals than we find recorded

of all former times; great droughts also in some quarters with resultant famines; and lastly – the disaster which wrought most harm to Hellas and destroyed a considerable part of the people – the plague.
Thucydides, 1. 23

The underlying cause of the war was the growth and projection of Athenian power after the Persian Wars, challenging traditional Spartan dominance in military affairs; the immediate causes were interference by both cities in the affairs of each other's allies, such as Kerkyra, Potidaia, Plataia and Megara. The war was a classic conflict between a strong naval power and a fearsome land army.

Athenian strategy, devised by Perikles, one of the ten generals, was to abandon the countryside of Attica, have everyone move within the protection of the walls of Athens, and rely on the fleet both to provision the city and to prosecute the war all over the Aegean.

The Spartan plan was to bring its army into Attica in a series of annual campaigns, to destroy the crops and plunder the territory of Attica in an attempt to draw the Athenians into a pitched land battle.

Both sides suffered tremendous reverses. In 429 BC the overcrowded conditions in Athens aided the spread of a devastating plague which killed thousands of people, including Perikles. A large earthquake in central Greece in 426 caused the Spartans to withdraw from their annual invasion. In 425/4 a Spartan force of 420 warriors was trapped on the island of Sphakteria; many were killed and the 292 survivors surrendered, a tremendous blow to Spartan military prestige.

A fragile peace was observed in 421–415 BC, following which the Athenians sent a huge fleet against Syracuse, a Corinthian

colony in Sicily, on the pretext of helping the smaller cities of Egesta and Leontini. This force was trapped and wiped out, with its general, Nikias.

The flamboyant Alcibiades was then general for several years, with decidedly mixed results, until he went into exile in 406 BC. Finally, in 404 BC, the Spartan admiral Lysander destroyed an Athenian fleet at Aegispotamoi in the Hellespont and starved Athens into submission.

The grave stele of two Athenian warriors, Chairedemos and Lykeas, c. 420 BC, presumably killed during the Peloponnesian War.

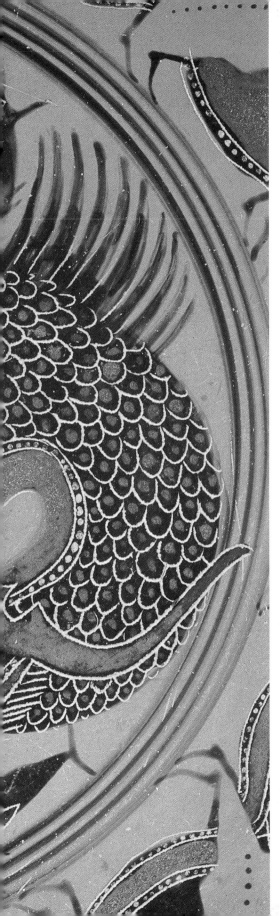

VII

GODS AND HEROES

Nearly all the names of the gods came to Hellas from Egypt. For I am assured by inquiry that they came from foreigners, and I believe they came primarily from Egypt.

Herodotus, 2. 50

AS WITH ALMOST ALL human societies, the Greeks felt that aspects of their lives were directed by forces well beyond their control and attempts were made to come to terms with them, to appease and placate them, and, if possible, to encourage their active support and beneficence. There are signs of matriarchal religious systems in pre-Greek religion, in the exaggerated fertility figurines of the Neolithic period and perhaps in the bare-breasted 'goddesses' of Minoan Crete. In the Linear B tablets of Mycenaean Greece we begin to find the earliest evidence of the pantheon of Olympian gods who were to reign supreme throughout the historical period.

In addition to these great gods, many of whom were attributed with control over natural phenomena, there was a host of lesser deities, demi-gods and local heroes; the Greeks followed a fantastically polytheistic religion.

As well as the full Olympian gods, the Greeks worshipped numerous demi-gods and heroes, and the favourite was probably Herakles. His adventures are depicted in statues, vase-painting and mosaics all over the Greek world – on this mid-sixth century BC vase from Tarquinia he is shown wrestling with a sea-monster.

SANCTUARIES, FESTIVALS AND SACRIFICES

GREEK SANCTUARIES could consist of huge marble temples or the simplest altar or outcrop of bedrock. Though there was considerable variety in the rituals, the focal point of a cult was usually the altar, set in the open air, where offerings were made; these could range from a whole bull or other animal down to a libation of wine and a honeycake. There are traditions and indications that early on, in times of trouble, human sacrifice was practised occasionally.

Many Greek sanctuaries were repositories of tremendous wealth. Expensive temples, built of lavish materials and richly decorated with sculpture were often erected, and votive offerings of pottery, sculpture, and a wide range of bronze, silver and gold objects would be dedi-

*(Right) Greek temples were
originally repositories of great
treasures dedicated by worshippers
to the deity. Most of these valuable
dedications have long since gone,
plundered in antiquity, so this gold
bowl found at Olympia is a rare
survival. It is inscribed in
Corinthian letters of the late
seventh century with the name
of the Kypselids.*

*The gods were offered sacrifices
of various sorts, such as the sheep
being led in this procession, painted
on a wooden plaque found in
a cave near Corinth and dated
c. 520–500 BC. Once sacrificed,
the meat of the animal was usually
cooked and shared between priests
and the celebrants.*

cated to the deity. The temples were plundered eventually and the wealth is usually long gone, but inscribed temple inventories survive to carry a record of these treasures. The sanctuary might also own large tracts of sacred land which would be leased out.

The security of the sanctuary and the god's protection made it a good place to store public and private wealth as well. The Athenian state treasure was housed in the Parthenon and the funds available in an emergency even included the sheets of gold on Athena's cult statue. In Sparta, private wealth was frowned upon and many Spartans therefore stored their personal wealth in the sanctuary of Alea at Tegea, just over the border in Arcadia, in an early instance of offshore banking. And the great sanctuary of Artemis at Ephesus was said to be the largest bank in Asia.

In the days before easy and ubiquitous entertainment, most Greeks relied largely on the spectacles associated with the great festivals to enliven their year: processions, athletic contests, singing and dancing, and feasting. Prometheus was credited with persuading the gods that they liked the smell of roasting meat but did not care too much what happened to it after the sacrifice. Festivals were therefore one of the few times in the year when a Greek could expect to eat meat, often at the expense of the state or a wealthy sponsor.

The practice of religion was very much a social occasion, for the entire city. The concept of a separation of cult and state was unheard of, and all activities, public or private, were carried out under divine auspices and, if possible, with divine approval. The gods were not arbiters of human morality and their own behaviour all too often left something to be desired. Individual gods had certain domains or activities which were their specific concern and they are recognizable by the attributes they carry which are appropriate to their specific character. As early as the seventh century BC these attributes allow us to recognize the principal gods in vase-painting and sculpture.

Most cult activity in the form of offerings and sacrifices took place outside the actual temple at open-air altars. The temple building housed the treasure dedicated to the deity and the cult statue. The artist of this clay vessel, dated to the fourth century BC, has attempted to show a temple in perspective, with the doors swung open to reveal the cult statue of Apollo inside, painted white to convey the impression that it was made of metal.

THE TWELVE OLYMPIAN GODS

THE TWELVE OLYMPIAN GODS take their name from Mt Olympus, the tallest mountain in Greece, thought to be their abode. According to early cosmographies, they seized power from their forebears, the Titans, and held it after a ferocious battle with the Giants – one of the favourite scenes in Greek art. Which twelve gods are to be included among the Olympians is not always clear.

ZEUS was regarded as the father of the gods and the most powerful, controlling the land and sky, while his brother Poseidon held the sea, and another brother, Hades, ruled the underworld. Zeus as supreme weather god is often shown carrying the thunderbolt with which he punished offenders. The oak was his sacred tree. His principal sanctuary was at Olympia, where there was a colossal statue of him, with important shrines at Dodona and Nemea as well.

HERA was the consort of Zeus, constantly contesting his enthusiasm for mortal women. Her stone temple at Olympia, where races for

women were held in her honour in separate games, is actually earlier than Zeus' and she had especially important sanctuaries at Argos and Samos.

POSEIDON, the brother of Zeus, held sway over the sea, earthquakes and horses. Like Zeus, he is shown as a powerful, heavily bearded figure, often holding a trident and accompanied by a dolphin. His primary sanctuary was at the Isthmus leading into the Peloponnese and at Sounion, on the southern tip of Attica, south of Athens (see p. 15).

DEMETER, goddess of vegetation, was credited by the Greeks with teaching mankind agriculture. She is often shown with sheaves of wheat or holding a torch, since her rites were secret and nocturnal. The seasons were explained by the Greeks as Demeter's withholding of her favours during the six months each year her daughter Persephone was compelled to live in the underworld with Hades/Pluto, who had abducted her. Demeter's primary sanctuary was at Eleusis, in the territory of Athens, where well-attended mystery rites were held (pp. 132–33).

ATHENA was the daughter of Zeus and Metis (goddess of wisdom), whom Zeus swallowed so she would not give birth to anyone smarter or stronger than himself. Nine months later, he had a terrible headache, which resulted in the birth of Athena from the head of her father. Goddess of wisdom as well as arts and crafts,

(Right) Zeus, the father of the gods, and Hera his wife, are depicted in rare harmony in this small Archaic carving of c. 620 BC found on Samos, where Hera had an important sanctuary.

(Above, right) Poseidon, the brother of Zeus, was god of the sea, earthquakes and horses. He is often shown brandishing a trident, as on this silver stater from Paestum (Poseidonia) dating to c. 510 BC.

Athena was also a warrior and is usually shown fully armed. The owl was her sacred bird, the olive her sacred tree, and she is often depicted with a snake, Erichthonios. Though she was extraordinarily popular throughout the Greek world, her primary sanctuary was without doubt the Acropolis of Athens.

ARTEMIS was the sister of Apollo and shares many of his sanctuaries. She, too, was an archer and huntress, often dressed in hunting gear, accompanied either by dogs or deer. Her largest sanctuary was the Artemesion at Ephesus, one of the Seven Wonders of the world, and she had substantial temples in Magnesia (Asia Minor) and Sardis (Lydia).

(Right) Demeter is the goddess of agriculture and vegetation. Her daughter Persephone was abducted by Hades (p. 150), god of the underworld, and lived for six months of the year in his kingdom – hence the burning summer months when her mother mourned her and nothing grows in the Mediterranean. This statue of Demeter is from Knidos, dating to c. 330 BC.

(Far right) Athena sprang fully armed from the head of her father Zeus, and she is often depicted as a warrior goddess, as here. However, she was also the goddess of wisdom and arts and crafts. This sculpture of Athena is from the west pediment of the Temple of Aphaia on the island of Aegina, dating to around 510 BC.

(Right) Artemis, the sister of Apollo and usually worshipped as a virgin huntress, had a secondary role, shown here in this relief from Achinos in Thessaly, as a protectress of women in childbirth. Here a child is presented to the goddess along with appropriate offerings. In the background hangs a full set of the new mother's clothing, dedicated to the goddess as a thank-offering for a successful birth.

147

APOLLO was the god of light and music and, like Athena, was worshipped all over the Greek world. He is recognizable by the bow he carries and his youthful appearance. The laurel (bay tree), once the nymph Daphne, is his sacred tree, and the tripod is one of his regular symbols. His most important sanctuaries were found at Delphi, Didyma (Asia Minor) and on the island of Delos.

APHRODITE, the goddess of love, seems to have come to Greece from the east. Born in the sea-foam, and often depicted nude or half-draped, she was worshipped at Paphos, on Cyprus, at Kythera and at Corinth. Her companion or son, Eros, is usually shown as a winged child.

HERMES was the messenger of the gods and the conductor of souls to the Underworld, recognizable by his wand with snakes (*caduceus*) and winged sandals. He was also the god of commerce and thieves. He rarely received a full temple, but his worship was common as he was one of the patron deities of the gymnasium; truncated statues of him (called herms) were also used to mark entrances in Athens and some other Greek cities.

(Opposite) Aphrodite on a swan; white-ground cup by the Pistoxenos Painter, c. 470 BC, found on Rhodes.

(Far left) Apollo, god of light and music, is usually depicted as a glorious youth, as here in this sixth-century bronze, found in an ancient warehouse in Peiraieus, the port of Athens. In his left hand he held a bow and perhaps a libation bowl in his right. Compare the Apollo shown on p. 145.

(Left) Hermes, messenger of the gods, with the infant Dionysos. Pausanias described such a statue by Praxiteles at Olympia, where this statue was found in 1897, but scholars are not certain whether this is the original or a later copy (see also pp. 176–77).

(Above) Hephaistos is shown here making a new set of armour for Achilles, at the request of Achilles' mother Thetis: 'First he fashioned a shield, great and sturdy, adorning it cunningly in every part, and round about it he set a bright rim, threefold and glittering, and from it made fast a silver baldric. The shield itself had five layers, and on it he wrought many curious devices with great skill' (Homer, Iliad 18. 478–82). Athenian red-figure cup by the Foundry Painter, found at Vulci, c. 480–470 BC.

(Above centre) Dionysos, surrounded by maenads and revellers. Athenian black-figure amphora by the Amasis Painter, c. 540 BC. Note the Boiotian high-handled drinking cup, as illustrated on p. 89.

HEPHAISTOS, god of the forge, comes originally from Lemnos, in the northeast Aegean, where metallurgy had early roots. He was the husband of Aphrodite. His worship was not grandly expressed in many places, though he shared the well-preserved temple overlooking the Athenian Agora with Athena (pp. 120–21).

ARES, god of war, was also worshipped under the name Enyalios. He was usually depicted as a fully armed warrior and had only a very limited number of attested sanctuaries.

HESTIA was a minor deity, the goddess of the hearth. As such, she was worshipped in the *prytaneion* (town-hall) of every Greek town, where an eternal flame was kept burning on her hearth or altar.

Other gods

Several other gods were important, though they did not originally qualify as Olympian.

DIONYSOS, god of wine, good times and theatre was perhaps the most important. He is often shown partying with a rowdy, drunken company of satyrs and maenads. He was thought to have come to Athens from Boiotia and at all times is shown with a recognizably

Boiotian winecup: a kantharos with generous high-swung handles. Honoured with rural festivals and theatrical performances all over Greece, one of his largest sanctuaries was at Teos, in Asia Minor, where there was said to have been a fountain which produced water tasting like wine.

HADES, god of the underworld, is also known as Pluto. He, too, is shown as a heavily bearded male, though he is not a popular figure in Greek art, nor are there many large sanctuaries dedicated to him. Various places in the Greek world had chasms reputed to be entrances to the Underworld: Cape Tainaron (Peloponnese), Ephyra (Epiros), Hierapolis and Nysa (Asia Minor), and Sicily.

PAN was perhaps the ultimate rural deity, the goat-footed, horned patron of shepherds and goatherds, keeping to mountains and living in caves, usually accompanied by an assortment of Nymphs.

THE ENTRANCE TO THE UNDERWORLD

the Plutonion is an opening of only moderate size, large enough to admit a man, but it reaches a considerable depth, and it is enclosed by a handrail, about half a plethron [15 m/50 ft] in circumference, and this space is full of a vapour so misty and dense one can hardly see the ground. Now to those who approach the handrail anywhere around the enclosure the air is harmless, since the outside is free from that vapour in calm weather and the vapour stays within; but any animal that passes inside meets instant death. At any rate bulls that are led into it fall and are dragged out dead; and I threw in sparrows and they immediately breathed their last and fell. But the Galli, who are eunuchs, pass inside with such impunity that they even approach the opening, bend over it, and descend into it to a certain depth, though they hold their breath as much as they can.

Strabo, 629–30
on Hierapolis

(Far left) Hades/Pluto, god of the underworld, carries off Persephone (Kore), the daughter of Demeter; a Hellenistic terracotta from Taranto.

(Left) Aphrodite fends off Pan, with the help of Eros; marble statue group found on the island of Delos, c. 100 BC.

Heroes

IN ADDITION TO THE FULL GODS, the Greeks had a host of demi-gods or heroes, some as important or popular as many Olympian deities. Several, such as Herakles or Asklepios (pp. 160–61), had an international appeal and their cults are widespread throughout the Greek world. Many more, such as Theseus, were primarily important local heroes, wor-shipped only in one city. Sacred calendars indi-cate that there were literally hundreds of less significant local heroes, worshipped within a single township or village.

Heroes for the most part were thought to have been born mortal, but achieved divine status through extraordinary acts of strength or courage. They were chthonic, or of the

HERAKLES

The premier hero of antiquity was surely Herakles, whose cycle of Twelve Labours was a favourite theme for artists for centuries; he is depicted in sculpted reliefs, free-standing statues, mosaics and on vases. The son of Zeus and the mortal Alcmene, Herakles was a man of prodigious strength and appetite. He is one of the few heroes to achieve the status of fully fledged god and several scenes show his introduction to Mt Olympus. He was widely worshipped throughout Greece, though usually just with a simple sanctuary rather than a formal temple. He was also, appropriately enough, a patron deity of the gymnasium, and statues and dedications for him are often found there.

Driven mad by a jealous Hera, Herakles killed six of his own children; in expiation, he was ordered by the Delphic oracle to serve King Eurystheus at Tiryns for twelve years, carrying out whatever tasks he assigned. About half his Labours are set close to home, in the Peloponnese. Many involve the control of water, which is interesting in view of several large-scale water-management projects which can be dated to Mycenaean times (a dam near Tiryns, dykes at Arcadian Orchomenos and Pheneos, and the draining of the Copaic basin). The order of the Twelve Labours given in the literary texts (Apollodorus, Diodorus Siculus and others) varies somewhat from that shown on the mosaic from Elis:

1. The Nemean Lion was the first Labour. Herakles wrestled with the beast and strangled it, using its pelt as his cloak.

2. The Lernean Hydra was a monster with a dog-like body and nine snaky heads which grew back double when severed. Eventually Herakles seared each stump to prevent new heads from growing back. Gall from the monster's entrails was used to make Herakles' arrows deadly poisonous.

3. The Erymanthian Boar had to be captured alive, so Herakles drove it into a snow field where it became tired out.

4. The Kerynean Hind, with bronze hooves and golden horns, was sacred to Artemis. It also had to be captured and brought back alive, a task accomplished by tracking it for a full year to the far north and back, until it was too exhausted to flee any further.

5. The Stymphalian Birds, sacred to Ares, were a flock of bronze-beaked, bronze-clawed, man-eating birds, which had settled in the great marsh in the plain of Stymphalos. Driving them out of the swamp with castanets, Herakles was able to shoot them with his arrows.

6. Hippolyte's Girdle had to be fetched from the land of the Amazon queen, on the northern shores of the Black Sea. Having killed Hippolyte, Herakles returned to Mycenae after many adventures and handed over the girdle to

underworld, since they died like other mortals. Offerings to heroes therefore consisted of poured libations or other gifts deposited in pits in the ground, rather than the burnt offerings common for the Olympians, the smoke and good smells of which wafted up to them in the skies.

In some ways these local heroes seem to have had a more regular and popular appeal than the Olympian gods, as do the many saints of the Catholic church today.

Theseus carries off the Amazon Antiope. This is the central acroterion from the roof of the temple of Apollo Daphnephoros at Eretria, c. 500 BC.

Eurystheus' daughter, Admete.

7. The Augean Stables in Elis, near Olympia, had not been cleaned for years, though Herakles achieved this task in a single day. His solution was to divert the waters of the Alpheios and Peneos rivers to flow through the farm and wash away all the dung.

8. The Cretan Bull, a fire-breather, was subdued and brought back to Mycenae, where it was eventually set free.

9. The Horses of Diomedes, from Thrace, were man-eaters. Herakles conquered their master, Diomedes, and fed them his flesh, thus assuaging their appetites sufficiently to allow him to control them.

10. The Cattle of Geryon belonged to a monster with three heads, three bodies and six hands, who lived out beyond Spain in the west. On his way, Herakles set up the Pillars of Herakles at the entrance to the Mediterranean.

11. The Capture of Cerberus, the three-headed dog which guards the underworld, had to be accomplished without his usual club or arrows; Herakles managed to choke it into submission.

12. The Apples of the Hesperides were from a golden tree in Hera's garden on Mt Atlas, guarded by the dragon Ladon. Atlas was persuaded to recover the apples with the help of his daughters, the Hesperides, and he was then tricked into resuming his task of holding up the world which Herakles had

undertaken for him while the apples were being stolen.

(Left) The Labours of Herakles, depicted on a mosaic of the third century AD, found in Elis. The Labours are shown anticlockwise from the top, starting with the Nemean Lion. In the centre are Herakles' club and bow and arrows, and a victor's crown.

Herakles returning with Cerberus, the three-headed canine guardian of the entrance to the underworld, while King Eurystheus cowers in horror in his hiding place in a pithos (storage jar). Black-figured hydria of the sixth century BC.

153

THE PANHELLENIC FESTIVALS

FOUR SANCTUARIES in the Greek world rose to a status far above that of local cults, primarily because of the athletic contests which were an important part of the festival programme: Olympia, Delphi, Isthmia and Nemea. Held only every four or two years, these four are known collectively as the Panhellenic games. Open to and attended by all the Greeks, a victor in all four, a *periodonikes*, was the equivalent of the modern winner of the Grand Slam in tennis or golf. Games were also held at literally hundreds of local festivals – by the early Roman period there were as many as 146 cities sponsoring 266 games – but these four were the only international events. Accompanied by a sacred truce, they provided occasions – often rare among the fiercely independent and combative Greek states – for diplomacy and for more informal business and social contacts.

Organized athletic games seem to have their origin in funeral rites. The earliest we hear of are those sponsored by Achilles at the funeral of his friend Patroklos, as recorded in the *Iliad*. And although they were held in sanctuaries of Olympian gods, all four of the large festivals did have a funerary aspect, often in honour of a local hero.

Greek games originated in funeral rites: this fragment depicts the funerary games of Patroklos; it was found near Pharsalos, Achilles' home, and dates to c. 580 BC.

Olympia, home of the earliest games

Olympia holds pride of place as the oldest and most prestigious of the athletic festivals. The

(Left) A stone halter (jumping weight) from Olympia, inscribed with the name Akmatidas of Sparta, c. 500 BC.

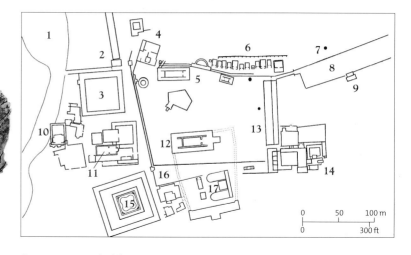

A discus-thrower; detail from an Attic calyx krater by the Kleophrades Painter, c. 500 BC, found at Tarquinia.

first games were held in 776 BC, some 200 years earlier than the others, which then largely followed the programme of events developed at Olympia. There are actually several traditions as to their foundation, some indicating that 776 was the occasion of a refounding of earlier games which had collapsed in the chaos of the Dark Ages.

The games were held in a sanctuary of Zeus and for almost 50 years the only event was a race to light the fire on the altar. In terms of prestige, this race was the premier event, at least officially – victors' names were used as part of the dating formula: 'In the 12th Olympiad, when so-and-so won the *stade*'. In Greek athletics the standard course was 183 m (600 ft) long, a distance of measure known in Greek as a *stade*, from which comes our word stadium. One

Plan of the site of Olympia.

1 River Kladeos
2 Gymnasium
3 *Palaistra*
4 *Prytaneion*
5 Temple of Hera
6 Treasuries
7 Altar
8 Stadium
9 Judges' box
10 Baths
11 Workshop of Pheidias
12 Temple of Zeus
13 Stoa
14 Roman baths
15 Leonidaion
16 Processional entrance
17 *Bouleuterion*

Imaginative reconstruction (Paris, 1889) of the sanctuary of Zeus at Olympia, with the large Doric temple of Zeus (c. 460 BC) in the centre. There is no evidence for the hole in the roof.

ATHLETICS

Athletics, as practised by the Greeks, have been handed down to us in the form of the Olympic Games, resurrected in their modern guise in Athens in 1896. Many of the supposed aspects of ancient organized sports admired and emulated at least in theory today were not in fact much practised in antiquity. Fair play, amateurism and team-work – all worthy goals – are largely the romantic invention of nineteenth-century scholars; the world of ancient Greek athletics was an intensely competitive one, far closer to the reality of modern sports. There was a distinct, perhaps aristocratic, emphasis on personal achievement and success; all the events were for individuals, not teams, and a prize was awarded for first

One of the characteristic features of Greek athletics is that the participants practised and competed naked. Here three youths are shown training on the base of a funerary statue of c. 510 BC.

of the foundation myths concerning the Olympic games was that they were held in honour of Pelops, and that Herakles laid out the course. As Herakles' feet were large, the *stade* at Olympia was longer – 192 m (630 ft) – than anywhere else. Other events were added over time and the prize was a wreath taken from Zeus' sacred olive just behind the temple dedicated to the god. This temple, built c. 470 BC and now in ruins, housed the great gold and ivory statue of Zeus, by Pheidias, one of the Seven Wonders of the ancient world (p. 176).

The sanctuary at Olympia has been excavated since the 1870s by the German Archaeological Institute. The sacred grove with temples of Hera and Zeus, has been found, along with a sanctuary of Pelops and the bases for hundreds of statues of victorious athletes.

A stadium, gymnasium, *palaistra* (wrestling ground) and bath have all also been uncovered just outside the sanctuary,

A seated boxer, weary and battered, is depicted with great realism in this Hellenistic bronze sculpture found in Rome and dating to the third–second century BC. His arms and hands are still bound up for the fight.

place only. This competitive ethos, of course, put tremendous pressure on the athletes and cases of bribery and cheating are not unknown:

At the terrace stand bronze statues of Zeus. These statues were made from the fines imposed on athletes who deliberately violated the rules of the games. The first were set up in the 98th Olympiad [398 BC], for Eupolis of Thessaly bribed the boxers who presented themselves. They say that this was the first offence committed against the rules of the games and Eupolis and the men he bribed were the first who were fined by the Eleans…. After Eupolis they say that Kallippos, an Athenian, a competitor in the pentathlon, bribed his antagonists, and that this happened in the 112th Olympiad…. The images next to those are two in number and were dedicated from the proceeds of a fine imposed on wrestlers.

Pausanias, 6.21

The only official prize offered was a wreath of leaves, taken from the sacred tree of the deity in whose honour the games were held: olive at Olympia; laurel at Delphi, pine at Isthmia and celery at Nemea. In theory, athletes competed for honour alone. In reality, they could expect to be richly rewarded by their home city; awards of cash, free meals for life in the town hall, poems written and performed in their honour, and statues set up both at the sanctuary and back home were among the rewards for success in the games.

Athletics originated in the rites that accompanied funerals, such as those in honour of the dead Patroklos sponsored by Achilles in the *Iliad*, our earliest reference to athletics. These games are interesting because they differ so much from the later games of the historical period. The first

major difference is that there are prizes of value: bronze cauldrons, skilled slave women, animals, gold, silver, iron, armour and weapons, in contrast to the Panhellenic games, where the only prize was a wreath. Interestingly, the commonest early prize was a metal vessel of some sort – reminiscent of the silver vessels handed out at contests large and small today. Also unusual, Achilles lays out prizes for more than just first place – as many as five for the five teams entered in the chariot race. In the Panhellenic games there was just one prize, everyone else was a loser and came away empty-handed.

The son of Peleus [Achilles] set out other prizes for fleetness of foot: a mixing bowl of silver, well made; six measures it held, and in beauty was far the best in all the earth, since Sidonians, well skilled in handiwork, had crafted it cunningly, and men of the Phoenicians brought it over the murky deep and landed it in harbour, and gave it as a gift to Thoas …

Homer, *Iliad* 23. 740–45

Organized competitive athletics as we know them in the historical period were dated by the Greeks to 776 BC, the year of the first Olympic games. Early in the sixth century BC, several other sanctuaries arose as venues for prestige games, mimicking, but never overshadowing, Olympia. Delphi, the oracular site of Apollo, sponsored the Pythian games, also held every four years; here the programme included musical and singing contests as well. The sanctuary of Poseidon at Isthmia and of Zeus at Nemea also held similar games, every two years.

The Olympic programme as it developed was the model for most subsequent athletic festivals. Events eventually came to include the *stade*, double *stade* (*diaulon*), long-

distance runs (*dolichos*), wrestling, boxing, *pankration* (all-out fighting), pentathlon (five contests: running, wrestling, discus, long jump and javelin), and horse and chariot races.

A characteristic feature of Greek athletics is that both training and competitions were held in the nude. Indeed the word 'gymnasium' derives from the Greek word γυμνός (naked), and this practice was a defining aspect of Greek culture for non-Greek cultures, such as the Romans and the Jews. Athletic festivals were confined largely to the Greek parts of the Roman world; the Romans themselves borrowed little from pure Greek athletics, preferring the more spectacular gladiatorial games borrowed from the Etruscans, and wild animal hunts.

The one event which was tremendously popular in both cultures was the chariot race, which survived until the end of antiquity. And for the Romans, the gymnasium was somewhere primarily to bathe and socialize, rather than exercise.

The Greek gymnasium was a building designed for athletic training, equipped with running tracks and a wrestling ground (*palaistra*), as well as bathing facilities and storerooms for the oils and powders or dusts used by the athletes (see also p. 173). The

earliest gymnasia go back to the sixth century BC. Gymnasia could be public buildings, though often they were built and endowed by wealthy citizens; in later times they might have a full staff of trainers and instructors. In many cities they were used to instruct young men in the skills necessary for successful warriors: wrestling, javelin, archery, and the like.

Gymnasia were the ideal location to instruct the groups of young men gathered to train their bodies in other disciplines as well, and they became very much like schools; it is no accident that the two great philosophical schools of Athens, the Academy and the Lyceum, were both founded in gymnasia (pp. 138–39).

Later gymnasia include special lecture halls (*ephebeia*) for the young men (*ephebes*) under instruction. Even today, the word in Germany and Greece for a middle school is 'gymnasion', and we should perhaps add the concept of a formal education encouraged by the state as another legacy from ancient Greece.

The stadium at Olympia where the Olympic games were held: the starting line for the athletes is visible in the foreground.

The palaistra *at Olympia,
surrounded by Doric columns: this
large, square open space was where
athletes wrestled and trained.
Various rooms of different
functions originally surrounded
the square.*

(Below) *Statue of a charioteer
from a victory monument for the
Pythian games at Delphi. The four-
horse chariot race (tethrippon)
was won by Polyzalos, tyrant of
Gela in Sicily, in around 474* BC;
*the prize and glory went to the
owner of the horses. For another
Sicilian charioteer, see p. 103.*

(Below right) *The stadium at
Delphi, in its final phase, dating
to the second century* AD.

while the hippodrome has been washed away by
the flooding of the Alpheios river.

A building identified by Pausanias as 'the
workshop of Pheidias' lies outside the sanctuary, west of the temple itself. It was a very tall
building and its plan reflected that of the interior of the temple where the great cult statue of
Zeus stood.

Delphi

Delphi was the site of the Pythian games, most
prestigious after those at Olympia. They were
also held only every fourth year, in the middle

of the Olympic cycle. The games celebrate the
death of the monster Pytho (hence Pythian) at
the hands of Apollo. They were instituted in
582 BC and the prize was a crown of laurel. The
programme was similar to Olympia, with one
important addition: singing and musical contests were also held, beginning early on as
simple hymns in honour of Apollo, god of
music. The words and musical notations of one
such hymn have been found inscribed on the
wall of the Athenian treasury in the sanctuary.

The French excavators at Delphi have
uncovered the theatre for the musical contests,

a gymnasium and bath, and the stadium, which is well preserved. An early inscription records a fine of 10 drachmas for anyone bringing wine into the stadium, with half the fine going to the informer. The hippodrome was down at the base of Mt Parnassos, in the Pleistos river valley; its exact location has not been identified. Statuary erected to commemorate Pythian victories has also been recovered, in particular a bronze charioteer of the 470s BC and the massive marble figure of the Thessalian pancratiast (all-out wrestling), Agias, set up in the 330s BC (p. 177).

Isthmia

Isthmia was the site of Poseidon's principal sanctuary and the venue for the Isthmian games, held every two years. Founded in 578 BC and under the administration of Corinth, they honoured the youth Palaimon/Melikertes, the son of an early king whose drowned body was brought to shore here by a dolphin. The prize was a wreath of pine boughs.

The American excavations have brought to light the remains of two successive stadia – one with an elaborate starting device – and a bath. No gymnasium has been uncovered thus far.

Nemea

Nemea was the site of the last of the Panhellenic games, held in a sanctuary of Nemean Zeus in honour of the infant Opheltes, son of an early king. An oracle had foretold his death if ever he was allowed to touch the ground and his nurse, Hypsipyle, was charged never to let this happen. The Seven Against Thebes passed through, on their way from Argos to attack Thebes, and asked her for water; she laid the child on a celery plant to comply and a huge snake appeared and devoured it. The prize at Nemea was therefore a wreath of celery. Like Isthmia, the games occurred every two years; they were administered at times by the nearby small town of Kleonai, at others by Argos.

American excavations have revealed most of the stadium, which has a tunnel giving access to the track, its walls covered by graffiti scratched by nervous athletes waiting their turn to compete. Just outside the tunnel is one of the few examples of an ancient locker room (*apodyterion*). A large bath has also been uncovered, but no gymnasium as yet.

(Above) A dedication by a successful Athenian athlete, recording his victories in (from left to right): the Panathenaia at Athens (an amphora for the prize oil); the Isthmian games (a wreath of pine); the Aspis games at Argos (a shield); and the Nemean games (a wreath of celery).

(Right) A Roman sarcophagus found at Corinth, showing the myth of Opheltes, the origin of the Nemean games. On the long side are the Seven against Thebes, while on the short side is Opheltes being devoured by a serpent (as foretold in an oracle) and his distraught nurse, Hypsipyle.

MEDICINE AND HEALING CULTS

CURES AT EPIDAUROS

14. *A man with a stone in his membrum. He saw a dream. It seemed to him he slept with a fair boy and when he ejaculated he ejected the stone and picked it up and walked out holding it in his hands.*

15. *Hermodikos of Lampsakos was paralysed. When he slept in the temple the god healed him and ordered him to bring to the temple as large a stone as he could. The man brought the stone which now stands before the Abaton.*

16. *Nikanor, a lame man. While he was sitting wide awake, a boy snatched his crutch and ran away. Nikanor got up and pursued him and so was cured.*

17. *A man had his toe healed by a serpent. He, suffering dreadfully from a malignant sore on his toe, fell asleep. A snake then came from the abaton and healed the toe with its tongue and then went back inside.*

IG IV, fourth century BC

DOCTORS ARE ATTESTED since the time of the *Iliad* and throughout the subsequent historic period. Indeed, modern professionals still honour Greek medicine with the Hippocratic Oath, attributed to a famed doctor who lived in the fifth century BC. Generally, however, the Greeks wisely relied on divine intervention when their good health was under threat. The primary healing deity was Asklepios (Aesculapius in Latin), originally a hero who was the son of Apollo and a mortal woman, Koronis. Like Herakles, Asklepios is one of the few heroes to merit promotion to full-fledged god. Almost every Greek town had an Asklepieion, a sanctuary dedicated to the health of its citizens. Sacrifices, prayer, rest, fresh air and clean water were all part of the regimen, and the god either healed directly or appeared in a dream and informed the suppliant what measures were necessary for a cure. Small votive offerings showing the afflicted part were often dedicated; examples in precious metals are listed in the temple inventories though for the most part only versions in stone or clay survive. If local treatment proved insufficient, a visit could be arranged to one of the great shrines of Asklepios: Epidauros, Kos or Pergamon.

Votive relief of the fourth century BC, showing scenes of healing by the hero Amphiaraos (left) and a snake (right). The inscription reads: 'Archinos dedicated this to Amphiaraos'.

Epidauros

Though his cult originates in Tricca in northwest Thessaly, Asklepios' primary sanctuary was in the territory of Epidauros, in the eastern Peloponnese. Greek excavations here have revealed a large sanctuary, with a temple, a mysterious and lavishly built round building (*tholos* or *thymele*, p. 170), a dormitory (*abaton*) for the sick, and a hostel for those accompanying the afflicted. Inscriptions record dozens of miracle cures carried out by the god. Athletic and musical contests were both part of his festival, and a stadium, bath, gymnasium and theatre have been uncovered.

The theatre, the best preserved in the ancient world, seats 15,000 people, an indication of the popularity of the god and his festival (p. 172). The sanctuary lies 8 km (5 miles) from the modest city of Epidauros, with no settlement nearby, yet the theatre holds almost as many people as the one in Athens (about 17,000), built for the largest city in the Greek world. The other indicator of Asklepios' popularity is the tenacity of his cult. Long after the worship of other pagan gods was stamped out, as late as the sixth century AD the Christians were still trying to wean people away from Asklepios.

Kos

The second great centre for the worship of Asklepios was on the island of Kos, which Hippocrates made his headquarters. The sanctuary here, built on three terraces outside the town, was provided with temples and abundant springs of fresh water.

Pergamon

Pergamon in northwest Asia Minor, was the third great cult centre of Asklepios. Begun in the Hellenistic period, it flourished especially in Roman times, when a huge complex was constructed, comprising a circular temple, a large round curing establishment provided with fresh water, a theatre, a library and several colonnaded walkways. Aelius Aristides, a notorious hypochondriac, visited frequently and describes the sanctuary at its height during the second century AD.

Other deities

Other deities, often more local in character, were also thought to have healing powers. Among the most significant perhaps was

Amphiaraos, one of the Seven Against Thebes, who was worshipped at Oropos, between Athens and Thebes. His sanctuary was embellished with buildings and was the scene of a popular festival. Like Asklepios, he starts out as

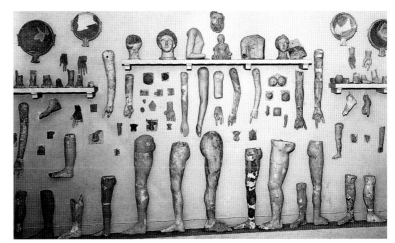

a hero and eventually rises to full god, as the result of a decision by the senate of Rome. The Roman *publicani* (tax-collectors) were trying to tax the people of Oropos, who claimed immunity because their land was sacred to Amphiaraos, a god. The *publicani* argued he was only a hero and therefore not tax-exempt, and the dispute was adjudicated (in favour of Oropos) by a senatorial commission, which included the orator Cicero, sent out from Rome in the first century BC.

Hygieia was also a healing deity, worshipped with Asklepios.

Votive body parts of terracotta, found in the sanctuary of Asklepios at Corinth. Most external parts and many organs are represented; lists from Athens of more precious silver dedications suggest that the most frequent afflictions involved the eyes.

MEDICINE

Statue of Asklepios, or one of his physician sons who served in the Trojan War: Machaon or Podaleirios. Snakes were thought to have healing powers.

The influence of Greek medicine on modern times is most obviously seen in the Hippocratic Oath, still taken by physicians today. Another constant reminder is the vocabulary of medicine, almost entirely Greek in its technical terminology.

At all times the Greeks turned to their divine healer, Asklepios, and every Greek city had an Asklepieion. His sons Machaon and Podaleirios, were physicians and fought in the Trojan War.

Greek society had need of doctors and several inscriptions honouring their efforts on behalf of individual cities survive. The Greeks were fascinated with the human body and it was the subject of intense scrutiny by artists, athletes, philosophers and, eventually, doctors.

Hippocrates, the 'father of medicine', was regarded as the first to separate medicine from philosophy. He lived in the fifth century BC (469–399 BC) and worked on the island of

Kos, where there was an important sanctuary of Asklepios. Numerous writings, many dated to the fifth and fourth centuries, are collected under his name. These include physicians' case notes, a collection of aphorisms, essays on the effects of environment on health, on prognosis, on the treatment of acute diseases, on fractures, on epilepsy, on the nature of children, and a description of the heart.

Another famous name in ancient Greek medicine is that of Galen, who lived in the second century AD. He was from Pergamon originally and began his career as a doctor for gladiators, where business must have been brisk and the opportunities for autopsy plentiful. He travelled widely

and studied in Alexandria and Greece, before becoming the court physician for the emperor Marcus Aurelius in Rome. He wrote extensively, recording and adding to the body of medical information on pharmacology, diet, physiology and anatomy.

The growth of plants forms an excellent parallel to the study of medicine. Our characters resemble the soil, our masters' precepts the seed; education is the sowing of the seed in season and the circumstances of teaching resemble the climatic conditions that control the growth of plants. Industrious toil and the passage of time strengthen the plant and bring it to maturity.

Canon of the Hippocratic corpus

ORACULAR SHRINES

(Right) King Aegeus, father of Theseus, consults the Pythia. The tripod which serves as her seat was placed over the chasm from which the vapours arose. It is therefore a symbol both of Delphi and Apollo. Athenian red-figure cup.

(Below) View of the temple of Apollo at Delphi, site of the oracular responses by the Pythia. The present Doric temple, dating to 360–325 BC, is the sixth one to stand on this spot.

THE GREEKS OFTEN TURNED to the gods for advice and insight into the future, and many sanctuaries were oracular in nature. Apollo was the primary deity who told the future, while the means of divination varied from site to site.

Delphi

The sanctuary of Apollo at Delphi, on the southern slopes of Mt Parnassos, was the most famous oracle of antiquity. It was thought to be the centre of the world and one of its sacred symbols was the *omphalos* (navel or belly button; see p. 69). The sanctuary is almost unique in Greece in that it is truly international; though it lay within the territory of ancient Phokis, it was administered by a committee (known as the *amphikteony*) made up of 24 representatives from twelve Greek cities.

The Delphic oracle had a major role in the concept of Hellenism by virtue of the active part it played in the colonization of the Mediterranean and Black Sea in the eighth to sixth centuries BC. The many dedications and treasuries from Greek cities all over the Mediterranean attest to its central role in the rise of a national identity. It was considered to be infallible, having been tested by King Croesus of Lydia.

The answers given were usually ambiguous, so that if events did not turn out as foreseen the fault lay with the interpretation of the applicant and not the god. Oracular responses were produced by the Pythia, a specially chosen woman who went into some sort of trance and was thought to have been possessed by Apollo. There are literary references to a cleft in the rock from which vapours emerged, sending her into a frenzy. Her ravings were recorded and often survive as a line or two of neat hexameter verse. The French excavations have failed to reveal a cleft underneath the temple, though the area is very active tectonically and any such chasm may have closed up since antiquity.

Dodona

The oldest oracle in the world, mentioned in the *Iliad*, was thought to have been that of Zeus at Dodona, in Epiros, in northern Greece. Originally the oracular responses were produced by the sound of the wind in the sacred oak tree, and later by the vibrations of a series of bronze tripod vessels set side by side in a circle. Greek excavations have revealed a modest temple, rebuilt several times, a large theatre, a racetrack and several other minor buildings. They have also uncovered a series of lead tablets, on which the applicant wrote his question; they concern both high matters of state ('Is the harsh winter caused by some impure individual

THE ORACLE AT DELPHI

They say that the seat of the oracle is a cave that is hollowed out deep down in the earth, with a rather narrow mouth, from which arises vapour that inspires a divine frenzy; and that over the mouth is placed a high tripod, mounting which the Pythian priestess receives the vapour and then utters oracles in both verse and prose, though the latter too are put into verse by poets who are in the service of the temple.

Strabo, 419

THE OMPHALOS

For it is almost in the centre of Greece taken as a whole and it was believed to be in the centre of the inhabited world, and people called it the navel of the earth, in addition to fabricating a myth, which is told by Pindar, that the two eagles sent by Zeus met there, one coming from the west and one from the east. There is also a kind of navel to be seen in the temple; it is draped with fillets and on it are two likenesses of the birds of the myth.

Strabo, 419–20

(Above) The temple and oracle of Zeus at Dodona, in Epiros, excavated by the Archaeological Society of Athens. The tree is a replanting of the original oracular oak.

(Left) Inscribed lead tablet containing a request of the oracle at Dodona.

living among us?'), to the intensely personal ('Is the boy really my son?').

Didyma and Claros

Two other important oracular shrines to Apollo are found in Asia Minor, at Didyma, in the territory of Miletus, and at Claros, in the territory of Kolophon. Didyma is the site of one of the largest temples in the Greek world – a giant with a double row of Ionic columns, so large it was not roofed and took centuries to build without ever being completed (pp. 98–99). A paved sacred way, lined with votive statues of marble as well as other smaller sanctuaries, connected the temple to the city of Miletus, some 18 km (11 miles) away.

Claros is noteworthy for the rare use of the Doric order for a temple in Ionia, as well as an elaborate underground arched oracular chamber below the temple's cult statues. Hundreds of inscriptions record delegations to the oracle, particularly in the Roman period, and dozens of bases with rings to secure the sacrificial victims line the area in front of the altar.

Other oracles

Boiotia was once especially rich in oracles, including the sanctuary of Ismenion Apollo at Thebes and the oracle of Apollo Ptoos at nearby Akraiphnia.

Among the most famous was that of the hero Trophonios at Leibadia. Pausanias, travelling and writing in the second century AD, provides us with our fullest account of one visit to the oracle, the procedures that had to be followed and the mental state of the applicant. Despite Pausanias' precise description, the actual location of the oracle of Trophonios has not be discovered.

Another means of telling the future was a visit to the underworld, and in Epiros in northwest Greece there was a *nekromanteion* (oracle of the dead) on the Acheron River. This was an entrance to the underworld and an old site, since Homer knew it as a source of particularly potent poison (*Odyssey* 1. 259–62).

Coin of Alexander the Great; the ram's horn appears after his visit in 330 BC to the oracle of Zeus at Siwa in the western desert of Egypt (map p. 194), where he was declared the son of Zeus Ammon.

VIII

GREEK ART AND ARCHITECTURE

THE ART OF GREEK culture is one of the most influential and enduring legacies from the past. In architecture, sculpture, painting, ceramics, metalwork and gem-carving, the Greeks set standards admired and emulated from Roman times to the present day. Greek art is evolutionary rather that revolutionary. It is a process of refinement, of working within long-established traditions and changing very slowly. Novelty for the sake of novelty seems not to have been greatly admired. In architecture, the Doric and Ionic orders were codified by the seventh century BC and used with little change for almost a thousand years. In sculpture, the nude male figure – at rest or in motion – was the theme which artists strove for centuries to perfect. Black-figured vase-painting persisted for 150 years, and the red-figured style for 200. The channelling of so much energy and creativity along well-defined paths led to masterpieces which have stood the test of time in all fields of artistic expression.

These incremental changes of long-established forms permit a general development through time to be discerned, whether in architecture, sculpture or pottery, and allow a stylistic chronology to be proposed when outside evidence for the date of an object is lacking.

The initial inspiration for both monumental architecture and sculpture can be found in the earlier civilizations of Egypt and the Middle East, which the Greeks had been in contact with for centuries.

Interior two-storey Doric colonnades of the temple of Hera II at Paestum, southern Italy, mid-fifth century BC.

ARCHITECTURE

MONUMENTAL GREEK ARCHITECTURE is firmly based on a post-and-lintel system, with vertical columns and horizontal architraves. Early on, columns and the superstructure they supported were given a set form which was used over and over again. The combination of architectural elements which appear repeatedly together are known as an 'order'. In Greek architecture, there were two principal orders, the Doric and the Ionic: minor variations, particularly in the capitals, were added later. The two orders developed in the two halves of the Greek world during the seventh century BC, the Doric in the west, and the Ionic in the east. A well-established series of proportions and ratios determined the size of the individual elements which made up each order.

Doric

The Doric order seems to have its origins in stone in the northeast Peloponnese in the seventh century. The earliest examples are found at Corinth and Isthmia, and also at Olympia. The columns have no base, shallow

(Right) Restored drawing of the temple of Aphaia on Aegina, 510–500 BC, showing the principal elements of the Doric order.

(Below) Temple of Apollo at Bassai, near Phigaleia in Arcadia, 420s BC. Pausanias reports that the temple was designed by Iktinos, the architect of the Parthenon in Athens.

flutes and a simple capital with a flaring element (*echinos*) supporting a square top (*abacus*). Above is the architrave (*epistyle*), which spans the columns and supports the frieze. The frieze consists of alternating *triglyphs*, divided into three vertical sections, and *metopes*, panels which could be sculpted, painted or left plain. Above, an overhanging cornice (*geison*) protects the façade. The top of the architrave and the underside of the cornice are decorated with knob-like protrusions known as *guttae*. They look for all the world like the ends of wooden pegs, and this, along with other considerations, leads to the conclusion that the Doric order developed out of wooden prototypes. When a stone version was first created, representations of the pegs were included and what started life as a functional element became a decorative one, persisting for centuries, throughout the life of the Doric order. This same transformation from functional to decorative can be paralleled in several other instances in Greek architecture.

The various elements are built in proportion to one another: a metope is usually square, and a triglyph is two-thirds the width of a metope, while the columns fall directly under every other triglyph in the frieze. Because these proportional relationships are so regular, it requires only a tiny fragment or two to restore an entire Doric façade with confidence.

The Doric order was especially prevalent in the Peloponnese and in the Western Greek colonies of south Italy and Asia Minor, where dozens of examples survive, dating from the sixth to the fourth centuries BC. The Doric order was used for only a handful of large temples in the eastern Aegean, as at Assos, Claros and Troy.

Ionic

The Ionic order developed, as the name suggests, in Ionia, centre of the East Greek world and is found in stone in Asia Minor and the Aegean islands as early as the seventh century. It is a lighter, more ornate style than Doric. The columns are tall and thin and have elaborate bases and capitals with carved mouldings and ornamental volutes. The entablature above is also lighter than its Doric counterpart and originally consisted only of architrave and cornice, with no intervening frieze. The decorative mouldings used to highlight the edges of courses or the transitions from horizontal to vertical surfaces were carved and painted, rather than just painted as was the norm for Doric mouldings. The frieze is a continuous band of stone, which could be carved along its entire length without any breaks for triglyphs.

Historically Ionia flourished particularly in the Archaic period, when the great temples of Ephesus, Samos and Didyma (Miletus) were under construction. In the Classical period Athens controlled the Aegean and limited

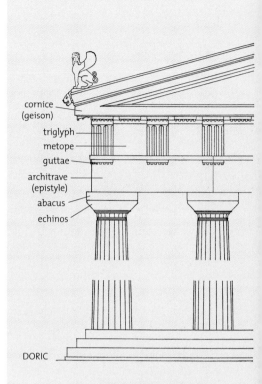

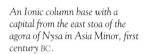

An Ionic column base with a capital from the east stoa of the agora of Nysa in Asia Minor, first century BC.

One of the most enduring legacies of the Greek world to modern times is monumental architecture in stone, particularly the three columnar orders: Doric, Ionic and Corinthian. Large public buildings all over Europe and the United States are readily recognizable from their façades, adorned with massive columns carrying architraves, friezes and pediments. Banks, lawcourts, palaces and parliaments, all use the vocabulary of Greek architecture to convey the message of stability, power, authority and security.

In historical antiquity the first use of external columns in Greece appears, appropriately enough, in temples of the gods. The two principal orders developed in the two halves of the Greek world – Doric in the west, Ionic in the east.

The Doric order is the more austere, with heavier proportions, simpler forms and less ornamentation. Almost certainly, it derives from wooden prototypes. Embedded

THE ARCHITECTURAL ORDERS

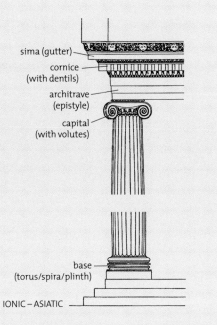

sima (gutter)
cornice (with dentils)
architrave (epistyle)
capital (with volutes)
base (torus/spira/plinth)
IONIC – ASIATIC

antefixes
sima (gutter)
cornice (geison)
frieze
architrave
capital (acanthus leaves)
Attic base (torus/scatia/torus)
CORINTHIAN

in its decorative scheme in stone are elements which must have been functional in a wooden structure: the ends of beams, rafters and wooden pegs.

The earliest stone Doric temples appear in the seventh century BC in the Peloponnese, particularly in the area around Corinth. From there the order spread rapidly westwards, to the Corinthian colony of Syracuse in Sicily, and to the other cities of south Italy.

Once established, the proportions and modules used in Doric architecture resisted significant change for centuries – close to a thousand years – with only the slightest modifications introduced over time. This refinement of traditional forms is what drove and guided Greek artists towards perfection.

The Parthenon is not one man's genius, it is the result of 250 years of building Doric temples in stone. The proportional relationships between elements are described

for us by the architectural historian Vitruvius; the names of the elements come from ancient Greek contracts or building specifications preserved on stone, or from Vitruvius.

The Ionic order developed out of eastern influence. The marble-workers of the island of Naxos had great faith in their material and there is less obvious evidence of any wooden prototype for the order.

Sculptural decoration in Doric is usually confined to the metopes of the frieze and the triangular pediments at the ends. The Ionic order was far more experimental in the placement of sculpture, and examples at the bottoms (Ephesus) and tops (Smintheion) of column shafts, on the architraves (Didyma), on the face of the gutter (*sima*, at Ephesus) and in the coffers of ceilings (Priene, Belevi) are known. Eventually a frieze was added and it, too, might carry sculpture on an Ionic building (Athens, Halicarnassus).

The Corinthian order is little more than the Ionic order with the addition of a more elaborate floral capital of acanthus leaves, the origin of which is described for us in a tale told by Vitruvius (p. 170).

Other styles were used on occasion, in particular in northwest Asia Minor in both the Archaic and Hellenistic periods, but the Doric, Ionic and Corinthian orders were favoured by the Romans and thus transmitted to western Europe.

Observation and measurements show that proper use of the orders includes the repeated use of ratios and proportions, both in the building as a whole (length to width, width to height, etc) and between the individual elements (spacing of columns, metope width to triglyph width, etc). The principles are laid out for us again by Vitruvius, though the specific ratios and proportions he cites are applicable only to the early Roman period.

The planning of temples depends upon symmetry: and the method of this architects must diligently follow. It arises from proportion [Greek analogia]. Proportion consists of taking a fixed module, both for the parts of the building and for the whole, by which the method of symmetry is put into practice. Without symmetry and proportion no temple can have a regular plan; that is, it must have an exact proportion worked out after the fashion of the members of a finely shaped human body. For Nature has so planned the human body that the face from the chin to the top of the forehead and the roots of the hair is a tenth part; and the palm of the hand from the wrist to the tip of the middle finger is the same.

Vitruvius, 3.1

THE CORINTHIAN ORDER

The third order, which is called Corinthian, imitates the slight figure of a maiden, because girls are represented with slighter dimensions because of their tender age and admit of more graceful effects in ornament. Now the first invention of the capital is said to have happened thus. A girl, a native of Corinth, already of age to be married, was attacked by disease and died. After her funeral, the goblets which delighted her when living were put in a basket by her nurse, carried to the grave and placed on top. To keep them there, she covered the basket with a tile. As it happened, the basket was placed on the root of an acanthus. In spring the acanthus put forth leaves and shoots. The shoots grew up the sides of the basket, and, pressed down at the corners by the weight of the tile, formed the curves of volutes at their ends. Then Callimachus, who for the elegance and refinement of his marble carving was known as katatecnos *by the Athenians, was passing the monument and saw the basket and the young leaves. Pleased with the style and novelty of the grouping, he made columns for the Corinthians on this model and fixed the proportions.*

Vitruvius, 4. 1

construction was undertaken in Ionia itself, though the Athenians used the order in the fifth century for the Erechtheion and Propylaia (interior), and at Sounion and Delphi. In the fourth century, power and influence shifted eastwards once again and the architect Pytheos set a new canon for the Ionic order with the Athena temple at Priene. In the late third century further adaptations to the order were introduced by Hermogenes at Magnesia and Teos and were to become very influential in the Roman borrowing of Greek architectural forms.

Other orders

Closely related – indeed almost identical – to the Ionic order, is the Corinthian, which is first used in interiors only as late as the fifth century BC and not for exteriors until the fourth century. The characteristic feature and only real difference is the basket-shaped capital covered with carved representations of acanthus leaves and plant tendrils. This results in a capital which has four identical sides, unlike Ionic, with its distinct sides and ends, which are a problem on corner columns. Corinthian capitals became especially popular throughout the Roman world.

The Aeolic style also resembles the Ionic in most ways, though the capitals have two large

volutes which spring from below. It was developed in northwest Asia Minor, fell out of favour, and was rarely used after the sixth century BC.

Other capitals featured long leaves of water plants as their decorative motif, apparently borrowed from Egyptian prototypes; and composite capitals, combining two different sorts of decoration, are found from the second century BC.

Public buildings

A wide variety of building types served the various needs of the public, communal lifestyle of the Greeks. In general they were well suited to the Greek climate, with the open colonnades of temples and stoas or the interior peristyle courts of market buildings and gymnasia offering shelter from the elements. Over time, specific plans were developed to accommodate specific functions and the form of a Greek building, even at foundation level, usually gives some idea of its intended use.

The costs of public buildings varied tremendously, depending on size and material used. Temples were the most expensive structures; other buildings were often more modest. Both the state and wealthy individuals are known to have financed public buildings. Surviving contracts and specifications written on stone tell us

(Below) An Aeolic capital from the sixth-century temple of Apollo at Neandreia, in northwest Asia Minor. Similar capitals have been found at sites in the eastern Aegean ranging from European Thrace in the north to the Halicarnassus peninsula in the south.

(Right) Elaborate floral capital of the Corinthian order, used in the interior of the tholos of Epidauros, c. 360–320 BC (p. 160).

a lot about the economics of construction and often include enough detail to allow us to restore a public building which does not actually survive, even in ruins.

Another source for much of what we know about Greek architecture is Vitruvius, a Roman architect who lived and wrote during the reign of Augustus (first century BC/AD). His ten books in Latin describe the orders, building materials, many different public buildings, and the innovations and achievements of specific Greek architects. He cites numerous references, indicating that many ancient architects wrote treatises describing their buildings.

The very identity of a city as being Greek could be stated in architectural terms, and every city could be expected to have at least one example of each of the following building types.

Temples

Temples are the most common type of public building to survive, with many examples found in every city. The most lavish would be ringed with columns (peripteral), while giant Ionic temples (Ephesus, Samos, Didyma) would sport a double row (dipteral). Within was the room which held the cult statue (cella or naos), often approached through a front porch (pronaos) and provided with a back porch (opisthodomos) as well. The purpose of a Greek temple was to house the cult statue and to store votive offerings; it could therefore be very small. All the liturgy – involving priests, assistants, crowds of onlookers and sacrificial victims – took place outside, at the open-air altar in front of the temple. Greek temples usually faced east towards the rising sun, though many Artemis temples (Ephesus, Magnesia, Sardis) faced west.

BUILDING ACCOUNTS

Gorgias took the contract for polishing the pavement in the colonnade and smoothing the outer face of the cella walls, for 821 drachmas, 2 obols; his guarantors were Oliphidas and Alexos.

For gold for the stars: 64 drachmas, 1 obol.

To Euphraios for tiles, 140 drachmas.

Chairis took the contract for dressing down the foundation steps for 64 drachmas.

Hektoridas took the contract for half the pediment sculptures, for 1,610 drachmas; his guarantors were Philokleidas and Timokleidas.

Journey money to Sotairos, 4 dr. To the herald Aischinas, 12 dr. To Damophanes, for a lock and key, 12 dr....To Antilochos for painting coffers, 36 dr. 4 ob. To Isodamos for ironwork of the doors, 22 dr. 3 ob. To Euklinos for wax, 2 dr. 1 ob. To Sortairos for lead, 23 dr. 4 1/2 ob. For carting 3 dr.

Building accounts for the temple of Asklepios at Epidauros, fourth century BC

The recently discovered sixth-century BC temple at Metropolis, Thessaly. The plan is unusual, with five columns across the front and a central colonnade within. The Romans destroyed the building in the mid-second century BC: excavations produced a thick layer of destruction fill, including the sixth-century bronze cult statue, found in two pieces tumbled off its base (see also p. 174).

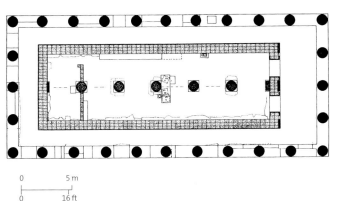

The Stoa of Attalos (159–138 BC) in the Agora of Athens, reconstructed in 1953–56.

Stoas

A stoa is any long colonnaded building. The simplest had a single row of columns set parallel to a wall, with the area between roofed. Fully developed, the more complex stoas had as many as three storeys, with double colonnades and rooms behind. Stoas were the ideal public buildings for the Mediterranean climate, providing ample light and air for a huge number of people, while sheltering them from the strong summer sun or wind and rain in winter. They served a multitude of functions: markets, public offices, magistrates' headquarters, storerooms, display of paintings or votive offerings (i.e. museums), and simply as places to stroll and meet others. They are accordingly found wherever large numbers of people gathered: in sanctuaries, agoras and near theatres.

Theatres

Theatrical performances in honour of Dionysos, Apollo and Asklepios were an integral part of Greek life, and large well-built theatres were a feature of the urban design. Usually they were set into a hillside, often at the base of the acropolis itself, taking advantage of the natural slope to create tiers of seats. In large cities the theatres provided seating for as many as 15,000 to 24,000 spectators.

The performance originally took place in the orchestra, a large level area at the bottom of the auditorium; here the choruses, with their

The theatre at the sanctuary of Asklepios at Epidauros, c. 300 BC. Seating about 15,000, the auditorium is almost intact, its remote location having spared it from being plundered in later times for building material. As Pausanias wrote in c. AD 150: 'In the Epidaurian sanctuary there is a theatre which in my opinion is most especially worth seeing. It is true that in size the theatre of Megalopolis in Arcadia surpasses it, and that in splendour the Roman theatres surpass all other theatres in the world, but for symmetry and beauty what architect could vie with Polykleitos? For it was Polykleitos who made this theatre and tholos.' (Pausanias, 2. 27. 5.)

singing and dancing, were the focal point. As Greek drama developed, however, the emphasis shifted to the actors, who performed on a raised stage which was moved forwards over time, impinging on the old dancing-ground of the orchestra. Many Greek orchestras are in the form of circles or half-circles – thought to have developed out of circular dancing; recent research suggests that the primitive orchestra was rectilinear, however, perhaps used originally for military drill and precision marching. A modest structure in the background initially carried painted panels to set the scene. This became increasingly elaborate as the stage became more prominent, with the addition of a colonnaded façade, and by the Roman period scene buildings were three storeys high, incorporating all three architectural orders – Doric, Ionic and Corinthian – and often lavishly decorated with sculpture.

A variant of the theatre, dating to Hellenistic times, was the *odeion* or concert hall, designed specifically for musical performances (*ode* = song). These are smaller than theatres and are usually roofed.

Assembly halls: *bouleuteria*

While the theatre or agora served as the place of assembly for all the citizens, most Greek cities had smaller deliberative bodies which were housed separately. These small buildings were set in or near the agora and were square in plan with a level floor for benches, capable of seating 500 to 1,200 people. In the Hellenistic period they were given banked rows of stone seats, either rectilinear or curved, the latter close in appearance to *odeia*. The major difference is the floor level of the 'orchestra', which in an *odeion* is usually sunken, and access from the façade, which is usually restricted in an *odeion*.

An early local variant may be seen in Sicily and south Italy (Akragas, Poseidonia/Paestum and Metapontum), where the assembly halls are in the form of a full circle or oval, with stone benches and a very slight declivity.

Gymnasia

Greek military training and education were inextricably linked to the gymnasium, which is attested as an institution as early as the sixth century BC. A large city would have several examples. Essential components were the *palaistra* (wrestling ground), usually a courtyard open to the sky with colonnades and rooms around all four sides, and the running tracks. The rooms of the *palaistra* served a variety of functions;

some were lecture halls, others were given over to the application of oils and dust or powder, and some were used for bathing. The tracks were a *stade* (183 m/600 ft) long, and there would be two side by side, one open, the other covered, like a stoa. By the Hellenistic period the arrangement of the rooms was well established.

The Roman borrowing of the Greek gymnasium involved a shift in emphasis, with far more expense and effort devoted to the bathing and socializing, and far less on the actual facilities for exercise. The gymnasium and the practice of exercising nude was for the people of the Mediterranean a defining feature of the Greeks. At Ai Khanoum in Afghanistan, the Hellenistic city there was provided with a gymnasium, overseen by the usual divine patrons, Hermes and Herakles.

Other buildings

Other public buildings were also found in Greek cities and numerous examples have been brought to light by excavation. The *prytaneion* served as the town-hall, a dining-room for high magistrates and official guests, as well as the place where an eternal flame was kept burning at the altar or hearth of Hestia. Fountain-houses and public baths were a feature of most Greek towns, though the water had to be brought in a gravity line; the pressure lines which allow water to be raised seem not to have been developed until the third century BC. Most Greek cities made their own coins and a handful of mints have been recognized in excavations. Basilicas, amphitheatres and public latrines are Roman additions to the urban scene.

THE ELEMENTS OF A GYMNASIUM

Although the building of the palaistra is not a usual thing in Italy, the method of construction has been handed down. It seems good therefore to explain it and show how the palaistra is planned among the Greeks. Square or rectangular peristyles are to be made, some two stades in length. Three sides should have single colonnades, the fourth one, facing south, is to be double, so that rain may not reach inside. On the other three sides large exedras [niches] are to be planned with seats where philosophers, teachers of rhetoric, and other studious folk can sit and discuss. The following provisions are to be made for the double colonnade. In the centre there is to be the ephebeion, three times as long as wide; on the right the coryceum [punching bag room]; next to this the conisterium [powder room], and at the corner the cold bath called in Greek the loutron. At the left of the ephebeion is the elaeothesium [oiling room]; then the cold room from which the furnace room is entered in the corner. Next to this, inside and on a line with the cold room, is a vaulted sweating-room twice as long as broad, with a Laconicum [domed sweat chamber] in the corner, and a warm bath opposite.

Vitruvius 5. 11

These little Greeks [graeculi] must have their gymnasia.

The Emperor Trajan to Pliny, governor in Bithynia, c. AD 111
Pliny, *Letters* 10. 40

SCULPTURE

(Below) Bronze cult statue of Apollo, sixth century BC, as found recently in the destruction debris of the temple at Metropolis, in Thessaly. The full height of the statue is about 0.80 m (2.6 ft).

(Right) A rare example of a gold and ivory (chryselephantine) statue, found buried under the sacred way at Delphi. Lifesized and dating to late sixth century BC, it was apparently kept in a treasury which burned down in the fifth century BC, discolouring the ivory.

(Opposite above) Zeus carrying off Ganymede: a terracotta sculptural group from the roof of a treasury at Olympia (c. 480–470 BC), 1.1 m (3.6 ft) high. The use of such figures was a feature of Etruscan temple decoration, and this one may have been from the treasury of a Western Greek city.

(Opposite below) Marble statues making up a centauromachy in the west pediment of the temple of Zeus at Olympia, c. 460 BC.

THE GREEKS produced large amounts of sculpture and used it to adorn their cities, both as decoration on buildings and as free-standing monuments; statues were dedicated in sanctuaries of the gods as thank-offerings for success or good fortune, or decorated tombs. Literally tens of thousands of pieces have been recovered and are displayed in museums around the world. Sculptures were made in a variety of materials: marble, bronze, gold and ivory, wood and terracotta. Most statues were brightly painted and probably would have seemed quite garish; perhaps fortunately, only rare examples of polychromy survive.

Terracotta and marble statues tend to survive most frequently. Bronze statues could be and were melted down, so fewer pieces exist, usually chance finds from the bed of the sea (p. 178). The cuttings and sockets found on a statue base, however, usually indicate whether the statue which was attached was of marble or bronze, and hundreds of examples show that bronze was at least as common as marble. It was presumably quicker and cheaper; a lifesize marble figure would take one man about a year to

carve. Gold and ivory (chryselephantine) were used for cult statues and are known primarily from literature, though parts of two or three were found burned and buried under the sacred way at Delphi.

Many Greek sculptors are known to us by name (e.g. Pheidias, Polykleitos, Praxiteles, Lysippos) and attempts have been made to associate specific works with famous artists. Rarely, however, can surviving masterpieces such as the Riace Bronzes (p. 178) or the Motya Charioteer (p. 103) be safely attributed to named sculptors, nor have many works by the masters survived from antiquity. Their names are preserved particularly in the writings of Pliny (late first century AD) and Pausanias (second century AD), and there are hundreds of surviving artists' signatures on stone.

The Romans were great collectors of Greek sculpture; they plundered vast amounts during conquests and occupations in the third to first centuries BC, hired Greek artists to come to work in Italy and commissioned numerous copies or adaptations of Greek originals. These Roman copies have traditionally played a major role in attempts to interpret the style of individual Greek masters.

Certain cities became known for their schools of sculptors and the ancient sources are often careful to tell us which sculptor was a pupil of which master. Athens, Argos and Sikyon were all prominent in the Classical period, whereas Rhodes was a great centre of production in Hellenistic times, when the workshops and family genealogies of sculptors can be traced on the surviving statue bases. Rhodes was also the home of one of the largest and most famous statues of Hellenistic times, a colossal figure of Helios, the patron deity of the island – the Colossus of Rhodes, one of the Seven Wonders of the world.

Architectural sculpture

From the very beginnings of stone architecture in the seventh century BC a primary use of sculpture was to adorn temples. On a Doric building it occurs in the triangular pediments at either end, in the metopes of the frieze and on the apex and corners of the roof. The use of sculpted metopes may well have developed first in the western colonies. The Ionic order is far more experimental and varied in the use of sculpture, especially early on; in addition to the pediments and frieze (for instance the Siphnian treasury at Delphi), sculpture might be used to

THE COLOSSUS OF RHODES

Calling for admiration before all others was the colossal statue of the Sun at Rhodes made by Chares of Lindos, pupil of Lysippos. This statue was 70 cubits [33.5 m/110 ft] high, and 56 years after its erection was overthrown by an earthquake, but even lying on the ground it is a marvel. Few people can make their arms meet around the thumb of the figure, and the fingers are larger than most statues. Where the limbs have broken off enormous cavities yawn, while inside are seen great masses of rock with which the artist steadied it as he erected it. It is recorded that it took 12 years to complete and cost 300 talents [1,800,000 drachmas], money raised from selling the siege machines of King Demetrios which he abandoned when he tired of the long siege of Rhodes.

Pliny, *Natural History* 34. 41

MASTER-SCULPTORS OF ANTIQUITY

Several names of sculptors occur repeatedly in the ancient sources, indicating that their works were both admired and influential in the development of Greek sculpture. Most of them date to the fifth and fourth centuries BC.

Polykleitos of Argos was credited with perfecting the sculpting of the human figure. He was active in the middle years of the fifth century BC, a period when sculptors had broken free of the stiff striding pose borrowed from Egypt and used by Greek sculptors throughout the sixth century for *kouroi*, the statues of naked young men (p. 70).

Polykleitos of Sikyon, pupil of Hageladas, made a statue of the Diadoumenos ['hair-binder'], a soft-looking youth, famous for having cost 100 talents, and also the Doryphoros ['spear-bearer'], a manly-looking boy. He also made what artists call a canon or 'model statue', since they draw their outlines from it as

though from a standard; and he alone of mankind is deemed in a single work to have embodied the principles of his art…. Polykleitos is thought to have perfected this science of statuary and to have refined the art of carving sculpture, just as Pheidias is considered to have revealed it. A discovery that was all his own is the art of making statues with their weight thrown on to one leg.

Pliny, *Natural History* 34. 19

Working increasingly in bronze, sculptors such as Polykleitos experimented with showing the human form in motion and in a variety of poses. One of the best-known examples of the trend, preserved only in marble copies of the Roman period, is the 'discus-thrower' by **Myron**, from Eleutherai, in Boiotia. Marble sculpture of the period, such as the pediments of the temple of Zeus at Olympia (*c.* 460 BC), show a similar interest and growing skill in rendering movement and action.

Statue of Zeus at Olympia, by Pheidias.

Pheidias was the creative genius behind the Periklean building programme on the Acropolis of Athens (450–430 BC). It is

assumed the Parthenon sculptures give some idea of the 'Pheidian' style of sculpture, with idealized faces and elaborately decorative folds of drapery. He was also famed for his monumental cult statues in gold and ivory, in particular the Athena Parthenos in the Parthenon and the colossal statue of Zeus at Olympia.

Praxiteles, an Athenian, was active in the years around 360–330 BC and was known for his marble statues and his ability to show emotions. His most famous statue, known only from copies, is of a nude Aphrodite, dedicated and displayed in a round building in a sanctuary at Knidos. Modelled on his mistress, Phryne, the statue is one of the first to show the goddess nude and caused something of a

(Above left)
The Doryphoros
(spear-bearer)
of Polykleitos
(Roman copy).

The Diskobolos
(discus-thrower)
of Myron
(Roman copy).

Aphrodite of Knidos, by Praxiteles (Roman copy).

scandal at the time. One of the longest-running controversies in sculptural studies concerns a statue at Olympia he either did or did not carve. Pausanias, describing the interior of the temple of Hera, records a statue by Praxiteles he saw there of Hermes holding the infant Dionysos. German excavators found just such a statue within the temple ruins (p. 149). Despite this close correlation of archaeology and the text of Pausanias, several features have prevented many scholars from accepting the statue as an original of the fourth century BC: the struts and tree-trunk support are more common in Roman copies and perhaps suggest a bronze original, some of the tooling and the highly polished surfaces have bothered others, while the sandal worn by Hermes is hard to parallel in the fourth century. Regrettably, the base carries no inscription to guide us, and the assessment of the statue has passionate adherents on both sides.

Lysippos, from Sikyon in the Peloponnese, was active in the second half of the fourth century BC. He was a prolific sculptor, mostly in bronze, and is said to have produced 1,500 statues. He was the court sculptor of Alexander the Great, who especially approved of Lysippos' portraits of him. He was admired for the slender proportions of his figures. A marble statue set up at Delphi in 338–334 BC of the athlete Agias is thought to reflect Lysippos' style closely and may be by him. The poetic inscription on the base of the statue at Delphi is identical to that found on a second base for a statue of Agias in Pharsalos, the athlete's Thessalian home town. The Pharsalos base (though not the one at Delphi) also carries the signature of Lysippos, perhaps suggesting that both statues were products of Lysippos' workshop.

A sculpted metope from the interior frieze of the temple of Zeus at Olympia (c. 460 BC): Athena, Herakles and Atlas with the apples of the Hesperides.

The Agias from Delphi, original of c. 335 BC, perhaps by Lysippos.

adorn the top or bottom drum of a column (at Ephesus and Chryse), the architrave (Didyma), the *sima* (roof gutter: Ephesus), or the roof itself, a location favoured by the Etruscans.

The themes depicted were also varied and the connection of a given scene with the deity whose temple it adorned is not always obvious. Scenes of mythology are common,

ETRUSCAN SKILLS

Varro … says that the art of clay modelling was brought to perfection in Italy, especially in Etruria. He says too that Vulca was summoned from Veii to receive from Tarquinius Priscus a contract for the statue of Jupiter to be consecrated on the Capitol, this Jupiter being made of clay and so regularly painted with cinnabar; also, that the four-horse chariots on the ridge of the temple were made of clay.…

Pliny, *Natural History* 35. 45

The base and sculpted Ionic column from the fourth-century BC temple of Artemis at Ephesus (see p. 101).

WARRIORS FROM THE SEA

The Zeus/Poseidon from Artemision.

Much of the best Greek sculpture was of bronze and most of it was plundered, melted down and reused. Only a handful of pieces survive, usually chance finds from shipwrecks, dragged up off the seabed in a fisherman's net. Two of the most spectacular recoveries, by coincidence, are of roughly the same date and depict similar figures.

Zeus/Poseidon

In 1927 a magnificent statue in bronze was found off Cape Artemision, the northernmost tip of the island of Euboia. It depicts a heavily bearded naked male figure striding forward, about to throw an object, now missing, from his right hand. The complex pose, the treatment of the musculature, the use of bronze and the details of the hair have led most scholars to date the figure to the transitional period between Archaic and Classical sculpture, known as the Severe style (c. 480–450 BC).

Other questions are harder to answer. Who does the figure represent? Most believe it must be a god, and Zeus or Poseidon, god of the sea, are the favoured candidates, depending on what is restored in the right hand. If Zeus, a thunderbolt is the usual weapon, though in small figurines he usually throws it like a baseball, with the arm cocked by the ear, rather than fully extended. A long-shafted weapon, like Poseidon's triple-pronged trident, fits the pose better, though the head of the weapon would then obscure the god's face. Where the piece once stood is also unknown; it seems likely it was a votive, dedicated in some sanctuary, if not the actual cult statue itself. Where

it was headed when the ship that was carrying it went down is again uncertain, though it may well have been destined for the Roman market; found with it was a magnificent horse and jockey of much later date,

suggesting that the ship carried a mixed load of sculpture plundered or purchased from Greece.

Riace Bronzes

In the 1980s, an Italian diver swimming off the coast of the toe of Italy saw what looked like an arm protruding from the sandy seabed. It turned out to be just that, though belonging to a bronze statue, not a human. Recovery operations produced two magnificent bronze statues of nude warriors, but not the shipwreck from which they presumably came. A long process of study and restoration has been carried out on both figures. The treatment of the head of one of them suggests that he was wearing a helmet, while the pose of the arm indicates that he once carried a shield.

Considerations of style lead to a date in the early to mid-fifth century BC. As with the Artemision god, the original location of these statues remains a subject of debate, some thinking they must be from well-known sculptural groups of heroes from an important sanctuary in Greece. Who may have sculpted them is also a matter of speculation. Presumably they, too, were on their way to Rome when they were lost.

With the Artemision and Riace bronzes we are faced with the irony that we can say little with certainty about the sculptors or original locations of three of the few surviving masterpieces of Classical Greek sculpture, and we are reminded that some of the finest treasures from antiquity come from chance encounters rather than archaeological investigation.

One of the Riace bronzes.

Part of the gigantomachy decorating the Great Altar of Zeus at Pergamon, c. 180–160 BC, now in Berlin.

A kore (female figure) from the Acropolis of Athens, sixth century BC. This is one of more than a dozen such maidens, beautifully carved and painted, dedicated to Athena.

while three battle scenes in particular seem to predominate: between gods and giants (gigantomachy); Greeks and Amazons (amazonomachy), and Lapiths and Centaurs (centauromachy). On some of the Classical temples (Parthenon, Nike temple, Olympia, Delphi) there is a tendency to show a relatively calm scene on the eastern pediment, and a battle scene on the west.

Votive sculpture

Every temple had at least one statue dedicated to its patron deity. Originally they were of wood and crudely carved; by the Classical period they could be of gold and ivory, richly adorned with glass and jewels. In addition to these cult statues, sanctuaries such as the Athenian Acropolis might be filled with other sculptures dedicated to the god or goddess by individuals. In Athens, the favoured dedication was a *kore*, a handsomely draped young female figure usually shown holding out a small offering to the goddess. Male deities tended to receive a male statue, a *kouros*, a striding naked youth showing stylistic affinities with early Egyptian sculpture, but adapted to Greek tastes (see p. 70). The Egyptian prototype showed the pharaoh in kilt and headdress; the Greek version did away with the kilt, while the triangular form of the headdress became a mantle of hair falling on to the shoulders. *Kouroi* have been found in particularly large numbers at the sanctuary of Apollo on Mt Ptoon in Boiotia and at the sanctuary of Poseidon at Sounion, in Attica.

The Panhellenic sanctuaries of Delphi and Olympia were full of votive statues put on display to impress visitors from all over the Greek world. Pausanias says Delphi was stripped of 500 statues by Nero alone and then goes on to record dozens of offerings still standing in his day, a century later. Often they are associated with a particular event, such as victory in battle, in which case the sculpture represents a tithe or tenth of the value of the spoils. Numerous examples of dedications by cities, composed of groups of statues, were reported by Pausanias as he climbed the sacred way at Delphi. Individual achievement was also the occasion for a rich sculptural dedication, especially for successful athletes. Pausanias devotes an entire book to a description of the statues of winning athletes set up in the sanctuary of Zeus at Olympia, and several monuments of winners in the Pythian games have been excavated in Delphi.

Funerary sculpture

A major class of Greek sculpture was that used to mark graves. Stone stelai showing hunting and battle scenes were erected over Mycenaean shaft graves (p. 45). In the Dark Ages, when monumental sculpture did not exist, graves were marked with large vases (p. 60). Both relief sculpture and sculpture in the round were used to mark graves beginning in the seventh century BC.

BURIAL CUSTOMS, FUNERALS AND GRAVES

Proper disposal of the dead was a concern throughout antiquity, and funerary laws and rituals have been a rich field of study. Mortuary practices changed over time and varied in different parts of the Greek world: burial as opposed to cremation, orientation of the body, the location of cemeteries inside or outside the settlement, the specific assemblage of grave goods required, and single or multiple graves are just some of the cultural markers which distinguish various groups of Greeks in either space or time.

Some belief in the afterlife is perhaps implied by the grave goods regularly deposited with the deceased, and the size of a tomb and the lavishness of its preparation seem to be an indicator of wealth and status. Indeed, in democratic Athens, strict limits were placed on grave monuments at various times in order to limit ostentatious display by the aristocracy.

Though often plundered, even in antiquity, many tombs survive in a good state of preservation and are among the most impressive surviving

(Above) Grave stele of Dexileos, a young Athenian cavalryman, aged 19, killed in battle at Corinth in 395 BC. A very rare example of a grave inscription recording both date of birth and death.

(Left) An old woman, showing the tendency of Hellenistic sculptors to portray figures realistically.

Kouroi were often a favourite choice early on, or some animal such as a lion or a sphinx. Later, stelai with reliefs were preferred, showing a warrior or the deceased bidding farewell to family members (pp. 140–41). Such markers were expensive and provided an opportunity for ostentation by the wealthy. In democratic cities like Athens such displays were offensive and attempts were made from time to time to limit the amount of money a family could spend on a tomb. One such law took force in the late fourth century BC, ending with the stroke of a pen an entire field of Athenian sculpture.

(Below left) A cavalryman rides down a Greek warrior on this Greco-Persian sarcophagus recently found in northwest Asia Minor, c. 400–375 BC. Compare the scene with the contemporary stele of Dexileos (opposite above).

(Right) Large marble sarcophagus, recently found north of Troy: the sacrifice of Polyxena by Neoptolemos at the grave of his father, Achilles, c. 530–510 BC.

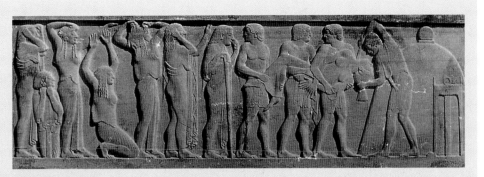

monuments of antiquity. One thinks, for example, of the tholos tombs of the Mycenaean world (p. 42), the heroon of Dark Age Lefkandi (p. 61), or the Mausoleum of Halicarnassus (p. 191).

Unplundered cemeteries provide some of the best evidence for archaeologists, as most burials represent time-capsules containing a related group of artifacts untouched since antiquity. Royal or aristocratic burials (the shaft graves at Mycenae (p. 40), the Macedonian tombs at Vergina (pp. 192–93)) have produced many outstanding examples of Greek art and workmanship.

Funerary scenes on vases of the eighth century BC are among the earliest expressions of Greek art. They often show the body laid out on a bier or wagon, surrounded by women in unmistakable poses of mourning (pp. 58–59). From the Classical period hundreds of sculpted marble grave stelai survive, usually showing the deceased and one or more family members, accompanied by servants or a favourite pet. Small lekythoi (oil jars) made especially as grave goods are often decorated with scenes of the tomb (p. 183).

Elaborately painted and/or sculpted caskets for the burial of important personages, though rare, are a feature of Greek art which can be traced through the ages and throughout the Mediterranean. The earliest examples are known from Minoan Crete, the most ornate being the clay larnax or sarcophagus from Aghia Triadha (pp. 48–49), painted with scenes of ritual, including the sacrifice of a bull and a procession of figures bearing offerings to a deity or statue. The tradition is transferred to and carried on in mainland Greece, in Boiotia, where a Late Bronze Age cemetery was found in Tanagra, not far from Thebes, full of painted clay caskets. Mourning women are generally shown, and one larnax has scenes of bull-leaping (p. 51).

The Dark Ages have no such boxes in the tenth and ninth centuries, but the huge burial urns of the eighth century, used to mark graves, are decorated with funerary scenes and stand at the beginning of an unbroken tradition of representational art in Europe.

From the Archaic period we have a magnificent sculpted marble sarcophagus recently discovered not far from Troy. Dating to around 530–510 BC, it shows scenes of the sacrifice of Polyxena, watched by a full complement of distraught women, while the other long side has armed warriors dancing before an enthroned woman with attendants.

The same area of Asia Minor has even more recently produced a Classical sculpted sarcophagus, with brightly painted scenes of hunting and battle. The same themes are found on one of the most famous decorated sarcophagi of antiquity, the so-called Alexander sarcophagus of the late fourth century BC, found in the last century at Sidon and now in the Istanbul museum.

Sculpted stone sarcophagi become increasingly commonplace in the Roman period, and centres like Aphrodisias produced hundreds of examples which were exported widely throughout the Mediterranean. Many show favourite scenes from Greek mythology and from the epics (p. 159), and several identical copies survive. The same scene of Priam ransoming the body of Hector from Achilles, for instance, appears in Bithynia in northwest Turkey, in Ioannina in northwest Greece and in the Capitoline museum in Rome.

Marble sarcophagus, c. 330–320 BC, showing Alexander fighting the Persians. Found in the tomb of a royal family of Sidon (in modern Lebanon), it is now in Istanbul.

POTTERY

'...she that raised her glorious trophy at Marathon invented the potter's wheel and the child of clay and the oven, noblest pottery, useful in house-keeping'. And in fact Attic pottery is held in high esteem.

Athenaios, *Deipnosophistai* 28C (quoting Critias)

EPITAPH FOR A POTTER

Of those who blend earth, water, fire into one by art, Bakhios was judged by all Hellas first, for natural gifts; and in every contest appointed by the city he won the crown.

Athenian tombstone, fourth century BC

(Above left) Corinthian vase with mythical creatures, sixth century BC (see also p. 92).

(Above right) The François Vase, a krater (mixing bowl) signed by the painter Kleitias, with several bands of decoration showing scenes of Greek mythology: the Calydonian boar hunt is in the uppermost register. Found in an Etruscan tomb at Chiusi, it dates from c. 575 BC (c. 0.66 m/2 ft high).

GREEK POTTERY is the most enduring survival from the past, which explains why it receives so much attention from archaeologists. You can drop an intact vase and it will break into a dozen pieces; you can then jump up and down on those pieces and you will end up with a hundred fragments, but it takes phenomenal effort to turn that pot to dust. Scraps survive in virtually every level excavated, they are readily recognizable and they are the primary dating tool on many prehistoric and most historic sites. Just as a Coca-Cola bottle – or even a fragment of one – tells us we are no earlier than the late nineteenth century, and a Coca-Cola can no earlier than the second half of the twentieth, so, too, much of Greek pottery serves as an indication of date.

Similarly, the specific function of a Greek vase is often known, just as we understand today that beer is not usually consumed from a teacup. Imports are also recognizable, by shape and/or fabric. Thus the pottery found within a given layer may well provide the date, the activities and the foreign contacts for the building within which it is found. Hence the enthusiasm for pottery by archaeologists; it is literally a mine of information, and usually an abundant one.

Clay was the primary material used for containers in antiquity, fulfilling the role, among others, of glass, paper, metal and plastic today. As a result, several dozen shapes were in use at any one time: jugs and pitchers of all sizes for the table (amphoras, hydrias, olpai), drinking vessels (kylikes, skyphoi, kantharoi), mixing bowls (kraters), plates, mortars, basins, lamps, condiment containers, feeding bottles, perfume flasks, oil jars (lekythoi, aryballoi, alabastra), cosmetic boxes (pyxides), chamber pots, storage jars (pithoi) and transport amphoras. Though produced in great quantities, these vases represent outstanding examples of the potters' skill and on many occasions they would sign their work.

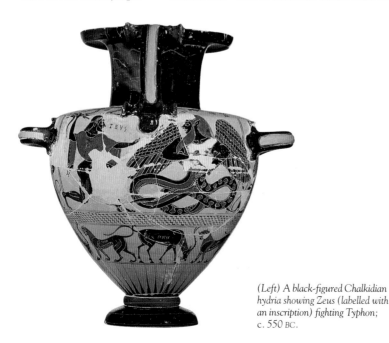

(Left) A black-figured Chalkidian hydria showing Zeus (labelled with an inscription) fighting Typhon; c. 550 BC.

There is a long tradition of painted decoration on Greek pottery, going back to the Bronze Age, when marine and floral motifs were favoured. In the Dark Ages the design was restricted to Geometric ornament: triangles, circles, swastikas, meanders, dog's teeth, zigzags, and the like. Horses, birds and human figures only became common again in the eighth century, still surrounded by Geometric ornament. The seventh and sixth centuries were a time of great experimentation and local variations, with Corinthian and then Athenian pottery gradually becoming dominant. Both in antiquity and in modern times Attic (Athenian) pottery has been judged the finest.

By the sixth century the so-called black-figured style was favoured, showing figures in black glaze on the lighter natural background of the clay, with the anatomical and other details drawn with thin incised lines. Numerous examples were exported throughout the Mediterranean and today adorn the museums of the world. In the years around 520 BC the red-figured style was developed, essentially the same technique, but reversed, using the natural reddish colour for the figures, set against a black background. The figures thereby stand out more sharply, and the interior details can be rendered more effectively in sinuous glazed lines rather than by incision. This style proved tremendously popular and vessels were extensively exported from Athens, especially to Etruria and elsewhere in Italy, as well as the Black Sea. They are often signed by the artists, and in many instances the style of a given painter is so distinctive that a number of pots can be assigned to his hand even when there is no signature. The quality of the painting varies tremendously and so, presumably, did the prices of individual vases. Figured pottery was generally available and affordable, to judge from the material found in relatively modest Athenian houses.

Scenes from a wide selection of Greek myths were favoured, as well as generic scenes of battle, workshops, sports and dining and revelry. Later, in the fifth century, domestic settings involving women and children became more common, and red-figured scenes are often used to illustrate various aspects of Greek daily life. They also give some indirect idea of the arrangement and quality of large-scale paintings, now lost, which once adorned public buildings and temples throughout Greece.

A special class of Greek vase-painting was reserved for funerary vases and high-quality votives in sanctuaries. This involved setting the scene on a white background. Several sanctuaries have produced cups in this style, and white-ground lekythoi (oil jars) were very popular in Athenian burials during the fifth and fourth centuries BC.

(Above left) Achilles kills the Amazon Penthesileia; an Athenian black-figured vase by Exekias, c. 540–530 BC.

(Above) Priam ransoming the body of his son Hector from Achilles (Iliad, 24. 468ff.); Attic red-figured skyphos by the Brygos Painter, c. 480–470 BC, from Cerveteri.

A white-ground lekythos, by the Bosanquet Painter, c. 450–425 BC, found at Eretria. A warrior visits a tomb: note the dedication of numerous lekythoi, traditional grave goods, left on the steps of the tomb depicted. (See p. 148 for another example of white-ground painting.)

183

PAINTING

*A nice story is told of him in
connection with Protogenes,
who was living in Rhodes.
Apelles sailed there, eager to
see the works of a man known
only to him by reputation, and
went at once to his studio.
Protogenes was out, but a
solitary old woman was keeping
watch over a large panel on an
easel, who asked his name.
'Here it is', he said, and
snatching up a brush, Apelles
drew a very thin line across the
panel. When Protogenes
returned he declared that the
visitor must be Apelles, for no
one else could draw such a
delicate line. He then drew a
still finer line on the first, in
another colour, and went away,
telling the woman to show it to
Apelles should he return. As
expected, Apelles returned and
drew a third line down the
length of the other two, leaving
no room for further refinement.
Protogenes admitted defeat and
hurried to the harbour to find
his visitor; they agreed to hand
the painting as it was to
posterity, a marvel to all, but
especially artists. It perished in
the fire of the house of the
Caesars on the Palatine.
Before, we could look at it, its
wide surface disclosing nothing
except lines which eluded sight,
and among the numerous works
by excellent painters it was like
a blank, and it was precisely
this which lent it surpassing
attraction and fame.*

Pliny, *Natural History* 35.36

*Four colours only were used by
Apelles, Aetion, Melanthios
and Nikomachos in their
immortal works; illustrious
artists, a single one of whose
pictures the wealth of a city
was hardly enough to buy,
while now that purple covers
even our walls and India
contributes the ooze of her
rivers and the blood of dragons
and of elephants, no famous
picture is painted.*

Pliny, *Natural History* 35.32

UNTIL RECENTLY, GREEK PAINTING was only known indirectly. Descriptions preserved in the writings of Pliny and Pausanias make it clear that monumental painting was as developed and important to the Greeks as sculpture and architecture, but very few examples from antiquity have been preserved. Famous paintings adorned the public buildings of Athens and the sanctuaries of Greece. Certain cities, such as Sikyon, were known for their schools of painters, and successful artists found commissions all over the Greek world.

The earliest wall-paintings survive mainly in tombs, where the atmosphere is stable, and come from the fringes of the Greek world. In Asia Minor, a few handsomely painted tombs in Lydia and Phrygia give some idea of the sophistication of Archaic and early Classical painting. In the west, the painted tombs of the Etruscans show strong Greek influence, and the Tomb of the Diver from Poseidonia (Paestum) provides an example from the fifth century (p. 106).

With the active excavations carried out in Macedonia, in northern Greece, the picture has changed radically in recent years. Numerous tombs dating from the fourth to second centuries BC have been found, many with wall paintings surviving in good condition, comple-

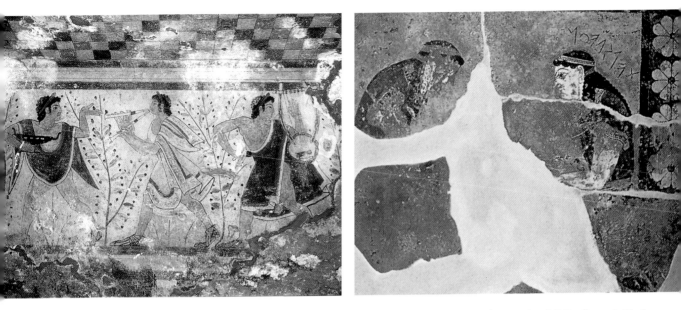

menting the literary evidence that Macedonian kings hired the best Greek artists to adorn their palaces. Only a handful of examples were known previously and the new paintings increase both the numbers and range of subjects. Warriors, women, animal hunts and scenes from mythology have all been found, as have architectural embellishment, *trompe l'oeuil* painting to make a flat surface look moulded, shading

and attempts at perspective. As these are the elements of the Pompeian styles in Italy, and as the Romans were active militarily in Macedonia during the second century BC, it seems probable that we have here the inspiration for much of Roman wall-painting. As with architecture and sculpture, the Romans would have borrowed extensively from this branch of Greek art as well.

(Above left) Revellers in the Tomb of the Leopards, at Tarquinia in Etruria, early fifth century BC. There is a strong Greek influence in the numerous scenes found in Etruscan painted tombs of the sixth to fourth centuries BC, which are also where many of the finest examples of Athenian red- and black-figured pottery were found. The Greeks and Etruscans shared certain conventions in painting: a strong ground line with sparse indications of setting, gender-specific skin colours of red for men and white for females, and a mix of frontal and profile views of figures.

(Opposite above) A painted grave stele of Demetrios of Olynthos, third century BC, from Demetrias in Thessaly, a Macedonian dependency.

(Left) A drunken reveller on a funerary couch from Potidaia, late fourth century BC, showing the full skill and sophistication of Macedonian painting.

(Right) Perseus rescues Andromeda; Roman wall painting from Pompeii, before AD 79. While Roman innovations in painting included more complex backgrounds, perspectives and poses, many panels at Pompeii were signed by Greek artists.

(Above) Painted terracotta revetment plaque or metope from Thermon in Aetolia, c. 620 BC, with an inscription reading 'Chelidon'. This stands at the beginning of a long tradition of painted architectural decoration.

THE PAINTER PARRHASIOS
He [Parrhasios] painted an ingenious personification of the Athenian Demos [people], discovering it as fickle, passionate, unjust, changeable, yet exorable, compassionate and pitiful, boastful, proud and humble, bold and cowardly, in a word, everything at once.

Pliny, *Natural History* 35.36

185

Metalwork

Maenad at rest on the shoulder of a huge gilded bronze krater (mixing bowl) found in a tomb at Derveni, outside Thessaloniki and dating to c. 350–320 BC.

METALWORKING had been well-established in Greece in the Bronze Age. Examples abound from the Mycenaean centres of beautiful bronze daggers inlaid with scenes executed in gold and silver (p. 40), and delicate appliques in gold were a feature of many rich tombs. The Dark Ages saw the introduction of iron, used espe- cially for weapons, and fine bronze-working was reintroduced to Greece from the East, perhaps through Crete. The earliest examples are large bronze tripod cauldrons with their rims deco- rated with elaborate animal heads (protomes). Soon there- after came all sorts of weapons and armour, much of it ornately decorated in relief

A silver bull of the fifth century BC, from a treasury at Delphi, found in a pit under the Sacred Way together with other rare items (see p. 174). Bronze strips inside show that thin silver sheets were nailed to a wooden frame.

or with incision. Many fine examples were given as votives in sanctuaries, especially Olympia.

Because metal can be melted down and reused, only a relatively small number of pieces have been recovered, usually from unplundered tombs of the fourth century BC. From Derveni, in northern Greece, we have an outstanding example of a huge mixing bowl elaborately adorned with carvings and relief figures. And the tomb at Vergina, often identified as that of King Philip II of Macedon, was full of wonders of metalworking: wreaths of golden oak leaves

and acorns, beautifully chased silver drinking cups, and a bronze lantern, among others.

On a much smaller scale, exquisite gold jewelry, with fine filigree work and granulation, was made by Greeks from as early as the ninth century BC until well on in the Hellenistic period. Mostly recovered from graves, the usual items of personal adornment are found: necklaces, bracelets, earrings, pins, rings and diadems. Floral elements, mythical beasts, erotes, lions and snakes were the favoured decoration.

(Below left) A Greek bronze krater (sixth century BC) found in a Celtic grave at Vix in central France; it is over 1.5 m (5 ft) tall and weighs 204 kg (450 lb).

(Below) A selection of gold jewelry from Athens: (left to right) gold earrings of the ninth century BC, found in a cremation burial together with the pottery shown on p. 62; a Mycenaean seal ring; and two earrings in the form of Eros (early Hellenistic).

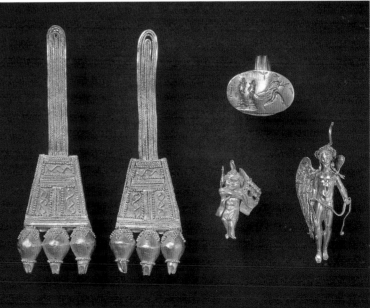

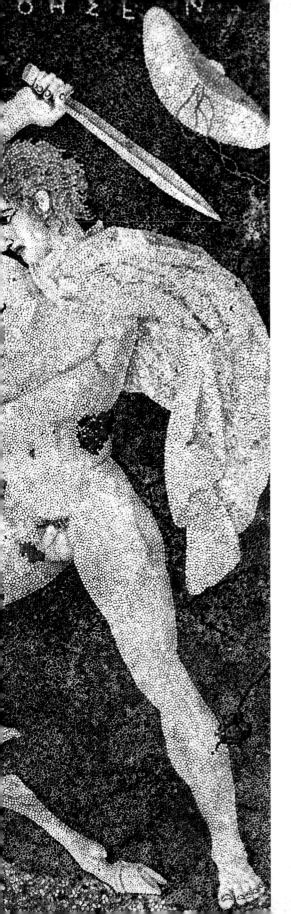

ALEXANDER AND THE HELLENISTIC WORLD

F OLLOWING THE CONQUEST of Greece by Philip II, his son Alexander led the Macedonian army across Asia to India. The result of this conquest was a homogeneous spread of Greek culture across the known world. During the centuries between Alexander and the rise of Rome in the east, his successors ruled large kingdoms in Greece, Asia Minor, Syria and Egypt. Quite distinct artistically, socially, militarily and politically from the earlier Classical world, this time is known as the Hellenistic period.

The Hellenistic world was founded on and by the Macedonians, who were regarded by other mainland Greeks as semi-barbarian: an oracle from Delphi had been necessary to establish their right to participate as Greeks in the Olympic games. Theirs was a tribal society, with a constitutional monarch who ruled by strength and the consent of other chieftains. Hunting and fighting were actively pursued and are common themes in the paintings, mosaics and sculptural groups commissioned by Macedonian rulers. Large palaces dominated their cities (Pella, Aigai, Naoussa and Demetrias in Thessaly), with huge peristyle courts surrounded by dining rooms for intense feasting after the fight or hunt was over. In general, with their palaces and aristocratic society, their emphasis on hunting and warfare, their fondness for luxury goods of gold, silver and ivory, and their preference for large burial chambers with elaborate façades buried under huge mounds of earth, the Macedonians seem to reflect a return to, or a survival of, the heroic times of the Mycenaean world.

A mosaic floor from Pella, capital city of Macedonia, depicting a stag hunt and signed by the artist Gnosis; early Hellenistic.

HISTORICAL BACKGROUND

BY THE FOURTH CENTURY BC both Athens and Sparta had been exhausted by war and other claimants to the hegemony of Greece arose. At first Thebes was dominant for a short period (371–362 BC) under Epaminondas. Further north, in Thessaly, Jason and then Alexander of Pherai contended with the Thebans for control of the mainland.

In southwest Asia Minor a Persian satrap (governor) by the name of Mausolus (Maussollos) unified the area known as Caria, making Halicarnassus (modern Bodrum) his new capital and exerting his influence along the coast of Ionia and in the adjacent islands. On his death in 353 BC he was interred in an elaborate grave monument, deemed one of the Seven Wonders of the world, which gave its name – the Mausoleum – to all such future grandiose burial structures. The monument is described in some detail by Pliny and other authors. It rose 36.5 m (120 ft) high, had a pyramidal roof crowned with statues, and was decorated on all four sides with friezes sculpted by the best Greek artists available. It was damaged by earthquakes but

THE CITY OF HALICARNASSUS

At Halicarnassus, also, although the palace of the mighty king Mausolus had all parts finished with Proconnesian marble, it has walls built of brick. Nor was it

for lack of means the king did this, for he was enriched by enormous revenues when he ruled over all Caria. Though born at Mylasa, he observed at Halicarnassus a place

naturally fortified, a suitable market, and a useful harbour, and there he established his palace. The setting is like a natural theatre. The agora is placed at the lowest level, along

the harbour. Midway up this natural amphitheatre is a street of ample width, in the middle of which is the Mausoleum, of such splendid workmanship it is numbered

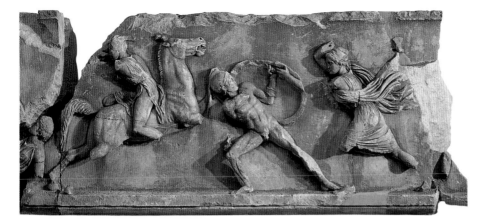

A fragment of the Amazonomachy, one of the friezes that decorated all four sides of the Mausoleum, c. 350 BC.

One possible reconstruction of the Mausoleum, with four tiers of statues, a frieze and a four-horse chariot on the summit.

among the Seven Wonders of the world. In the middle of the top of the citadel is a temple of Ares with a colossal statue with marble extremities, made by Leochares or Timotheos. On the right at the top is a temple of Aphrodite and Hermes, by the fountain of Salmacis. This fountain is mistakenly thought to afflict those who drink of it with an aphrodisiac disease.... On the left side is the royal palace which King Mausolus had built to his own plan. From it there is seen on one side the agora and harbour, and the whole circuit of the walls; on the other side there is a secret harbour lying hidden under high ground....

Vitruvius, 2. 8

Then to Halicarnassus, the royal residence of the dynasts of Caria. Here is the tomb of Mausolus, one of the seven wonders, a monument built by Artemesia in honour of her husband. And here is the fountain of Salmaci, which has the slanderous reputation of making effeminate all who drink from it.

Strabo, 656

Halicarnassus, capital of Caria; the crusader fort occupies the site of Mausolus' palace, while the Mausoleum was built in the centre of the town, between the theatre and the harbour.

THE MAUSOLEUM AT HALICARNASSUS

The Mausoleum is largely destroyed, but we have some descriptions from antiquity:

And on these two [Satyros and Pythios, architects of the Mausoleum] good fortune conferred the greatest and highest good. For their works are judged to have a merit famous throughout the ages and of unfading freshness, and they employed distinguished artists for their works. For on the several sides, different rival craftsmen took a share in decorating and competing: Leochares, Bryaxis, Skopas, Praxiteles, and some add Timotheos. The outstanding excellence of their work caused the fame of the Mausoleum to be included in the seven wonders of the world.

Vitruvius, 7 praef. 13

Bryaxis, Timotheos, and Leochares were rivals and contemporaries of Skopas and must be mentioned with him, as they worked together on the Mausoleum. This is the tomb erected by Artemesia in honour of her husband Mausolus of Caria, who died in the 2nd year of the 107th Olympiad [351 BC], and its place among the seven wonders of the world is largely due to these great sculptors. The length of the north and south sides is 163 feet, the two façades are shorter, and the whole perimeter is 440 feet. Its height is 25 cubits [11.5 m/37.5 ft], and it has 36 columns. The sculptures on the east are carved by Skopas, those on the north by Bryaxis, those on the south by Timotheos, and those on the west by Leochares. The queen died before the work was finished, *but the artists carried it through to the end, judging that it would be an abiding monument of their own glory and the glory of art. A fifth sculptor also worked on the monument. Above the colonnade is a pyramid, as high as the lower structure, consisting of 24 steps rising to a peak. On the apex stands a chariot and four horses in marble, made by Pythis. Including this, the height is 140 feet.*

Pliny, *Natural History*, 36. 4

A colossal figure, once identified as Mausolus himself, one of dozens of freestanding sculptures which adorned the Mausoleum.

---

survived until 1501, when it was quarried for building material by the Knights of Rhodes (later the Knights of Malta) for the castle of St Peter and St Paul which still guards the harbour of Bodrum. Sculptures found in excavations of the site in the 1860s and others removed from the castle walls are now on display in the British Museum.

In Macedonia, Philip II became king in about 359 BC and gradually consolidated his power in the north. His expansion brought him into conflict with Greek cities lying on Athens' vital sea routes to the Black Sea and he intervened actively in central Greece during a Sacred War fought over control of Delphi. In 338 BC, at Chaironeia in Boiotia, with his son Alexander he defeated a combined Athenian and Theban army and gained effective control of Greece. At Olympia he erected an elaborate round building, within the sacred enclosure, housing gold and ivory statues of himself and his family; as these materials were generally used for cult images of the gods, we are close here to the origins of ruler-worship by the Greeks.

Philip was assassinated soon thereafter, in 336 BC, and his kingdom fell to the young Alexander, just 20 years old. An unplundered tomb found in 1977 at Vergina has been identi-

(Above) A miniature ivory head from Tomb II at Vergina, identified as a portrait of Philip II.

(Right) Exterior of Tomb II at Vergina, with a Doric façade surmounted by a painted frieze of an animal hunt. It was identified by the excavator as the tomb of Philip II himself, and therefore dated to c. 335 BC.

Gold gorytus (quiver) with battle scenes in relief, from Tomb II at Vergina.

fied by many as the tomb of Philip. Buried within a huge earlier mound was a small temple-like building, its façade decorated with a painted frieze showing a hunt involving numerous hunters and animals. Within was a rich burial, the cremated bones wrapped in purple cloth embroidered with gold and placed in a golden casket. Grave goods included a gold wreath, weapons, an iron cuirass, a shield covered with gold and ivory decoration, a couch inlaid with gold, ivory and glass, and dozens of bronze and silver vessels. So rich was the tomb in metalwork that very little pottery – the usual indicator of date – was included; the few pieces there are, however, seem to date late in the fourth century, perhaps too late for Philip, and it may be the tomb actually houses the remains of a later Macedonian king.

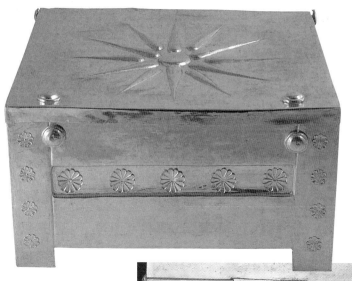

A gold casket from Tomb II at Vergina, with the lid embossed with a twelve-pointed star. Inside (right) was preserved a gold and purple cloth used to wrap the cremated remains and then placed in the casket; c. 335–325 BC.

THE CONQUEST OF ASIA

PORTRAITS OF ALEXANDER

The statues that give the best representation of Alexander's person were those by Lysippos (who alone was allowed to make his image); those peculiarities which many of his successors and friends afterwards tried to imitate, the inclination of the head a little toward the left shoulder and the melting eyes, have been expressed by the artist exactly.

Plutarch, *Alexander* 3

THE YOUNG ALEXANDER was put to the test immediately as Thebes revolted at the news of Philip's death. His response and its message were clear: the city was besieged, taken and utterly destroyed. With Greece now secure, Alexander turned his attention to the great project envisioned by his father, the conquest of the Persian Empire. An army of about 40,000 men was assembled and in 334 BC Alexander crossed over into Asia to begin what was, and still remains, one of the most extraordinarily successful military campaigns in history. In just eleven years he and his army fought and marched across Asia Minor, the Levant, Egypt and the Middle East, as far as India. On foot, he and his army conquered and occupied the modern countries of Turkey, Syria, Lebanon, Israel, Egypt, Jordan, Iran, Iraq, Saudi Arabia, Yemen, the Gulf States, Afghanistan and Pakistan. The campaign is one more chapter

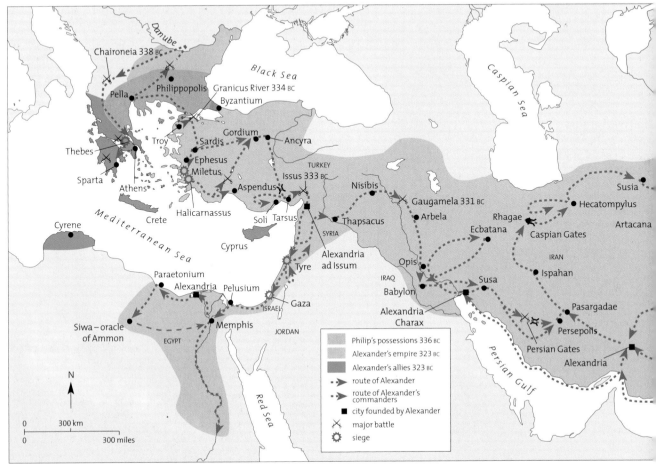

in the conflict between East and West played out in this part of the world over thousands of years and documented since the Trojan War. Memories in this part of the world are long. When he burned the Persian capital of Persepolis, Alexander declared that it was in revenge for the Persian destruction of the Acropolis of Athens, 150 years earlier, in 480 BC.

Alexander died of a fever in Babylon in 323 BC, before he had time to consolidate his vast empire. None the less the conquest had a profound impact. This was not simply a punitive or plundering expedition, Alexander had the future clearly in sight. One of his policies was to found cities, frequently named after himself, and populate them with a mixture of Greek and native elements. By far his most successful foundation was Alexandria in Egypt, but dozens of other cities were created in his wake. He also encouraged assimilation, marrying a local princess himself and arranging for thousands of his soldiers to take local women as wives. The result was the spread of a relatively homogeneous Greek culture from India to Spain, and from Egypt to South Russia, bound by a common language, shared religions and a wide range of similarities in the material record: pottery, sculpture, coinage and architecture. This Hellenistic civilization, as it is called, thrived throughout the third and second centuries BC until it was overwhelmed by the rising power of Rome.

(Above left) A portrait of Alexander the Great.

(Above) Alexander (left) attacks Darius, the Persian king, at the battle of Issus in 333 BC. This Roman mosaic from Pompeii (c. 100 BC) is thought to be a copy of a Hellenistic painting.

(Left) Map showing the campaign of conquest by Alexander and his army, 334–323 BC.

ALEXANDER'S ARMY

His army, by the computation of those who favour the fewest, consisted of 30,000 foot and 4,000 horse, while those who make the most of it, speak of 43,000 foot and 5,000 horse.

Plutarch, *Alexander 15*

THE HELLENISTIC KINGDOMS

THE CITY OF ALEXANDRIA

Polybios at least, who visited the city, was disgusted with its condition at the time [2nd century BC]. He says it is inhabited by three classes of people, first the native Egyptians, an acute and civilized race; secondly by the mercenaries, a numerous, rough and uncultivated set, it being an ancient practice there to maintain a foreign armed force which, owing to the weakness of the kings, had learned to rule rather than obey; thirdly, there were the Alexandrians themselves, a people not genuinely civilized for the same reason, but still superior to the mercenaries, for though they are mongrels they came from a Greek stock and had not forgotten Greek customs.

Strabo, 797

UPON HIS DEATH, no one individual was strong enough to lay claim to Alexander's vast empire. Numerous claimants arose and wars of succession went on for generations; Hellenistic history is accordingly a complex field of study, with no well-defined focal points. Eventually several generals were able to control large territories and these became the bases of royal dynasties: the Ptolemies in Egypt, the Seleucids in Syria and the Near East, the Attalids in western Asia Minor and the Antigonids in Greece.

Ptolemaic Egypt

In Egypt, Ptolemy I, a general in Alexander's army, founded one of the most successful and long-lived of the Hellenistic kingdoms. Ptolemy established his claim to the succession by carrying off the body of Alexander as it was being taken from Babylon back to Macedonia for burial. His capital was Alexandria, founded by Alexander in 333 BC on the coast of Egypt and destined to become one of the great cities of antiquity – a port through which passed the riches of Egypt. Much of the ancient city lies under the modern – and below the sea in the harbour – but ancient written sources and chance finds give some idea of its magnificence.

Ptolemy was responsible for the construction of the Pharos, a huge lighthouse set at the entrance to the harbour which came to be regarded as one of the Seven Wonders of the world. His successor, Ptolemy II, established a library which became the largest in the world, with some 50,000 works. The associated Mouseion (sanctuary of the Muses) was a great centre of learning and scholarship as well as science. Wealthy, powerful and cautious, the dynasty lasted 300 years, down to Ptolemy XII and his sister Cleopatra (VII), who captivated both Caesar and Mark Antony in the first century BC.

The Egyptian cults of Isis and Sarapis were enthusiastically adopted by the Greeks and spread rapidly throughout the Greek world. Already by the 330s there was a sanctuary of Isis in Peiraieus, the port of Athens, and Apollo's sacred island of Delos had three separate sanctuaries to the Egyptian gods. These proved the most popular of the many deities assimilated by the Greeks as a result of Alexander's conquests of the East.

(Above right) Roman imperial coin showing the Pharos (lighthouse) of Alexandria, one of the Seven Wonders of the world.

(Right) A diver confronts a sphinx in the waters off Alexandria, where much of the ancient city lies submerged.

The Seleucids

The Seleucid dynasty was founded by Seleukos I, who built his capital city at Antioch, modern Antakya in Turkey. He originally controlled much of Anatolia, Syria and most of the Levant, though he was hemmed in by other kingdoms. He also fell heir to the easternmost parts of the empire, insofar as they could be held, and the Seleucids were responsible for the great spread of Greek culture. The dynasty was embroiled in numerous wars and distinguished itself by the use of elephants in battle. Seleukos' successors were active opponents of Roman expansion, and Antiochos III (the Great) fought several extensive campaigns against them, losing at Thermopylai in Greece in 191 BC, and at Magnesia in Asia Minor in 190 BC. He was forced thereafter to cede the western half of Asia Minor to the Attalids of Pergamon and to the island of Rhodes.

The Seleucids were active builders in the areas they controlled. As well as in the Levant, numerous cities were founded in Asia Minor: Stratonikeia, Nysa, Laodiceia and Antiocheia on the Maeander were destined to become large important centres over the centuries, adorned with huge public buildings. Long-established sanctuaries with giant temples drew Seleucid attention as well; they contributed to the building of the temple of Apollo at Didyma, the temple of Artemis at Sardis, and the Olympieion at Athens.

In the Seleucid east, excavations at Failaka (ancient Ikaros), an island near Kuwait at the head of the Persian Gulf, have produced Greek temples and inscriptions. And the site of Ai Khanoum, on the banks of the Oxus river in Afghanistan, has revealed a gymnasium (p. 173), Greek inscriptions and papyri, a fountainhouse with dolphin-head waterspouts, and a theatre capable of holding 6,000 people.

A coin of Seleukos, showing his use of war elephants.

(p. 173)

A GREEK INSCRIPTION IN AFGHANISTAN

These wise sayings of famous men from early times are set up at Holy Pytho [Delphi]; from there Clearchos copied them carefully to set them up, shining from afar, in the precinct of Kineas: 'When a child, be well-behaved; When a young man, well-controlled; In middle age, just; As an old man, a good counsellor; At the end of your life, free from sorrow.'

Greek inscription from Ai Khanoum, Afghanistan

The temple of Olympian Zeus at Athens, begun by Antiochos IV of Syria (174–165 BC), and only finished by Hadrian 300 years later.

PERGAMON
Pergamon, which is a famous city, and for a long time prospered along with the Attalid kings.... Now Pergamon was a treasure stronghold of Lysimachos, who was one of the successors of Alexander, and its people are settled on the very summit of the mountain; the mountain is like a cone and ends in a sharp peak. The custody of this stronghold and the treasure, which amounted to 9,000 talents [over 50 million daily wages], was entrusted to Philetairos, who was a eunuch from boyhood.... Attalos was the first to be proclaimed king, after conquering the Gauls in a great battle. Attalos not only became a friend of the Romans but also fought on their side against Philip along with a fleet of Rhodians.... The Kaikos flows past Pergamon, through the Kaikos plain, as it is called, traversing land that is very fertile and about the best in Mysia.

Strabo, 623–24

HELLENISTIC LIBRARIES
The Attalid kings, impelled by their delight in literature, established for general perusal a fine library at Pergamon. Then Ptolemy, moved by boundless jealousy and envy, strove with no less industry to establish a similar library at Alexandria.

Vitruvius, 7, praef. 4

The Attalids

The Attalid dynasty was founded by Philetairos – he was established in the fortress of Pergamon by the general Lysimachos, as the guardian of a treasure of 9,000 talents. On the death of Lysimachos, Philetairos founded a separate kingdom in northwest Asia Minor, which was handed on to his nephew, Attalos I. Pergamon, perched upon an impregnable crag and heavily fortified, was his capital city. Excavations have revealed palaces with painted walls and mosaic floors, granaries and huge piles of catapult balls on the top of the hill; agoras, sanctuaries, gymnasia and private houses cover the lower slopes.

The early years of the dynasty were spent attempting to repel the Gauls, who had crossed over from Europe in 278 BC. Victories over these barbarians were celebrated in sculpture and with festivals, and the Pergamenes saw and promoted themselves as the saviours of all the Greeks, just as the Athenians had saved Greece from the Persian threat 200 years before. In other ways, too, the Pergamene kings saw themselves as the successors of the Classical Athenians. They established a large library, earlier than that in Alexandria, and they encouraged a flourishing school of sculpture. An example of the ornate 'baroque' Pergamene style may be seen in the gigantomachy frieze adorning the ' Great Altar' dedicated at Pergamon in the second century BC, and now in the Berlin Museum (p. 179).

In architecture, the Attalids did not invest their money or efforts in large, flashy temples; even in Pergamon itself, the Hellenistic temples are remarkably modest and small. Instead, the Pergamenes were masters of the stoa, especially those built on sloping ground. Pergamene architects were well trained, for the acropolis of Pergamon itself is among the steepest in the Greek world. Double colonnades with rooms behind on two and even three storeys were not unknown, and well-preserved examples can be seen at Pergamene dependencies such as Assos and Aigai. Lavish gifts were made to the city of Athens by Attalos I, Eumenes II and Attalos II (p. 172), who studied there under the philosopher Karneades. Appropriately enough the gifts were large stoas and sculptural groups, including a battle against the Gauls. Delphi also was given a stoa by Pergamon. These were hands-on benefactions – the Pergamenes did not apparently believe in just sending funds. The stoa of Eumenes at Athens was made in pieces in Pergamon of local marble and then brought to Athens and assembled. And painters and 30 labourers were sent to Delphi to work on the stoa and to repair the theatre. Pergamene engineers seem also to have been among the first in the Hellenistic world to be able to carry and raise water under pressure; long aqueducts carried water up to the top of the citadel. Before the third century BC all Greek water lines had been gravity-flow channels.

The Pergamene kings adhered to a foreign policy of accommodation with the rising power of Rome. This reached an extraordinary conclusion when, in 133 BC, there being no suitable

The acropolis of Pergamon: a view along the sacred way which led to the sanctuary of Asklepios.

heir to the royal house, the entire kingdom was willed to the city of Rome. Pergamon – the great imitator of Classical Athens – should thus perhaps be seen as the primary means of transmission of Greek art and culture to the Romans, their close allies for generations.

The Antigonids

The wars of succession in Macedonia and mainland Greece were especially complex, though eventually Antigonos and his son Demetrios established a royal dynasty. Their capital was at Pella, in Macedonia, where large palaces have been excavated. Other Macedonian palaces have been excavated at Vergina, and at Demetrias in Thessaly, a Macedonian dependency. To judge from fragments and from the remains of better preserved houses, the palaces were decorated with handsome mosaic floors and the walls were brightly painted. Many of the rooms can be identified as dining rooms and it is clear that the Macedonians put great emphasis on hunting and fighting, followed by lots of feasting and drinking. They buried their dead in large subterranean tombs filled with lavish gifts of gold, silver and bronze. Though separated by centuries, these aspects of a warrior society are paralleled by those of the Mycenaeans, with their palaces decorated with hunting and battle scenes and their elaborate and rich burials. It may be more than coincidence or myth that the Macedonians believed that their royal family were originally Temenids, who in early times migrated north to Macedonia from the Argolid, centre of the Mycenaean world.

The various wars between these dynasties and the leagues of independent Greek cities in Aetolia and Achaia eventually drew Rome into the picture. As early as the early third century BC one of the dynasts, Pyrrhos of Epiros, had meddled in southern Italy and been driven out by the Romans, and by the late third century Greek Sicily had been largely annexed. Successive wars with the Macedonians (196 BC), the Aetolians and Antiochos III (191/190 BC), the Macedonians again (167 BC), and the Achaians (146 BC) finally led to the destruction of Corinth, capital of the Achaian League, in 146 BC and the annexation of Greece, which was then ruled as though a Roman province. As noted, soon thereafter (133 BC) Pergamon was willed to Rome and Greek Asia Minor also fell under Roman sway.

In the West, the city of Syracuse flourished in the early Hellenistic period, during the long reign of Hieron II (c. 271–216 BC). It was the

home of Archimedes and was adorned with handsome public buildings, including the theatre and an immense altar, over 180 m (600 ft) long. Other benefactions to the Ptolemies of Egypt as well as monuments in Rhodes and Olympia attest to Syracusan contacts with the eastern Greek world. Hieron's successors fell foul of Rome during that city's conflicts with Carthage, however, and Syracuse was besieged and taken in 211 BC. One casualty of the siege was Archimedes, despite the orders of the Roman general, Marcellus, to make sure he was taken alive. The capture of Syracuse also afforded one of the earliest instances of Greek plunder making its way in large quantities to Rome, the next Mediterranean power.

Remains of the large houses at Pella, capital of Macedon. Provided with large dining rooms decorated with handsome mosaic floors (p. 188), such houses were designed for the elaborate feasting that was an important part of Macedonian life.

THE ANTIGONIDS

However, this house [the Antigonids] was almost the only one which kept itself pure from crimes of this sort for many generations, or, to be more specific, Philip was the only one of the descendants of Antigonos who put a son to death. But almost all the other lines afford many examples of men who killed their sons, and of many who killed their mothers and wives. And as for men killing their brothers, just as the geometricians assume their postulates, so this crime came to be a common and recognized postulate in the plans of princes to ensure their own safety.

Plutarch, *Demetrios* 3

Mosaic floor from the island of Delos, site of an important cult of Apollo and a large Hellenistic town favoured by both the Antigonids and the Ptolemies. Depicted here is a late Panathenaic prize vase showing a chariot race (see pp. 130–31).

X

ROMANS AND CHRISTIANS

After this [Paul] left Athens and went to Corinth. There he met a Jew named Aquila, a native of Pontos, and his wife Priscilla; they had recently arrived from Italy because Claudius had issued an edict that all Jews should leave Rome.

Acts of the Apostles, 18

GREEKS AND ROMANS were aware of one another from very early times and there are interesting coincidences in the timing of the development of their societies. The traditional date of the founding of Rome, 753 BC, took place not long after the formal organization by the Greeks of the Olympic games in 776 BC, and the Romans abolished their monarchy and established a republic in 510 BC, just three years before the Athenians drove out their tyrants and established their democracy. The Phokaian settlers of Massalia in southern France established close ties with the Romans which lasted for centuries, and there are Roman dedications at Delphi as early as the beginning of the fourth century BC. Conflict between the two did not begin until the third century BC, when Roman expansion in Italy impinged on the old Greek colonies first in south Italy, then in Sicily. A series of wars against Greek leagues and Hellenistic monarchs drew Rome eastwards in the early second century BC, and her authority was firmly established in Greece and Asia Minor in the second half of the century. Though some cities maintained a nominal independence, most areas fell under a *pax Romana*; few Greek city walls can be dated to the second century or later, and they do not appear again until the collapse of security in the third century AD.

The Romans admired much in the more advanced culture of the Greek world and they borrowed a great deal, especially in the realm of art, theatre and philosophy. Roman armies, like their Hellenistic predecessors, were exposed and receptive to an array of eastern religions. One of these, Christianity, spread slowly but inexorably through Greco-Roman world.

Rome struggles to maintain her hold on the East. Historical reliefs on the Arch of Galerius in Thessaloniki, early fourth century AD.

ROMAN PHILHELLENISM

THE ROMANS absorbed the Greek world gradually over time, a kingdom here, a city there, throughout the third to first centuries BC. The individual fates of cities depended on their actions and attitudes towards Rome. Some were treated harshly and eradicated (all those of Epiros, Haliartos), others were destroyed and eventually rebuilt (Corinth, Pella, Thisbe), others were punished and then forgiven (Athens), and some enjoyed consistent goodwill and a nominal independence (Aphrodisias).

In general, the Romans were admirers, collectors and imitators of many things Greek, in particular sculpture, painting and architecture. Greek philosophy and rhetoric were admired also, as was the Greek language. Greek artists, teachers and philosophers were in great demand; many were enticed to Rome, while many Romans travelled east to seek them out.

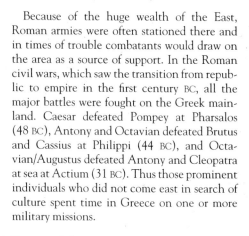

A lifesize bronze equestrian statue of the Roman emperor Augustus (27 BC–AD 14), pulled up in a fisherman's net in 1979, somewhere in the northern Aegean, northeast of the island of Euboia.

Because of the huge wealth of the East, Roman armies were often stationed there and in times of trouble combatants would draw on the area as a source of support. In the Roman civil wars, which saw the transition from republic to empire in the first century BC, all the major battles were fought on the Greek mainland. Caesar defeated Pompey at Pharsalos (48 BC), Antony and Octavian defeated Brutus and Cassius at Philippi (44 BC), and Octavian/Augustus defeated Antony and Cleopatra at sea at Actium (31 BC). Thus those prominent individuals who did not come east in search of culture spent time in Greece on one or more military missions.

Roman Athens

More often than not, when the Romans came to Greece it was to Athens, which maintained a reputation as the cultural and particularly the educational centre of the Mediterranean for centuries. Based on the schools established in the gymnasia and stoas of the city in the fourth century BC, Athens held pride of place by virtue of the antiquity of her educational traditions. Despite her loss of political, military and economic significance, Athens flourished throughout the Hellenistic period in educational matters, maintaining her prominence over important new centres of learning such as Alexandria, Antioch and Pergamon.

The depth of Roman reverence for Athens can be seen when we set it against Athenian political acumen; four times in the course of the first century BC Athens guessed wrong when required to pick sides in a conflict involving Rome. In 86 BC she sided with Mithradates, king of Pontos, in his revolt against Rome, then favoured Pompey over Caesar, Brutus over Antony and Octavian, and Antony over Octavian/Augustus.

With that record any other Greek city might well have been expected to disappear entirely from the map of Roman Greece, but not Athens – the city was besieged and taken, hundreds of Athenians killed, but it was not destroyed.

Many prominent Romans are known to have spent time in the city or to have provided money for her adornment in the first century BC: Caesar, Pompey, Octavian/ Augustus, Antony, Agrippa,

The Greek East

The Greek cities of Asia Minor also fared remarkably well under Roman administration, flourishing despite the Mithradatic wars (86–69 BC), occasional unauthorized military forays (Labienus in 40 BC) and earthquakes (AD 17, AD 60). Both the old cities of Ionia and Caria as well the new Hellenistic foundations were thriving, to judge from the material remains. Almost all these cities boast huge stone theatres, agoras with long and ornately decorated marble colonnades, monumental fountain-houses (Nymphaia) lavishly full of sculpture, stadia with stone seats, immense gymnasia and baths, and marble temples dedicated either to the gods or to deified Roman emperors. The architectural embellishment of these eastern Greek cities far surpasses anything on the mainland or in the western Greek world. Many of them, such as Aphrodisias in Caria, Miletus, and Ephesus, reach their absolute high-point in the first and second centuries AD.

Cicero, Horace and Varro, to name the best known. Roman benefactions continued for several centuries and the new monuments – concert halls, libraries, gymnasia, schools and lecture-halls – reflect Athens' role in the Roman world.

(Above) The library of Celsus (c. AD 115) and the agora gate (c. 4 BC) at Ephesus give some idea of the wealth and splendour of the Greek cities of Asia Minor for much of the Roman period.

(Left) Coin of Mithradates VI of Pontos, who led a long, bitter and ultimately unsuccessful revolt against Rome, involving most of the cities of Greece and Asia Minor.

APHRODISIAS

The Greco-Roman city of Aphrodisias lies in an upland plain, in the highlands of Caria, south of the Maeander river valley. Built on the site of a prehistoric mound in use throughout the Bronze Age, the city began flourishing in the third and second centuries BC.

The city's primary attraction was an important cult of Aphrodite. The late

Portrait of a magistrate from Aphrodisias, c. AD 410.

Hellenistic version of her temple is a handsome marble peripteral building in the Ionic order.

Aphrodisias followed a policy of friendship and accommodation with Rome. This stance served the city well over the centuries, allowing her to maintain a nominal independence.

One of the most lavish monuments of the city, consisting in part of long colonnades and hundreds of large sculpted reliefs, was the Sebasteion, a temple complex

built early in the first century AD and dedicated to the Imperial family in Rome. The wall of the eastern *parodos* (entrance passageway) of the theatre serves as an archive, carrying inscribed copies of correspondence and imperial decisions relating to the status of the city.

Throughout the first and second centuries AD the city was adorned with an array of handsome public buildings: a theatre, a huge bath, an agora, a temenos (boundary wall) around the Aphrodite temple

and a vast stadium. Nearby quarries of excellent white marble allowed the city to develop as the centre of a great school of sculptors which flourished for centuries. The site itself has produced hundreds of fine examples, and pieces signed by Aphrodisian artists have been found throughout the Mediterranean world.

The city's relatively remote location seems to have saved Aphrodisias from much of the turmoil of the early years of the collapse of the Roman empire

in the third and fourth centuries AD, and the city, seen through its public monuments and sculpture, remained untroubled until the sixth or seventh century.

Sculptors continued to produce pagan works in the fourth and fifth centuries, though the great temple of Aphrodite was converted into a Christian basilica.

Excavations of this rich Greek city of the Roman world have been carried on since the mid-1960s by American archaeologists from New York

University. It promises to be one of the great excavations of the twenty-first century, rivalling the uncovering of Ephesus, Miletus and Pergamon in the nineteenth century.

(Above) The ornamental gateway into the sanctuary of Aphrodite at Aphrodisias, second century AD. The remains of the temple, dated to c. 100 BC and rebuilt as a Christian basilica in the fifth century AD, are visible at rear right.

(Left) The stadium at Aphrodisias, built in the first century AD for at least 30,000 spectators.

(Right) Portrait of a magistrate, beginning of the fifth century AD.

HADRIAN AND THE GREEK WORLD

The temple of Hadrian at Ephesus, second century AD. Greek cities competed actively to become recognized centres of the official cult of the Roman emperors. Hadrian was also worshipped in a huge temple at Cyzicus and with Zeus in the Olympieion at Athens (p. 197).

THE REIGN OF THE EMPEROR HADRIAN (AD 117–38) in many ways represents the acme of Roman involvement in the Greek world. A great Philhellene and traveller, Hadrian visited Athens no fewer than three times, making the city the centre of his worship among a league of Greek cities known as the Panhellenion. He was also initiated into the Eleusinian mysteries and gave the city a library, a gymnasium and a Pantheon, as well as starting on an ambitious aqueduct project finished by his successor, Antoninus Pius. His attitude towards the

Greeks, and especially Athens, can be read on a remarkable series of imperial portraits which he allowed to be circulated in the Greek world (with examples from Athens, Peiraieus, Olympia and Hierapytna on Crete); his cuirass is decorated with a relief scene of Athena triumphant, being crowned by victories while standing on the back of the Wolf of Rome suckling Romulus and Remus.

Almost every city in Asia Minor has at least one large monument given by the emperor, and many temples were either built for or rededi-

cated to him (Ephesus, Claros, Cyzicus, Athens). Indeed, Pausanias records that the only Greek city Hadrian was unable to improve was the small town of Megara. Barbarian incursions into Greece start within a generation of Hadrian's reign, in the AD 170s, and the security provided by 200 years of Roman rule began to crumble.

(Above) A statue of Hadrian from Athens, showing Athena supported by the wolf of Rome.

(Above right) Arch of Hadrian at Athens (c. AD 132). Other honorary or commemorative arches for Hadrian are known from Ephesus, Nicaea and several other Greek cities.

A Roman mosaic of Pyramos and Thisbe from Paphos, Cyprus. Greek myths and language persisted throughout the eastern Roman empire. Late second century AD.

THE RISE OF CHRISTIANITY

A mosaic depicting St Paul from the Arian baptistery in Ravenna.

CHRISTIANITY AROSE IN JUDEA, the east Greek world, in an area ruled for centuries by the Seleucids. The large Jewish population there was supplemented by numerous Greeks. During Hellenistic times, Jews had dispersed across the Greek world, and active Jewish communities were to be found in many cities far from Palestine; Laodiceia and Corinth are just two examples.

St Paul in Greece and Asia

Christianity was spread only with great effort, much of which was provided by the apostle Paul, who attempted to convert people from among the Jewish communities in mainland Greece. His travels took him from Philippi and Berroia in northern Greece, to Athens, and then to Corinth. He had mixed success: at Philippi he was imprisoned, while the Atheni-

(Right) Map showing the travels of St Paul, as recorded in Acts. Much of his preaching took place in the Greek cities on the mainland and in Asia Minor.

(Below) Ancient Philippi: Paul's first conversion in Europe occurred here and the city became a pilgrimage site; several large basilicas were built in the fifth and sixth centuries AD. One is in the foreground, another is in the middle distance.

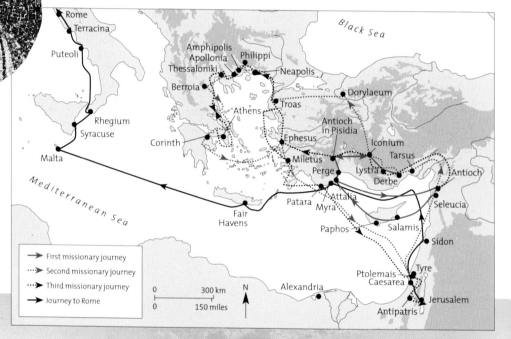

Map legend:
- → First missionary journey
- ⋯→ Second missionary journey
- ⋯⋯→ Third missionary journey
- → Journey to Rome

0 — 300 km
0 — 150 miles
N

Pagan and Christian in the catacombs of Rome: Herakles slays the Hydra (far left) and Abraham prepares to sacrifice Isaac (left). The continuing popularity of Greek myths into the early Christian period led to a conflation of the old images with the new values of Christianity. Via Latina catacombs, fourth century AD.

ans were strongly pagan and most resisted his message, and in Corinth his preaching caused disturbances which brought him to the attention of the civic authorities.

Small Christian communities grew up in Asia and all seven churches of the Apocalypse were to be found in Greek Hellenistic cities: Pergamon, Smyrna, Thyateira, Hierapolis, Laodiceia, Philadelphia and Kolossai. The struggles of the new religion in this part of the world are reflected in the correspondence between the Emperor Trajan (AD 98–117) and Pliny the Younger, his governor of Bithynia (northwest Asia Minor).

Greeks and Christianity

The rise and eventual success of Christianity was largely played out in the Greek world, and several sites were of great importance to the early church. Ephesus is one such, as it was here that St John brought the Virgin Mary to live after the crucifixion. He himself died here and was buried in a church which underwent several rebuildings, reaching a tremendous size under Justinian in the sixth century AD. The apostle Philip was buried at Hierapolis in Phrygia, and his grave became the focal point of a handsome martyrion dating from the fifth century AD (p. 211).

PLINY TO TRAJAN

Having never been present at any trials of the Christians, I am unacquainted with the method and limits to be observed either in examining or punishing them. Whether any difference is to be made on account of age, or no distinction allowed between the youngest and the adult; whether repentance admits to a pardon, or if a man has been once a Christian it avails him nothing to recant; whether the mere profession of Christianity, albeit without crimes, or only the crimes associated therewith, are punishable – in all these points I am greatly doubtful.

In the meantime the method I have observed towards those who have been denounced to me as Christians is this: I interrogated them whether they were Christians; if they confessed it I repeated the question twice again, adding the threat of capital punishment; if they still persevered, I ordered them to be executed. For whatever the nature of their creed might be, I could at least feel no doubt that contumacy and inflexible obstinacy deserved chastisement.

Pliny, *Letters* X. 96

The basilica of St Leonidas (fifth and sixth centuries) at Lechaion, port of Corinth. The outer courtyard (left) with fountain, the narthex (entrance hall), three-aisled nave and apse (curved end, right) are all features of a typical basilica. The total length of the building is 186 m (610 ft).

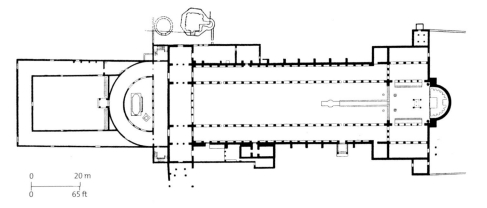

0   20 m

0   65 ft

TRAJAN TO PLINY

The method you have pursued, my dear Pliny, in sifting the cases of those denounced to you as Christians is extremely proper.... No search should be made for these people; when they are denounced and found guilty they must be punished; with the restriction, however, that when the party denies himself to be a Christian, and shall give proof that he is not (that is by worshipping our gods) he shall be pardoned on the ground of repentance, even though he may formerly have incurred suspicion. Information without the accuser's name subscribed must not be admitted ... as it is introducing a very dangerous precedent, and is by no means agreeable to the spirit of the age.

Pliny, *Letters* X. 97

(Below) The rotunda of St George, Thessaloniki, fourth century AD. The centralized round form goes back to the circular tombs of Augustus and Hadrian in Rome. This building may originally have been designed as a tomb, for the emperor Galerius, though he was eventually buried elsewhere.

Greek, too, is the common language of much of early Christianity; the chi-rho symbol or monogram stands for Christ, as does the symbol of the fish, ἰχθῦς in Greek ('Ιησοῦς Χριστός Θεοῦ Υἱός Σωτήρ: Jesus Christ, son of God, Saviour). The bitter controversies over the interpretation of the divinity of Christ are based on Greek terminology and the shift of a single letter. The Council of Nicaea in AD 325 was called to determine if Christ was ἀνόμοιος (not of similar substance to God), ὁμοιούσιος (similar substance), or ὁμοούσιος (the same substance) – one iota separates the last two terms in Greek.

Constantine and Constantinople

The history of the ancient world was radically altered during the reign of the emperor Constantine, who saw a vision of the Labarum (the chi-rho symbol of Christ) in AD 312, just before a crucial victory in the wars of succession; in AD 325 Christianity became a leading religion in the empire and Constantine himself convened the first church council in Nicaea. Almost equally important, in AD 330, Constantine established the city of Constantinople on the site of the old Greek *polis* of Byzantion (Byzantium), at the entrance to the Black Sea, and made it the capital of his empire. Power and influence shifted eastwards from Rome, back into the areas where Greeks had lived for centuries and where Greek culture was endemic.

This eastern Roman empire evolved into what is often referred as the 'Byzantine' empire, a made-up, scholarly term; the participants continued to refer to themselves as 'Romaioi' (Romans). Greek culture continued through the centuries in this guise, while the pagan worship of Olympian and other gods gave way only gradually to Christianity.

Set on a ridge which juts eastward into the Bosporus, the city of Constantinople was destined to become one of the great capitals of the world. The main street was laid out along the top of the ridge, as was the agora of the city. A large imperial palace was built at the eastern end, attached to the hippodrome, where the emperor could be seen by his people. Over the years the city was provided with more palaces, extensive fortification walls and numerous churches.

Early churches

Throughout the fourth to sixth centuries AD, churches were built all over the Greek world. Two basic plans were followed. One was the centralized plan, based on the *martyrion*, or grave of a saint. The building was likely to be round or polygonal in form, symmetrical on all sides and without a well-defined orientation. Often there would be an interior ambulatory and the focal point was the centre of the building. Santa Costanza in Rome is an example of such a plan, which is also found in early

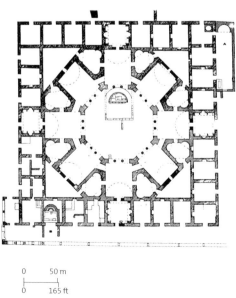

0   50 m
|—————|
0   165 ft

churches in Syria, Athens and Thessaloniki. Far more common was the basilica, which evolved out of Roman civic architecture.

A basilica was a large three-aisled building, the aisles defined and separated by colonnades or arches. The roof of the central aisle is higher than those of the sides so as to allow light into the centre of the building from upper windows set above the colonnades dividing the aisles. Basilicas are traditionally oriented east–west. A large courtyard and fountain for ablutions is usually found at the entrance, at the west end, separated from the body of the church by a wide entrance vestibule or narthex. The altar is found inside, at the east end, which almost always is curved or apsidal. Dividing the building into three longitudinally meant that the building could be made three spans wide, and there was virtually no limit on its length. Many early Christian basilicas are therefore huge. They appear in great numbers throughout the Greek world from the fourth century AD.

The pagan Olympian gods were not abandoned easily, however, and in the fourth and fifth centuries AD imperial legislation requiring the destruction of temples was passed in an ongoing attempt to crush paganism. In addition to building new churches, the Christians transformed existing temples into churches, and several prominent temples were turned into basilicas: the Parthenon, Erechtheion and Hephaisteion in Athens, the temple of Athena at Syracuse, and the temple of Aphrodite in Aphrodisias.

Justinian

Another high point of late Greek culture and Christianity occurred during the long reign of Justinian (AD 527–65). Byzantine civilization reached its maximum geographical limits during his tenure and he was a great builder. His crowning achievement was in Constantinople itself, a church dedicated to Divine Wisdom (Aghia Sophia). This was a huge domed church, which was a cross between the centralized plan and the basilica form. The dome was more appropriate to the centralized plan, whereas the clear orientation and use of side aisles, however truncated, derive from the basilica. Within, it was lavishly decorated with mosaics and highly coloured revetments of marble quarried from all over the empire. The dome was a feat of engineering, 35 m (115 ft) across and 50 m (165 ft) above the floor. The church stands at the pinnacle of religious architecture, the orthodox Christian equivalent of

The church of Aghia Sophia in Constantinople, built by Justinian (AD 527–65).

the Parthenon, Chartres cathedral or the mosque of Suleyman also in Istanbul.

Despite a history of 500 years and imperial recognition for over 200 years, Christianity was not yet fully established and it fell to Justinian to deal with remaining pockets of paganism. One of these was Athens, where the philosophical schools were still flourishing; with their origins in the gymnasia of the Classical city, adherents to these schools were still worshipping Hermes, Herakles, the Muses and the Nymphs. Their very success and popularity in a Christian world proved their downfall and in AD 529 Justinian forbade any pagan to teach philosophy in Athens. This move was matched in AD 532 by the foundation of the monastery of Monte Cassino in Italy, a great centre of Christian learning and scholarship.

With Justinian, the world of antiquity comes to an end and we stand at the threshold of the Dark Ages. Slavic invasions from the north started late in the sixth century AD, and the rise of Islam had a profound effect on the eastern Mediterranean from the seventh century on. The seventh and eighth centuries are times of uncertainty and danger, reflected by a severe drop in the level of material and intellectual culture in the Greek world. The language and traditions of the Greeks survived, embedded in all the cultures of the Mediterranean, but the world of the ancient Greeks had come to an end.

PERSECUTION ENDED

As we have long perceived that religious liberty should not be denied, but that it should be granted to the opinion and wishes of each one to perform divine duties according to his own determination, we have given orders that each one, and the Christians among the rest, have the liberty to observe the religion of his choice....
Therefore, we have decreed the following ordinance, as our will ... that no freedom at all shall be refused to Christians, to follow or keep their observances of worship.

'Edict of Milan', AD 313, issued by Constantine (and Licinius?), Eusebius, *Ecclesiastical History* V

(Opposite right) Martyrion/church of St Philip, the apostle, at Hierapolis, fifth century AD. An example of the centralized church plan based on the tomb of a martyr.

EPILOGUE: BYZANTINES, FRANKS AND OTTOMANS

DESPITE CHALLENGES in the Dark Ages, the Byzantine empire survived for several more centuries, its capital at Constantinople, with Thessaloniki as the second city of the empire. Both were provided with numerous handsome churches dating largely from the tenth to fourteenth centuries AD, as were the towns of Greece. The churches are much smaller than the huge basilicas of the fourth to sixth centuries. They were now a cross set within a square, or some similar strongly centralized plan. They were decorated with elaborate brickwork outside, and marble revetments and wonderful mosaics inside. By chance, several of the finest examples survive in Greece: Hosios Loukas near Delphi, Daphni near Athens and Nea Moni on the island of Chios.

In AD 1203 the Fourth Crusade set off from Europe. The Venetians, who provided the shipping, insisted that a stop be made first to plunder the wealth of Constantinople, even

(Below) The monastery of Hosios Loukas on the side of Mt Helikon, near the site of ancient Stiris, c. AD 1000–20.

(Right) The Pantokrator, a mosaic in the dome of the church at Daphni, near Athens.

(Opposite) The fortress and Byzantine town of Mystra (12th–16th centuries AD). All the Peloponnese was a battlefield for centuries between Byzantines, Franks, Venetians and Ottoman Turks (see also p. 91).

though it was a Christian city and not an obvious or appropriate target. The city was taken and occupied by the Venetians and Franks. The imperial court went into exile in Nicaea in northwest Asia Minor. Byzantine possessions were divided up and Greece was turned over to various Frankish knights. Large castles and high towers crowning hills all over the country remain as reminders of the centuries of Frankish occupation. The city of Constantinople was retaken in AD 1261, but Greece itself remained divided among Byzantines and Franks.

In 1453 Constantinople was captured by the Ottoman Turks and the Byzantine empire came to an end. Greece fell three years later in 1456 and remained Ottoman territory for almost 400 years, until the war of independence and the creation of the modern Greek state.

The world of the Greeks was the Mediterranean and its shores. An agonistic people, whether in athletics or on a political level, the competitive nature of the Greeks drove them to extraordinary achievements in a vast array of endeavours. The Parthenon, the plays of Sophokles, the bronze charioteer at Delphi, and hundreds of other examples have survived through difficult centuries to carry the memory of these astonishing people who established the standards in literature, politics and art against which our own times will be judged.

GAZETTEER

The following is a brief description of the principal sites and museums where the traveller may see many of the monuments and antiquities discussed in this book. As the logistics of travel change constantly, the reader is referred to the standard guidebooks available for Greece, Italy/Sicily and Turkey; those guides with a particular archaeological focus are listed below. Major, significant sites are in **bold**, those of lesser importance but still of interest are noted in *italics*.

GREECE

The *Blue Guide* for Greece, by Robin Barber, is excellent and is brought up to date regularly. Another guide is *Greece* by Christopher Mee and Antony Spawforth (Oxford Archaeological Guides, 2001). For the region around Athens, see *Athens, Attica, and the Megarid*, by H. R. Goette (London 2001). For central Greece and the Peloponnese the two-volume edition of Pausanias by Peter Levi (Penguin) is useful. For Northern Greece, see *Macedonia: History, Monuments, Museums*, by I. Touratsoglou (Athens 1995).

CENTRAL GREECE

This area is made up of several districts: Attica, Boiotia, Phokis, Thessaly and the long island of Euboia, just off the east coast.

ATHENS The ancient monuments lie surrounded by Greece's capital city, with a population now approaching four million people. The antiquities are well preserved and numerous, requiring two to four days to visit properly. **The Acropolis** (pp. 126–29) is the focal point, a steep outcrop of rock rising some 90 m (300 ft) above the city. Though the hill has been occupied for 5,000 years, the four surviving monuments all date to Periklean times (c. 450–420 BC), when Athens was politically, economically and artistically the foremost city of Greece. A monumental marble gateway (the Propylaia) gave access to the citadel, crowned with three temples dedicated to the goddess Athena, patroness of the city: the Parthenon, the Erechtheion and the Nike temple. The site museum, full of the Archaic sculptures and architecture destroyed by the Persians in 480/479 BC as well as sculptural remnants from the Classical buildings, is scheduled to be replaced by a larger one south of the Acropolis. The **Agora** (pp. 120–23) lies just north of the Acropolis; though not well preserved, it was the centre of town in almost all respects, especially commerce and politics. The restored Stoa of Attalos (159–138 BC) serves as the museum where hundreds of items used to run the Athenian democracy are on display: *ostraka*, weights and measures, water-clocks, allotment machines, ballots and magistrates' tokens. Also worth a visit are the Hephaisteion (Theseion), the best-preserved Doric temple in Greece (fifth century BC), and the little church of the Holy Apostles (AD 1000). Five hundred metres to the northwest are the German excavations of the **Kerameikos**, the principal burial-ground of Athens from 1000 BC to AD 500. It lies just outside the Dipylon, the main gateway through the city walls, which show several construction phases reflecting their long history. A small museum displays dozens of grave groups in a usefully chronological arrangement, as well as several of the sculpted gravestones.

East of the Agora is the monumental *library* built by Hadrian and next to that is the *market* built by Caesar and Augustus, along with the virtually intact marble sundial (second century BC) known from its sculpted frieze as the *Tower of the Winds*.

South of the Acropolis is the *theatre of Dionysos* (pp. 134–37), birthplace of Western drama and scene of the first performances of the tragedies of Aeschylus, Sophokles and Euripides, as well as the comedies of Aristophanes. Further to the southeast are the fifteen surviving Corinthian columns of the gigantic temple of Olympian Zeus (p. 197), which took close to 300 years to build.

The **National Archaeological Museum** houses one of the richest collections of antiquities in Europe; especially fine is the Mycenaean gallery, with material from the shaft graves at Mycenae, and the frescoes from Santorini/Thera. Also on display is an extensive array of sculpture and pottery from all over Greece.

Attica, the territory of ancient Athens, offers several day-trips well worth taking: the port of *Peiraieus*, with an excellent museum, the spectacular setting of the temple of Poseidon at *Cape Sounion* (pp. 14–15), the battlefield and museum at *Marathon* (pp. 110–12), the temple of Nemesis at *Rhamnous*, and the sanctuary of Demeter at *Eleusis* (pp. 132–33).

THEBES (pp. 88–90) The ancient city is buried under the modern and offers little to the visitor. The local museum, however, displays rich material from the Bronze Age citadel, the Cadmeia, found in rescue excavations all over the hill: frescoes, Linear B tablets, cylinder seals from all over the Middle East, carved ivories and pottery. Other material from the Boiotia region is also on display.

DELPHI (pp. 69, 158–59, 162) The setting of the oracular shrine of Apollo on the steep southern slopes of Mt Parnassos is one of the most spectacular in Greece. The site is well preserved, with a sacred way lined with votives winding up the hill to the temple. A small theatre and a stadium, both well preserved, lie higher on the hill. Below the main sanctuary is a gymnasium and sanctuary to Athena Pronaia, with its round temple, the tholos. The museum has some of the finest examples of Archaic sculpture in Greece, as well as the famed bronze charioteer.

VOLOS The museum has an outstanding and informative display of Neolithic material from nearby *Dimini* (ancient Iolkos?), *Sesklo* and other Thessalian sites (pp. 26–29). There is also a fine collection of painted grave stelai from Hellenistic Demetrias (p. 184).

EUBOIA The long off-shore island of Euboia has several important sites. Chalkis is totally hidden under the modern city, but there is a small museum with material from Manika, an extensive Cycladic site. The important remains of Lefkandi (pp. 60–61) are disappointing to visit, though the material from the site is displayed at the museum of Eretria, which has a variety of ruins studied by Swiss archaeologists.

NORTHERN GREECE

Northern Greece, lying north of Mt Olympus, consists largely of ancient Macedonia and Thrace. Intensive excavations in the past thirty years have made this area the most archaeologically active in Greece, resulting in many important new discoveries, especially of painted Hellenistic tombs.

DION was the religious and festival centre of Macedonia. Intensive excavations by the University of Thessaloniki have uncovered an altar of Zeus, a theatre, an odeion, a Roman bath, the city walls and a sanctuary of Isis. The museum is one of the handsomest in Greece.

VERGINA is thought by some to be the old Macedonian capital of Aigai. A palace, the theatre and the tombs in the great tumulus are all open to the public (pp. 192–93), as well as the rich finds from the tombs. Other painted tombs are to be seen at *Lefkadia*, near Naoussa, and at *Mieza* are the remnants of Aristotle's school for Alexander.

PELLA boasts the remains of large houses with rich mosaics (pp. 188, 199), as well as a huge agora destroyed early in the first century BC. Less well preserved on the hill above are the remains of the great palaces. The site museum has an excellent display of mosaics and objects recovered from the town.

THESSALONIKI, a Hellenistic foundation, was also the second city of the Byzantine empire. The rotunda of St George (p. 210) is well preserved and decorated with fine mosaics; nearby are the massive sculpted piers of the Arch of Galerius (pp. 100, 210). Pieces of the imperial palace, long stretches of the fortification walls, and several outstanding Byzantine churches are to be found throughout the modern city. There is an outstanding regional archaeological museum and a separate one for Byzantine antiquities.

Not far from modern Kavala are the remains of *Philippi* (p. 208), excavated by Greek and French archaeologists. The Roman forum, the Hellenistic/Roman theatre and several large early Christian basilicas have all been cleared.

PELOPONNESE

The Peloponnese is the large southern peninsula of the mainland, about the size of the state of Maryland. In antiquity it was divided into seven distinct areas, several controlled or heavily influenced by Sparta: the Corinthia, the Argolid, Laconia, Arcadia, Messenia, Elis and Achaia. **CORINTH** (pp. 90–93) guards the isthmus, entrance to the Peloponnese. The Archaic temple of Apollo, the forum area of the Roman city, and the Peirene fountainhouse (seventh century BC–fourth century AD) have been excavated by the American School of Classical Studies. The small museum has one room of Greek antiquities and another of Roman. Acrocorinth has wonderful medieval walls, but almost nothing survives of the famed temple of Aphrodite. A short drive to the east is the sanctuary of Poseidon at Isthmia; the museum houses finds from the excavation of the sanctuary and from Kenchreai, the eastern port of Corinth. Nemea (p. 159), home of Herakles' famed leonine opponent, lies just off the old road from Corinth to Mycenae. Excavations in the sanctuary of Zeus have revealed the temple, a Greek bath and a stadium connected to the locker-room by means of an arched tunnel. A well laid-out museum illuminates the history of the site and games.

MYCENAE (pp. 40–43) the palace site of Agamemnon, is the most impressive of the Bronze Age centres. The famed Lion Gate (p. 36) gives access through huge fortification walls to the citadel with Grave Circle A and the palace; at the far end of the acropolis is a subterranean staircase leading down to a secret cistern. Outside the walls is the 'Treasury of Atreus', the largest and best-preserved of all the tholos tombs of Greece.

Argos has a theatre, a Roman bath and part of the agora, all excavated by the French, while the museum includes material from prehistoric Lerna; the hill above the town has a handsome fortress with a commanding view of the Argolid. Across the plain are the remains of the Argive Heraion and Mycenaean Dendra. On the road to Nauplion are the impressive fortifications and remains of the palace of **Tiryns**. Nauplion, first capital of Greece and a Venetian gem, has a good regional museum housed in the old arsenal. Some 30 km (20 miles) to the east are the remains of the Asklepieion of **EPIDAUROS**, site of the best-preserved Greek theatre, along with the remains of a stadium, temple, hostel, gymnasium, bath and incubation hall (pp. 160, 172).

ARCADIA the mountainous, land-locked centre of the Peloponnese, produced numerous mercenaries. Tegea had a large fourth-century Doric temple of local marble, and Megalopolis was the federal capital of the Arcadians. The temple of Apollo at **Bassai** (p. 166), near ancient Phigaleia, is set in wonderful terrain high in the mountains, though the original effect is marred by the protective tent erected over the temple. SPARTA (pp. 84–87) has little in the way of ruins to tempt the hurried traveller: a Roman theatre, and the overgrown ruins of the sanctuary of Artemis Orthia. The museum has interesting fragments of sculpture, architecture and votive offerings from several sanctuaries. The valley of Laconia offers spectacular scenery under Mt Taygetos, and there are impressive medieval remains at Mystra, Geraki and Monemvasia. To the west of Taygetos is the fertile plain of ancient MESSENIA; its capital city, Messene, has some of the most extensive and best-preserved walls in Greece, along with a large stadium, gymnasium and sanctuary complex. On the southern coast are the fortresses of Koroni and Methone, built to protect Venetian shipping routes to the eastern Mediterranean. The town of Pylos overlooks the great bay of Navarino, scene of the pivotal sea battle in the Greek war of independence, and the island of Sphakteria, where Sparta suffered a significant defeat during the Peloponnesian War. A few miles inland is the site of the **Palace of Nestor** (pp. 38–39); the nearby village of Chora has a small museum with the frescoes and objects from the palace, as well as grave goods from numerous rich Bronze Age cemeteries in the area.

The main attraction of ancient Elis is **OLYMPIA** (pp. 68, 154–58), site of the Olympic games for over a thousand years. The German excavators have uncovered temples to Hera and Zeus, treasuries, the stadium, a gymnasium and numerous other monuments. The site museum has one of the richest collections of sculptures and bronze votives. Other remains in Elis include the slight remains of the ancient city and the well-preserved Frankish castle at Chlemoutsi (Castel Tornese).

ACHAIA active both in the Ionian migration and the colonization of the west, is a mountainous region along the south coast of the Corinthian gulf. The modern port of Patras occupies the site of a rich Roman city, with a restored odeion just below the medieval castle at the top of the hill. A small museum displays assorted finds from the city and surrounding area.

THE AEGEAN ISLANDS

The Greek island number in the hundreds and almost all have some archaeological remains and many have small museums. For antiquities, the most significant are Crete, Santorini and Delos.

CRETE (pp. 48–51) is by far the largest island in the Aegean. It was the home of the 'Minoan' civilization in the Bronze Age, and large palaces have been excavated at **KNOSSOS**, Phaistos, Mallia and Kato Zakro. Other important remains have come to light at Chania (ancient Kydonia), Archanes, Gournia and Palaikastro. The museum at **HERAKLEION** houses the most impressive collection of Cretan antiquities of all periods.

The volcanic island of **SANTORINI** (pp. 32–33), ancient Thera, is renowned for the Bronze Age remains of Akrotiri. Also of interest is the site of the later city, active from Archaic through Hellenistic times. **DELOS**, birthplace of Apollo and Artemis, was a major sanctuary. The island also has one of the most extensively excavated Hellenistic towns and the visitor can wander for hours through well-preserved houses, sanctuaries, a theatre, agoras, a gymnasium and a stadium. The site museum houses an excellent display of material from both the sanctuary and the town.

Other islands have antiquities of interest for the traveller with more time. An abbreviated list would include: Aegina (Temple of Aphaia, prehistoric town museum), Andros (Dark Age Zagoria, museum), Chios (archaic Emporio, museum), Kos (Asklepieion, city, museum), Lesbos (city, theatre, museum), Naxos (city, tower, sanctuaries, quarries, museum), Paros (city, quarries, museum), Rhodes (Crusader castle, acropolis, Lindos, museum), Samos (Heraion, Eupalineion, museum), Samothrace (sanctuary, museum), Thasos (walls, agora, acropolis, quarries, museum) and Tinos (sanctuary of Poseidon, museum).

ASIA MINOR

The ancient sites along the coast of Asia Minor are substantial and often very well preserved. Part of the terrain is mountainous, but the large plains of the Kaikos, Hermos, Kayster and Maeander rivers made the land fertile and rich, more so than the Greek mainland. All these sites are now in Turkey, including Constantinople. In addition to the standard guides, there are three archaeological guidebooks worth having along. George Bean's Aegean Turkey (London 1966) and Turkey Beyond the Maeander (London 1971) are both somewhat dated, but beautifully written and full of interesting material; E. Akurgal's Ancient Civilizations and Ruins of Turkey (Istanbul, multiple editions) is also very useful. **CONSTANTINOPLE** (pp. 210–11; modern Istanbul), founded as Byzantion (from Byzas, the founder) in the seventh century BC by settlers from mainland Megara, was destined to become one of the great cities of the world, capital of both the Byzantine and Ottoman empires. Greek Byzantion and early Christian Constantinople are poorly represented, except for the land walls, originally of the late Roman period; much of Justinian's city can be seen, however: the churches of Aghia Sophia and Saints Sergius and Bacchus, the cisterns, the hippodrome and the rich mosaics from the palace. The archaeological museum is one of the finest in the world, with antiquities from all over Turkey and the territories of the former Ottoman empire. **TROY** (pp. 52–53), though small and difficult to understand because of the complex stratigraphy, remains a sentimental pilgrimage site for anyone interested in antiquity and the history of archaeology. Walls, houses and gates of the prehistoric town survive, along with a few marble remains of Hellenistic/Roman Ilion. The museum at *Canakkale* has finds from Troy and elsewhere in the Troad, along with two recently discovered and beautifully sculpted sarcophagi (pp. 180–81).

Assos has one of the few archaic Doric temples in Asia Minor, along with some of the most impressive Hellenistic fortifications. Not far away are the remains of the temple of Apollo Smintheos (mouse god) at *Chrysa*, built in the third century BC, in the Ionic order with elaborate carved decoration.

PERGAMON (p. 198), Hellenistic capital of the Attalid dynasty, is among the best preserved sites in Turkey. In the lower city is the **Asklepieion** and the 'Red Court', an immense temple to the Egyptian gods. A stroll from the top of the acropolis brings the visitor past the sanctuary of Athena, the Great Altar of Zeus, the remains of palaces, granaries and arsenals, a temple to the emperor Trajan, a spectacular theatre, houses, sanctuaries, gymnasia, agoras and fortification walls. Many of the treasures of the site, including the sculpted friezes of the Great Altar (p. 179), are on display in the Pergamon Museum in Berlin. *SARDIS* (p. 73), capital of the Lydian empire, has a huge Ionic temple to Artemis, a heavily reconstructed Roman bath/gymnasium complex and one of the earliest synagogues in Asia Minor. A few kilometres to the north is *Bin Tepe* (thousand mounds), the royal cemetery with the huge tumuli over the graves of Alyattes and Gyges. Finds from the American excavations of Sardis are on display in the museum at Manisa.

EPHESUS (pp. 100–01, 203), excavated by Austrian archaeologists, is largely Roman as preserved, with numerous temples, houses, mosaics, wall-paintings, fountainhouses and colonnades. Restorations of the Library of Celsus and the gateway into the agora give some idea of the wealth of the city, as do the marble streets and a huge theatre. The site of the *Artemesion*, one of the Seven Wonders of the world, is a disappointing frog-filled mire. The *Basilica of St John* at Seljuk has been extensively restored in its Justiniac phase (sixth century AD). The museum at Seljuk has a large collection of material from Ephesus.

A twenty minute ride to the south brings one to *Magnesia on the Maeander*, with its tumbled remains of the Ionic temple of Artemis, attributed to the great Hellenistic architect, Hermogenes. Other partially excavated remains include a theatre, the agora, a stadium and large imperial baths.

PRIENE (pp. 80–81) is one of the most completely excavated ancient Greek cities. Though the dozens of excavated houses are now somewhat overgrown, the temple of Athena has been partially restored, and the theatre and the *ekklesiasterion* are among the best preserved from antiquity, as are the fortifications on the acropolis.

MILETUS (pp. 97–98), once the greatest city of Ionia, is now largely overgrown and partially flooded in the alluvium of the Maeander river. The most interesting surviving monuments are the Hellenistic/Roman theatre, the *bouleuterion* and the baths of Faustina (second century AD). Many important pieces of the site are on display in Berlin. The huge scale of the oracular temple of Apollo at **DIDYMA** (pp. 98–99), some 18 km (11 miles) to the south of Miletus, makes it one of the most impressive remains in Asia Minor.

Further south are several handsome, less-visited sites. *Herakleia*, with its spectacular setting below Mt Latmos on the shores of Lake Bafa, has a huge circuit wall in excellent condition (p. 78), along with the temple of Athena and a two-storeyed market building. Other sites in the vicinity include *Euromos* (Corinthian temple, much still standing), *Iasos* (seaside site excavated by Italians, all periods), *Labraunda* (sanctuary of Zeus in a lovely mountain setting), *Mylasa* (museum and Gumuskesen, an intact mausoleum with columns and pyramidal roof). Modern Bodrum sits atop ancient *Halicarnassus* (pp. 190–92); still visible are the circuit walls (fourth century BC), a theatre and the disappointing remains of the Mausoleum. The Crusader castle serves as a museum of underwater archaeology and has several excellent displays, including the material from the Uluburun wreck (p. 47).

SOUTHERN ITALY and SICILY

Several important Greek sites are found along the south and west coasts of Italy, and all around the coast of Sicily. Useful guides for South Italy are M. Guido, *Southern Italy: an Archaeological Guide* (London 1972) and *Magna Grecia* (Laterza Guides), by E. Greco (Rome 1995). For Sicily: *Sicily: an Archaeological Guide*, M. Guido (London 1967), *Sicilia* (Laterza Guides), F. Coarelli and M. Torelli (Rome 2000), and *Sicily* (Blue Guide, 5th ed.), A. Macadam (London 1999).

Ancient *Taras* (modern Taranto) was an important Mycenaean site and a rare Spartan colony (*c.* 706 BC); though little can be seen on the ground today, the museum has a first-rate collection of antiquities from the city and surrounding area. Along the instep of Italy are the sites of *Metapontum* (temple, museum), *Croton* and *Lokri*, and at the toe is *Reggio* with a fine museum displaying, among other things, the two bronze warriors found off Riace. **PAESTUM** (Greek Poseidonia, p. 106) is the best-preserved Greek site on the mainland, with three almost complete Doric temples, the remains of the city, and a fine local museum.

The many Greek sites in Sicily make up the third part of the triptych (with the Greek mainland and Asia Minor) of Greek occupation of the Mediterranean. **SYRACUSE** (pp. 104–05) has the spring of Arethusa, the temple of Athena (cathedral) and the early temple of Apollo on the island of Ortygia. On the mainland are the theatre, the great altar of Hieron, part of the residential district, the ancient quarries, the fortress of Epipolai and an excellent museum. Further west, GELA has a rare stretch of city-wall with a mudbrick superstructure, a Greek bath and a museum. **AKRAGAS/AGRIGENTUM** (p. 102) has the spectacular run of Doric temples along the ridge, the remains of the immense Olympieion, a *bouleuterion* and a good site museum. **SELINUS** (p. 103, modern Selinunte) also boasts several standing Doric temples, as well as houses, city walls and other sanctuaries. At the extreme west end of the island is the Phoenician settlement of *Motya*, on a small island; the marble charioteer is in the tiny site museum. **SEGESTA** on the north coast has a well-preserved Doric temple (p. 67), unfinished in antiquity, and a large theatre. Further east are the sites of *Himera* and *Tyndaris*. Beyond the straits of Messina on the east coast are the sites of *Taormina*, *Naxos* (the first Greek colony) and *Catania*, beneath the brooding presence of Mt Aetna, still an active volcano.

FURTHER READING

Chapter I: Who were the Greeks?
Biers, W. R., *The Archaeology of Greece*, Ithaca & London 1996.
Cartledge, P. (ed.), *The Cambridge Illustrated History of Ancient Greece*, Cambridge 1998.
Durando, F., *Greece. Splendours of an Ancient Civilization*, London & New York 1997.
Etienne, R. & F., *The Search for Ancient Greece*, London & New York 1992.
Green, P. *Ancient Greece. A Concise History*, London & New York 1975.
Hall, J. M., *Ethnic Identity in Greek Antiquity*, Cambridge 1997.
Lesky, A., *A History of Greek Literature*, New York 1966.
Levi, P., *Atlas of the Greek World*, Oxford 1980.
Stoneman, R., *A Literary Companion to Travel in Greece*, Malibu 1994.
Stoneman, R., *A Luminous Land: Artists Discover Greece*, Los Angeles 1998.
Talbert, R. (ed.), *Barrington Atlas of the Greek and Roman World*, Princeton 2000.

Chapter II: The First Greeks
Broodbank, C., *An Island Archaeology of the Early Cyclades*, Cambridge 2000.
Drews, R., *The Coming of the Greeks*, Princeton 1988.
Fitton, J. L., *Cycladic Art*, London & Cambridge, MA. 1989.
Getz-Preziosi, P., *Sculptors of the Cyclades*, Ann Arbor 1987.
Jacobsen, T. W., '17,000 Years of Greek Prehistory', *Scientific American*, 1976, pp. 76–87.
Jacobsen, T. W. & K. D. Vitelli (eds.), *Excavations at Franchthi Cave, Greece*, Bloomington, several volumes.
Perlès, C., *The Early Neolithic Period in Greece*, Cambridge 2001.
Renfrew, C., *The Emergence of Civilization*, London 1972.
Runnels, C. & Murray, P., *Greece before History*, Stanford 2001.

Chapter III: The Heroic Age
Bass, G., *National Geographic*, December 1987, pp. 692–733.
Cadogan, G., *The Palaces of Minoan Crete*, London 1976.
Chadwick, J., *The Decipherment of Linear B*, Cambridge 1967.
Chadwick, J., *The Mycenaean World*, Cambridge 1976.
Dickinson, O. T. P. K., *The Aegean Bronze Age*, Cambridge 1994.
Drews, R., *The End of the Bronze Age*, Princeton 1993.
Higgins, R., *Minoan and Mycenaean Art*, London & New York 1997.
Hooker, J., *Mycenaean Greece*, London 1983.
Mylonas, G. E., *Mycenae Rich in Gold*, Athens 1983.
Taylour, W., *The Mycenaeans* (2nd ed.), London 1993.
Vermeule, E., *Greece in the Bronze Age*, Chicago 1964.

Chapter IV: The Age of Expanding Horizons
Akurgal, E., *Alt-Smyrna I*, Ankara 1983.
Boardman, J., *The Greeks Overseas* (2nd ed.), London & New York 1980.
Boardman, J., *Persia and the West*, London & New York 2000.
Bonet, P. & C. Fernandez, *Los Griegos en Espana*, Madrid 1998.
Caratelli, G., *The Western Greeks*, London & New York 1996.
Coldstream, N., *Geometric Greece*, London & New York 1977.
Coulson, W. D. E., *The Greek Dark Ages*, Athens 1990.
Desborough, V. R., *The Greek Dark Ages*, London 1972.
Dunbabin, T., *The Western Greeks*, Oxford 1948.
Fagerstom, K., *Greek Iron Age Architecture (SIMA 81)*, Goteborg 1988.
Hodge, T., *Ancient Greek France*, London 1998.
Huxley, G., *The Early Ionians*, London 1966.
Joffroy, R., *Vix et ses Trésors*, Paris 1979.
Popham, M. R., P. G. Calligas & L. H. Sackett (eds), *Lefkandi II, The Protogeometric Building at Toumba*, BSA 1993.
Powell, B., *Homer and the Origin of the Greek Alphabet*, Cambridge 1991.
Snodgrass, A., *The Dark Ages of Greece*, Edinburgh 1971.

Chapter V: Polis: The Early Greek City
Bammer, A., *Ephesos, Stadt an Fluss und Meer*, Austria 1988.
Bammer, A. & U. Muss, *Das Artemesion von Ephesos*, Mainz 1996.
Bonacasa, N. & S. Ensoli, *Cirene*, Milan 2000.
Cartledge, P., *Sparta and Lakonia*, London 1979.
Cartledge, P. & A. Spawforth, *Hellenistic and Roman Sparta*, London 1989.
Dawkins, R. M., *The Sanctuary of Artemis Orthia at Sparta*, London 1929.
Demakopoulou, K. & D. Konsola, *Archaeological Museum of Thebes*, Athens 1981.
Ehrenberg, V., *The Greek State*, London 1969.
Finley, M. I., *Ancient Sicily*, London 1968.
Goodchild, R. G., *Cyrene and Apollonia*, Libya 1970.
Holloway, R., *The Archaeology of Ancient Sicily*, London & New York 1991.
Huxley, G., *Early Sparta*, London 1962.
Kyrieleis, H., *Führer durch des Heraion von Samos*, DAI Athens 1981.
Kleine, J., *Führer durch die Ruinen von Milet -Didyma - Priene*, Ludwigsburg 1980.
Kleiner, G., *Die Ruinen von Milet*, Berlin 1968.
Lazenby, J., *The Spartan Army*, Warminster 1985.
Papachatzis, N., *Ancient Corinth*, Athens 1978.
Pedley, J. G., *Paestum*, London & New York 1990.
Rhodes, P. J., *The Greek City-States: a Source Book*, London 1986.
Rumschied, F., *Priene*, Istanbul 1998.
Salmon, J. B., *Wealthy Corinth*, Oxford 1984.
Samos, the results of the German excavations, numerous volumes published by the DAI.
Sanmarti, E. & J. M. Nolla, *Empuries: Guia Itineraria*, 1988.
Voza, G., *The Archaeological Museum of Syracuse*, Syracuse 1987.
Waele, J. de, *Akragas Graeca*, Nijmegen 1971.
Westcoat, B., *Syracuse, The Fairest Greek City*, Rome 1989.
Wycherley, R. E., *How the Greeks Built Cities* (2nd ed.), London 1962.

Chapter VI: Classical Athens
Camp, J., *The Athenian Agora*, London & New York 1992.
Camp, J., *The Archaeology of Athens*, New Haven 2001.
Goette, H. R., *Athens, Attica, and the Megarid*, London 2001.
Hurwit, J., *The Athenian Acropolis*, Cambridge 1998.
Knigge, U., *The Athenian Kerameikos*, Athens 1991.
Mylonas, G., *Eleusis and the Eleusinian Mysteries*, Princeton 1961.
Neils, J. (ed.), *Goddess and Polis*, Princeton 1992.
Pickard, A. W., *The Theatre of Dionysos in Athens*, Cambridge, Oxford 1946.
Pickard, A. W., *The Dramatic Festivals of Athens*, Cambridge, Oxford 1953.
Travlos, J., *Pictorial Dictionary of Athens*, London 1972.
Travlos, J., *Bildlexikon zur Topographie des antiken Attika*, Tübingen 1988.
Wycherley, R. E., *The Stones of Athens*, Princeton 1975.

Chapter VII: Gods and Heroes
Bommelaer, J. F. & D. Laroche, *Guide de Delphes, Le Site*, Paris 1991.
Bruneau, P. & J. Ducat, *Guide de Delos*, Paris 1983.
Burkert, W., *Greek Religion Archaic and Classical*, Oxford 1985.
Farnell, L. R., *The Cults of the Greek States*, 1895, repr. 1971, Chicago.
Graves, R., *The Greek Myths*, Edinburgh 1955.
Olympia und seine Bauten, Munich 1972.
Parke, H., *The Oracles of Apollo in Asia Minor*, London 1985.
Parke, H. & D. Wormell, *The Delphic Oracle*, Oxford 1956.

Chapter VIII: Greek Art and Architecture
Barletta, B., *The Origins of the Greek Architectural Orders*, Cambridge 2001.
Berve, H. & G. Gruben, *Greek Temples, Theatres and Shrines*, London & New York 1962.
Boardman, J., *Athenian Black Figure Vases*, London & New York 1974.
Boardman, J., *Athenian Red Figure Vases*, London & New York 1989.

Boardman, J., *Greek Sculpture, The Archaic Period*, London & New York 1978.
Boardman, J., *Greek Sculpture, The Classical Period*, London & New York 1985.
Boardman, J., *Greek Sculpture, The Late Classical Period*, London & New York 1995.
Boardman, J., *The History of Greek Vases*, London & New York 2001.
Cook, R. M., *Greek Painted Pottery* (3rd ed.), London 1997.
Coulton, J. J., *Ancient Greek Architects at Work*, Ithaca, 1977.
Dinsmoor, W. B., *The Architecture of Ancient Greece*, New York 1975.
Dunbabin, K., *Mosaics of the Greek and Roman World*, Cambridge 1999.
Gruben, G., *Die Tempel der Griechen*, Munich 1980.
Koldewey, R. & O. Puchstein, *Die Griechischen Tempel in Unteritalien und Sicilien*, Berlin 1899.
Lawrence, A. W., *Greek Architecture* (5th ed., R. A. Tomlinson), New Haven 1996.
Lissarague, F., *Greek Vases*, Riverside Press 2000.
Osborne, R., *Archaic and Classical Greek Art*, Oxford 1998.
Pollitt, J. J., *The Art of Ancient Greece, Sources and Documents*, Cambridge 1990.
Ridgway, B. S., *The Archaic Style in Greek Sculpture*, Princeton 1977.
Ridgway, B. S., *The Severe Style in Greek Sculpture*, Princeton 1970.
Ridgway, B. S., *Fifth Century Styles in Greek Sculpture*, Princeton 1981.
Ridgway, B. S., *Fourth Century Styles in Greek Sculpture*, Madison 1997.
Ridgway, B. S., *Hellenistic Sculpture*, Madison 1990.
Robertson, M., *The Art of Vase-Painting in Classical Athens*, Cambridge 1992.
Sparkes, B., *Greek Pottery, an Introduction*, Manchester 1991.
Spivey, N., *Understanding Greek Sculpture*, London & New York 1996.
Spivey, N., *Greek Art*, London 1997.

Chapter IX: Alexander and the Hellenistic World

Ashley, J. R., *The Macedonian Empire*, London 1998.
Austin, M., *The Hellenistic World from Alexander to the Roman Conquest*, Cambridge 1981.
Bosworth, A., *Conquest and Empire, the Reign of Alexander the Great*, Cambridge 1988.
Charbonneaux, J., *Hellenistic Art 330–50 BC*, London & New York 1973.
Cohen, G., *The Hellenistic Settlements in Europe, the Islands, and Asia Minor*, Berkeley 1995.
Davis, N. & C. Kraay, *The Hellenistic Kingdoms; Portrait Coins and History*, London 1973.
Fraser, P., *The Cities of Alexander the Great*, Oxford 1996.
Green, Peter, *Alexander to Actium*, Berkeley & London 1990.
Gruen, E., *The Hellenistic World and the Coming of Rome*, Berkeley 1984.
Ling, R. (ed.), *Cambridge Ancient History, Plates to Vol. VII, pt. 1*, Cambridge 1984.
Long, A. A., *Hellenistic Philosophy*, London 1974.
Miller, S., *The Tomb of Lyson and Kallikles*, Mainz 1993.
Onians, J., *Art and Thought in the Hellenistic Age*, Princeton 1988.
Pollitt, J. J., *Art in the Hellenistic Age*, Cambridge 1986.
Rice, E. E., *Alexander the Great*, Stroud 1997.
Smith, R. R. R., *Hellenistic Sculpture, a Handbook*, London & New York 1991.
Walbank, F. ,*The Hellenistic World*, Sussex N.J. 1981.

Chapter X: Romans and Christians

Beckwith, J., *Early Christian and Byzantine Art*, London 1970.
Erim, K., *Aphrodisias, City of Venus Aphrodite*, London 1986.
Gough, M., *The Origins of Chritian Art*, London 1973.
Jones, R. H. M., *The Cities of the Eastern Roman Provinces* (2nd ed.), Oxford 1971.
Jones, R. H. M., *The Later Roman Empire 284–602*, Oxford 1964.
Krautheimer, R., *Early Christian and Byzantine Architecture*, London 1965.
Pharr, C., *The Theodosian Code*, Princeton 1952.
Ward-Perkins, J. B., *Roman Imperial Architecture*, London 1981.

SOURCES OF QUOTATIONS

For the most part the quotes used are translations from the Loeb Classical Library (Cambridge, MA, Harvard University Press), occasionally adapted slightly to match modern usage.

Aeschylus, *Persai*, H. W. Smyth, vol. I (1922, adapted): p. 29
Aeschylus, *Prometheus Bound*, H. W. Smyth, vol. I (1922, adapted): p. 112
Aristotle, *Politics*, H. Rackham, vol. XXI (1932): pp. 77, 99
Athenaios, *Deipnosophistai*, C. B. Gulick, vols I–VI (1927–41): pp. 108, 124, 181
Cicero, *Verrines*, L. H. G. Greenwood, vol. VIII (1935)
Diodorus Siculus, *Library of History*, C. H. Oldfather, vols I–XII (1933–67): pp. 102, 113
Herodotus, *The Persian Wars*, A. D. Godley, vols I–IV (1920–25): pp. 6, 56, 62, 63, 65, 71, 72, 73, 96 97, 107, 110, 125 143
Hesiod, *Works and Days*, H. G. Evelyn-White (1914): p. 74
Hesiod, *Theogony*, H. G. Evelyn-White (1914): p. 75
Homer, *Iliad*, A. T. Murray (vols I–II, 1978–85): pp. 37, 53, 72, 154, 157
Homer, *Odyssey*, A. T. Murray and G. Dimock, vols I–II (1919): pp. 50, 54
Pindar, *Pythian*, J. Sandys (1919, adapted): p. 113
Plato, *Epinomis*, W. R. M. Lamb, vol. XII (1927): p. 59
Plato, *Protagoras*, W. R. M. Lamb, vol. II (1924): p. 139
Pliny the Younger, *Letters*, W. Melmoth and W. Hutchinson (1915): pp. 173, 209, 210
Pliny, *Natural History*, H. Rackham, vols V & IX (1950, 1952): pp. 108, 175, 176
Pliny, *Natural History*, W. H. S. Jones, vol. VI (1951): p. 108
Pliny, *Natural History*, D. E. Eichholz, vol. X (1962): p. 166
Plutarch, *Moralia*, H. N. Fowler, vol. X (1936): p. 67
Plutarch, *Parallel Lives: Alexander*, B. Perrin, vol. VII (1919): pp. 194, 195
Plutarch, *Parallel Lives: Demetrios*, B. Perrin, vol. IX (1920, adapted): p. 199
Plutarch, *Parallel Lives: Lysander*, B. Perrin, vol. I, (1916): p. 72
Plutarch, *Parallel Lives: Pelopidas*, B. Perrin, vol. V (1917): p.90
Plutarch, *Parallel Lives: Perikles*, B. Perrin, vol. VIII (1916): p. 127
Polybios, *The Histories*, W. R. Paton, vol. V (1926): p. 101
Strabo, *Geography*, H. L. Jones, vols I–VIII (1917–32): pp. 11, 69, 73, 82, 88, 93, 151, 159, 163, 190, 196, 198
Thucydides, *History of the Peloponnesian War*, C. F. Smith, vols I–IV (1919–23): pp. 35, 56, 66, 140, 141
Tyrtaios, *Lyra Graeca*, J. M. Edmonds (1931): p. 85
Vitruvius, *On Architecture*, F. Granger, vols I–II (1931–34): pp. 64, 138, 169 170, 173, 190, 192, 198
Xenophon, *Hellenika*, C. L. Brownson, vols I–II (1918–21, adapted): p. 125
Xenophon, *Kynegetikos*, C. Marchant, vol. VII (1925): p. 160
Xenophon, *Lacedaimonian Constitution*, C. Marchant, vol. VII (1925): pp. 86, 87

Other sources and inscriptions
Archilochos, Fr. 3, *Greek Lyrics*, R. Lattimore (Chicago 1955): p. 74
Eusebius, *Ecclesiastical History*, X. V, C. F. Cruse (Grand Rapids, MI): p. 211
Herakleides/pseudoDikaiarchos, C. Müller, *Fragmenta Historicum Graecorum* II; trans. J. G. Frazer: pp. 79, 89
Herodotus, *The Persian Wars*, G. Rawlinson (Modern Library): p. 12
Hippocrates, *Hippocratic Writings*, trans. J. Chadwick and W. Mann, (E. LLoyd ed., Penguin 1978): p. 161
Homer, *Iliad*, 18. 478–82, R. Lattimore (Chicago, 1951): p. 154
Homer, *Odyssey*, I. 429–33, R. Fitzgerald (Doubleday, 1961): p. 54
Libanios, *Ekphraseis*, J.J. Pollitt, *The Art of Ancient Greece* (Cambridge 1990): p. 55
Pausanias, *Description of Greece*, J. G. Frazer (Macmillan, 6 vols, 1898): pp. 39, 78, 110, 127, 134, 157
Pliny, *Naturalis Historia*, K. Jex-Blake (1896): pp. 100, 177, 184, 185, 192
Thucydides, *History of the Peloponnesian War*, R. Crawley, *The Landmark Thucydides* (R. Strassler, ed., Free Press 1996): p. 25
p. 71: *A Selection of Greek Historical Inscriptions*, no. 7, R. Meiggs and D. Lewis (Oxford University Press, 1969)
p. 82 Attic Stelai, II, 71–80: J. Camp
p. 113: *A Selection of Greek Historical Inscriptions*, no. 17, R. Meiggs and D. Lewis (Oxford University Press, 1969)
p. 135: Agora I 7151: J. Camp
p. 144: Thorikos inscription: J. Camp
p. 160: IG IV^2 1, 121: E. J. and L. Edelstein, *Asclepius* (John Hopkins University Press, 1998)
p. 171: Epidauros building account: A. Burford, *Greek Temple Builders at Epidauros* (Liverpool University Press, 1969)
p. 181: gravestone: J. Beazley, *American Journal of Archaeology*, 1943, p. 456

ILLUSTRATION CREDITS

Abbreviations: ASCS – American School of Classical Studies at Athens; BM – British Museum, London; BSA – British School at Athens; DAI – German Archaeological Institute; EFA – École Française d'Athènes; HG – phoro Heidi Grassley, © Thames & Hudson Ltd, London; NMA – National Museum, Athens; PW – Philip Winton; JC – John Camp; RHPL – Robert Harding Picture Library; TAPA – Archaeological Receipts Fund, Athens; a – above; t – top; l – left; r – right; b – below; c – centre

1 BM, photo Hirmer; 2 HG, NMA; 6–7 Tony Gervis/RHPL; 8l BM, photo Edwin Smith; 8b Delphi Museum, photo Hirmer; 9 Martin Hürlimann; 10l AKG, London/Staatliche Antikensammlungen und Glyptothek, Munich; 10–11 Elizabeth Fisher; 11r BM; 12a Metropolitan Museum of Art, New York, Gift of George F. Baker, 1891; 12b BM; 12–13 PW; 14l National Archaeological Museum, Athens; 15–16 © Michael Jenner; 16l Othman Pferschy, Istanbul; 16r BM; 17 TAPA; 20 JC; 21a Biblioteca Ambrosiana, Milan; 21b Staatliche Antikensammlungen und Glyptothek, Munich; 22l L. Dupré, *Voyage à Athènes et Constantinople*, Paris 1825; 22r BM; 23 EFA; 24–25 John Bigelow Taylor, N.Y.C.; 26l JC; 26–27 Manolis Korres; 27r PW; 28al JC; 28ar PW; 28cl, cr, b NMA; 29l NMA; 29a Scala; 29b Volos Museum; 30l Benaki Museum, photo Edwin Smith; 30b BM; 31tl NMA, photo Josephine Powell; 31br, bc BSA, photos Josephine Powell; 31r BM; 32b Christos Doumas; 32–33 Photo Henri Stierlin; 33t JC; 33b Christos Doumas; 34a after A. J. B. Wace and F. H. Stubbings, *A Companion to Homer*, fig. 10; 34bl Archaeological Museum, Herakleion, photo Josephine Powell; 34bc Archaeological Museum, Herakleion; 34br Archaeological Museum, Herakleion; 35al Thebes Museum; 35ar photo Hirmer; 35bl ASCS, Frantz Collection; 36–37 HG; 38–39 ASCS, Frantz Collection; 39a Prof. C. W. Blegen, University of Cincinnati; 39b after C. W. Blegen, *The Palace of Nestor* I, fig. 64; 40a HG; 40bl NMA; 40c AKG London/Erich Lessing; 40br NMA; 41a after W. Taylour, *The Mycenaeans*, fig. 86; 41bl ASCS, Frantz Collection; 41br after A. Furumark, *Mycenaean Pottery*; 42–43 HG; 43a Martin Weaver; 43b NMA; 44a, b ASCS, Frantz Collection; 44ar after J. Chadwick, *The Decipherment of Linear B*, fig. 10; 45t EFA; 45c ASCS, Frantz Collection; 45b ASCS; 46t Christos Doumas; 46c Elizabeth A. Fisher; 46b JC; 46–47 Metropolitan Museum, New York, K. Wilkinson and M. Hill, 1983, cast; 47a, c Institute of Nautical Archaeology; 48a Archaeological Museum, Herakleion, photo Josephine Powell; 48l Archaeological Museum, Herakleion, photo Leonard von Matt; 48–49 ASCS, Frantz Collection; 49a Alison Frantz, Athens; 50a photo Peter Clayton; 50l BM, photo Peter Clayton; 50c after T. Sipahi, *Ist. Mitt.*, 2000; 50b M. Bietak, N. Marinatos, C. Palyvou; 51a D. and I. Mathioulakis, painting by Anna Menorinou; 51b Thebes Museum; 52a Naples Archaeological Museum, photo Hirmer; 52b JC; 53a Lloyd Townsend; 53b DAI, Athens; 54 TAPA; 55a ASCS, Agora; 55b BM; 56 The Oriental Institute, University of Chicago; 57a PW; 57b S. Gitin/T. Dothan; 58–59 NMA; 60l DAI, Athens; 60c, r, 61a, b Hugh Sackett, BSA; 62a ASCS, Agora; 62bl after Nicholls, BSA; 62br JC; 63 BSA; 64 PW; 65a photo Leonard von Matt; 65b DAI, Athens; 66 Staatliche Museen, Berlin; 66–67 PW; 67t JC; 68l Olympia Museum; 68r NMA; 68–69 photo Hirmer; 69a TAPA, Numismatic Museum, Athens; 69c after W. B. Dinsmoor, *Bulletin de Correspondence Héllenique*, 37, 1913; 70l Cairo Museum, photo Bildarchiv Foto Marburg; 70r NMA, photo Hirmer; 70–71 DAI, Athens; 71a Olympia Museum, photo DAI, Athens; 71b HG; 72a TAPA, Numismatic Museum, Athens; 72b ASCS, Agora; 72a Leu Numismatik; 73b JC; 74 Staatliche Antikensammlungen und Glyptothek, Munich; 75a Rheinisches Landesmuseum, Trier; 75b BM, photo Hirmer; 76–77 photo Elizabeth Pendleton; 78l PW; 78r JC; 79a PW; 79b ASCS, Agora; 80a PW; 80b JC; 81a JC; 81b BM; 82 Metropolitan Museum of Art, New York; 83a ASCS, Agora; 83b National Museum, Copenhagen; 84 BSA; 85l The Wadsworth Atheneum, Hartford, Conn.; 85r DAI, Athens; 86a BM; 86c, b BSA; 87a Bernisches Historisches Museum; 87b photo Hannibal; 88a JC; 88bl Rome, Vatican; 88br Leu Numismatik; 89a, bl DAI, Athens; 89br ASCS, Agora; 90a DAI, Athens; 90–91 ASCS; 91al JC; 91ar Leu Numismatik; 92b PW; 92–93 Archaeological Society of Athens; 93a ASCS, Corinth; 93c PW; 94l DAI, Athens; 94c PW; 94–95 DAI, Athens; 95al PW; 95ar Leu Numismatik; 95r DAI, Athens; 96a DAI, Athens; 96b DAI, Athens; 97al, r DAI, Athens; 97b JC; 98, 98–99 JC; 99b after H. Knackfuss, *Didyma*; 100a JC; 100b Leu Numismatik; 101a JC; 101bl F. Krischen, 1938; 101br JC; 102 Antonio Attini, Archivio White Star; 103a JC; 103bl Archaeological Museum Palermo, photo Scala; 103br Motya Museum, photo Roger Wilson; 104 photo Edwin Smith; 105a photo Leonard von Matt; 105bl Leu Numismatik; 105br Syracuse Museum, photo Hirmer; 106al Leu Numismatik; 106ar Paestum Museum; 106b JC; 107a JC; 107b, 108 Leu Numismatik; 108–09 Elizabeth Pendleton; 109bl NMA; 109br photo Hirmer; 111 Luisa Ricciarini; 111a BM, photo Eileen Tweedy; 111b Trireme Trust, photo Paul Lipke; 112–13 PW; 112al John Camp; 112ar *Guide de Delphes*, EFA; 113a BM; 114 DAI, Athens; 114–15 Villa Giulia, Rome; 115 BM; 116–17 JC; 118 Naples Archaeological Museum; 118–19 ASCS, Frantz Collection; 120l DAI, Rome; 120r BM, photo Martin Weaver; 120–21 ASCS, Craig Mauzy; 121a, c, b , 122a, b, 123 ACSS, Agora; 124a Antikenmuseum, Staatliche Museen Preussischer Kulturbesitz; 124b Musée du Louvre, Paris; 125 ASCS, Agora; 127l NMA; 126–27 ASCS, Frantz Collection; 128a BM, photo Susan Johnson; 128c BM, photo Edwin Smith; 129b Musée du Louvre, Paris, photo Hirmer; 129a HG; 129b ASCS, Agora; 130bl ASCS, Agora; 130a BM, photo Edwin Smith; 130br Detroit Institute of Art; 131a Mrs M. E. Cox; 131b BM; 132, 132–33 a, b JC; 133a PW; 134al ASCS, Agora; 134ar Museo Archeologico Nazionale Taranto, photo Leonard von Matt; 134ar Musée du Petit Palais, Paris; 134b Wagner Museum, Würzburg, photo Hirmer; 135l Naples Archaeological Museum, photo DAI, Rome; 134c BM; 135r Mantua Museum; 136–37 JC; 137 Craig Mauzy; 138l Naples Archaeological Museum; 138r Kunsthistorisches Museum, Vienna; 138–39 Staatliche Museen, Berlin; 139a Villa Albani, Rome; 139b Museo Nazionale, Rome, Farnese Collection; 140l Kerameikos Museum; 140r BM; 151 Art Archive/Archaeological Museum Piraeus/dagli Orti; 142–43 Museo Nazionale, Tarquinia, photo Hirmer; 144a Museum of Fine Arts, Boston, photo Raymond V. Schoeder, S.J.; 144–45 NMA; 145 Allard Pierson Museum, Amsterdam; 146l DAI, Athens; 146al BM, photo Hirmer; 146r photo Hirmer; 147ar Munich Glyptothek, photo Hirmer; 147b TAPA, Lamia Museum; 148 BM; 149l Art Archive/dagli Orti; 149r Luisa Ricciarini; 150l Berlin/Beazley; 150–51a Antikenmuseum Basel; 150–51b Museo Nazionale, Taranto, photo Leonard von Matt; 151r NMA; 152 N. Yialouris; 153a Chalkis Museum, photo Hirmer; 153b Musée du Louvre, Paris; 154a, c DAI, Athens; 154–55 V. Laloux and P. Monceaux, *Restauration d'Olympie*, 1889; 155al Museo Nazionale, Tarquinia, photo Hirmer; 155ar after C. Mee and A. Spawforth, *Greece*, Oxford, 2001; 156a Art Archive/ dagli Orti; 156b Terme Museum, Rome, photo Scala; 157 HG; 158l Delphi Museum, photo Hirmer; 158a HG; 158b ASCS, Frantz Collection; 159l JC; 159r DAI, Athens; 160 NMA; 161l Vatican Museums, photo DAI, Rome; 160r ASCS, Corinth; 162a Staatliche Museen, Berlin; 162b HG; 163a JC; 163c Archaeological Society of Athens; 163b Bibliothèque National, Paris; 164–65 photo Edwin Smith; 166–67 ASCS, Frantz Collection; 167 C. R. Cockerell, 1860; 168l JC; 168r after F. Krauss 1943; 169r PW; 170l JC; 170r Epidauros Museum, Bildarchiv Foto Marburg; 171 Ch. Intsesisoglou; 172a ASCS, Agora; 173 after CRAI, Bernard; 174l Ch. Intsesisoglou; 174r EFA; 175a DAI, Athens; 175b Olympia Museum, photo Hirmer; 176al Naples Archaeological Museum; 176ar after *Olympia II*, 1892; 176bl Terme Museum, Rome; 176br Vatican Museums, Rome; 177bl HG; 177a DAI, Athens; 177br BM; 178l HG; 178l Museo Nazionale Reggio Calabria, photo Scala; 179a Staatliche Museen, Berlin; 179r HG; 180a Kerameikos Museum, Athens, photo DAI, Athens; 180bl Metropolitan Museum, New York; 180br, 181a N. Sevinc, Canakkale Museum; 181b Archaeological Museum, Istanbul; 182al Musée du Louvre, Paris; 182ar Archaeological Museum, Florence; 182b Staatliche Antikensammlungen und Glyptothek, Munich; 183al BM; 183ar Kunsthistorisches Museum, Vienna, photo Erwin Meyer; 183b NMA; 184a ASCS, Frantz Collection; 184b TAPA, Thessaloniki Museum; 185al Archaeological Museum, Florence; 185ar NMA; 185b Naples Archaeological Museum; 186 Archaeological Museum, Thessaloniki; 187a EFA; 186bl Musée de Chatillonais-Châtillon-Sur-Seine; 187br ASCS, Craig Mauzy; 188–89 photo courtesy Ch. J. Makaronas; 190 JC; 191a BM; 191b PW; 192l BM; 192r Manolis Andronikos; 192c Ekdotike Athens; 193 TAPA, Thessaloniki Museum; 194a Acropolis Museum, Athens; 194–95 PW; 195 Naples Archaeological Museum; 196a Peter Clayton; 196b Photo Christoph Gerigk, © Hilti Foundation/ Discovery Channel /Franck Goddio; 197a Leu Numismatik; 197b ASCS, Frantz Collection; 198 JC; 199a photo courtesy Ch. J. Makaronas; 199b Photini Zaphiropolou; 200–01 photo Hirmer; 202 JC; 203a JC; 203b Leu Numismatik; 204l Archaeological Museum, Istanbul, photo Hirmer; 204–05 JC; 205a JC; 205b Archaeological Museum Istanbul, photo Hirmer; 206 JC; 207al JC; 207ar DAI, Athens; 208a Arian Baptistery, Ravenna; 208b Alison Frantz; 208c PW; 209 a Elizabeth Fisher; 209b after R. Krautheimer, *Early Christian and Byzantine Architecture* (London 1965); 210l photo Hirmer; 210r after D. Parrish (ed.), *Urbanism in Western Asia Minor* (Portsmouth, 2001); 211 JC; 212l JC; 212r photo Josephine Powell; 213 photo A. F. Kersting.